D1246247

Pumping Sunshine

A Memoir of My Rural Childhood

Susie H. Baxter

Susie H. Baxter

Grateful acknowledgment is made
for permission to reprint in the Author's Note p. xiii:
Excerpt from "Introduction" by William Zinsser from INVENTING THE TRUTH: The
Art and Craft of Memoir. Copyright © 1998 by William Zinsser. Reprinted by permission
of Houghton Mifflin Harcourt Publishing Company. All rights reserved.

Book designed by Jeanne B. Field
Fonts: Constantia and Goudy Old Style
Cover photo by Rob Uguccioni

ISBN 978-0-9980828-2-0
Library of Congress Control Number: 2017912775
1. Childhood memoir   2. Southern U.S. history
3. Coming of age   4. Childhood enuresis

Dedicated to my "big" sisters,
my teachers, Patsy and Anetha,
and in memory of Tommy, our protector

Other books by Susie H. Baxter

C.G. and Ethel: A Family History
2008

Write Your Memoir: One Story at a Time
2017

Acknowledgements

Thank you to my sisters, Patsy and Anetha, for your encourage-ment and assistance, and for reminding me time and time again how it *really* happened, even if we didn't always agree!

Thank you to everyone whose name appears in stories in this book, especially to friends and neighbors in Suwannee County and to relatives near and far. And a special thanks to Ellie and Emory for their helping hands.

Thank you to my husband, Gilbert, who proofed numerous stories before I felt comfortable sharing intimate details with others.

A big thanks to my critique pod mates, Wendy, Joan, Ann-Marie, Bonnie, and Kaye, for critiquing most of the tales in this book. Your questions and suggestions were invaluable. Thanks also to Hilda and Bev for your continued support.

Thank you to my daughters, Pamela and Jeanne. Thank you, Pamela, for saying, "I like this little girl" after reading the first three chapters. And Jeanne, you made my day when I saw you smile and chuckle as you read and edited the chapters before transferring them from Word to InDesign.

Thank you, Rob, for traipsing through the woods with camera in hand as the sun came up, in search of the cover photo you knew I wanted, one that reminded me of the rutted road that led to the moss-draped "backwoods" where my sisters and I grew up.

SUSIE H. BAXTER

Contents

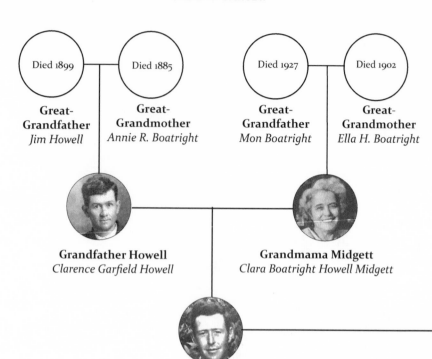

Died 1899

Died 1885

Died 1927

Died 1902

Great-Grandfather
Jim Howell

Great-Grandmother
Annie R. Boatright

Great-Grandfather
Mon Boatright

Great-Grandmother
Ella H. Boatright

Grandfather Howell
Clarence Garfield Howell

Grandmama Midgett
Clara Boatright Howell Midgett

Daddy
C.G. Howell

Our Family Tree

**Great-Grand-
father Rye**
*John Henry
Rye, Jr.*

**Great-Grand-
mother Rye**
Cora Newlan

**Great-
Granddaddy Tip**
Asberry Lanier

**Great-
Granny Dosia**
Theodosia Dees

Granddaddy Rye
Milton M. Rye

GrandmaRye
Delma Lanier Rye

Mama
Ethel Rye Howell

Patsy

Anetha

Tommy

Susanette

C. G. and Ethel Howell with Patsy and baby Anetha, 1943.
They just *thought* their family was complete.

Author's Note

How far back does our memory extend, and how much of our memory is from hearing stories told and retold? A few events described in this book occurred when I was only about three years old. Do I remember life without electricity? I know that I saw Mama light the oil lamp more than once, but was it only when the "current" went out during a thunderstorm?

As William Zinsser states in his book *Inventing the Truth: The Art and Craft of Memoir,* "Memoir is how we try to make sense of who we are, who we once were, and what values and heritage shaped us . . . . Memoir writers must manufacture a text, imposing narrative order on a jumble of half-remembered events. With that feat of manipulation, they arrive at a truth that is theirs alone, not quite like that of anybody else who was present at the same events."

I hope it's evident that the stories within are told from the perspective of a child—one who made plenty of mistakes—and you will forgive any inadvertent misrepresentations of facts.

My older sisters, Patsy and Anetha, tried to help me get the facts straight. For example, the story (page 300) about Marie Boatright's sprinkling black pepper into her mashed potatoes—peppered potatoes that Patsy refused to eat until Mama told her the black flecks were just "little bits of trash" that fell into the pot. Anetha insisted I had the facts wrong. "*You're* the one who wouldn't eat the food—and it was rice, not potatoes," she said. "*You* were the finicky eater!" But in my memory, Mama put Patsy's name in the story and said it was mashed potatoes, and I'm sticking with Mama's version. As *I* remember it.

Part I
At the End of a Dirt Road

1

Middle of the Night
North Florida, 1947

"Wake up, girls! Get outta bed!" Daddy yelled. Awakened from a nightmare, my half-awake eyes searched the cold, dark room. Dim moonlight shining through the bare windows helped me make out Daddy's flailing silhouette as he yanked quilts off my sisters and me. He grabbed my arm as I scrambled, trying to climb over Patsy and Anetha and off the cot we sisters shared. In my three years of life, I'd never been more scared. My heart pounded.

That night had started out like any other.

In the kitchen after supper, soapy water dripped from Mama's fingertips into the chipped enamel dishpan as she lifted her arm to brush loose strands of permed dark hair off her forehead. She couldn't stand hair in her face. Bangs like Patsy had would have annoyed Mama no end. Curls like mine that dangled to my eyes? Pure torture for Mama.

"C.G.," Mama called to Daddy. "How 'bout bringing in a washtub so the girls can take their baths by the fire?"

Through the kitchen doorway, I had a clear view of Daddy, sitting in a straight-backed chair by the hearth. Logs blazed. Daddy was studying a lesson in his Sunday school book that lay atop his open Bible. Expecting him to look up and answer Mama any second, I stared at the crown of his head. His hair was nearly as dark as Mama's, except when the sun or firelight hit it just right. Then, you could see sparkles of auburn. His barber clipped it short, as if Daddy still trained with the Florida National Guard. With his hair only an inch long, he didn't need to plaster it down with Brylcreem the way most men at church did theirs. Daddy didn't even need to comb his. You couldn't tell if he did or didn't.

He kept reading, not answering Mama. She rewarmed the dishwater with steaming water from the white enamel kettle on the oil stove and swished the dishrag around plate after plate before handing each to Patsy. We had our assembly line going. Patsy, who would soon start first grade, rinsed the dishes in another enamel pan before handing them to Anetha, the next oldest, who stood ready with a muslin towel. The dishes, pots, and pans ended up with me, the one everybody still called "the baby," even though I was already three years old. I put them away. If, that is, I could reach the proper shelf. Mostly, I couldn't, so I set the dishes and a few other things on the cook table for Mama to put away later. When we finished, Mama opened the kitchen shutter and tossed the dirty dishwater through the dark space onto frostbitten four-o'clock bushes in the backyard.

Daddy had been talking about adding a kitchen sink and pipes that would bring well water into the house and take it out again—"indoor plumbing," he called it. Our grandparents, who lived just up the road, had all that in their new house, built in 1944, the year I was born. They even had an indoor toilet!

"C.G.?" Mama called again.

Daddy was thumbing through the Good Book as if searching for a certain verse, but he finally looked up.

"Yeah, Ethel, I heard you. I'm studying my Sunday school lesson. I'll get the tub *to-reckly.*" To some people, that might mean *directly.* But from Daddy's lips, it meant "not right now."

The tub they were talking about was a #3 laundry tub that doubled as our bathtub. We had two. Each hung on a big nail in the open hall, or breezeway, that ran through the middle of our house. Later on, I learned that some people called ours a *cracker house*, but to me, it was just *home*.

Mama went out to the hall, brought the tub inside, and set it down hard in front of the fireplace near Daddy's feet. The tub's metal handles clanged against the side of the tub, sounding like a cowbell.

"Ethel, I told you I'd get that!" Daddy said, clearly annoyed, as he got up. He dropped his reading materials in his now empty chair, bumped the tub hard with one foot, and headed for the door. A few minutes later, he came back inside with a bucket of water in each hand. After

Home

he poured the cold water into the tub, Mama added hot from the kettle, then bent over and swirled the cold and hot water together.

"Who wants to go first?"

"Me! Me! Me!" we all said, since the first to get in the tub got the cleanest, warmest water. This night, Anetha got to go first. Later, dressed in our flannel nightgowns, we begged Daddy to put on a shadow show. With his hands positioned between the dangling overhead light bulb and the wall, he moved his fingers so the shadows looked like a barking dog, a scampering rabbit, and an eagle in flight.

"Show us a string trick!" Anetha said.

Daddy could loop a string, its ends tied together, around his fingers to make the outline of a cup and saucer, crow's feet—even a fancy Jacob's ladder.

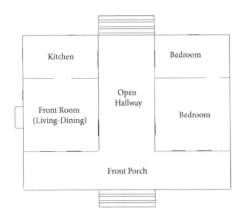

Floor layout

"Yeah! Do a string trick," I begged. I liked the one where he twisted a string around his fingers and pulled it a certain way, so it looked as if he'd cut off one of his fingers.

"No string tricks tonight," he said. "Time for bed."

Mama walked us to the bedroom we shared with her and Daddy. She reminded us to wee-wee if we needed to before we hopped into our bed, a metal Army cot that Daddy had lugged home from Camp Blanding when he left the Florida National Guard.

I pulled the enamel slop jar from under the crib—the baby bed I'd outgrown—and "went." The cot squeaked as I climbed up on the cotton-stuffed mattress and slid under the quilts between my sisters. Anetha slept next to the wall. Patsy had the choice, outside spot. If she reached her arms out, she could touch the footboard of Mama and Daddy's double bed.

As Mama tucked us into bed this chilly night, she leaned over and brushed hair from our faces. She then tugged the quilts to pull them up around our necks before kneeling beside our bed. We closed our eyes—well, I closed mine so I don't really know

Camp Blanding

During World War II, Camp Blanding (southwest of Jacksonville, FL) was one of the largest military training facilities in the U.S. It sprawled over more than 170,000 acres. From 1940 to 1945, more than 800,000 soldiers received all or part of their training there. *http://www.usfcam. usf.edu/CAM/exhibitions/1998_12_McCollum/supplemental_didactics/36.History.pdf*

5

about anybody else—and recited "Now I Lay Me Down to Sleep."

Mama was walking out the door when Patsy decided she wanted to move to the foot of the cot. Mama said okay, so Patsy switched ends. That put me in the choice spot, closest to Mama and Daddy's bed. As I closed my eyes, I hoped I wouldn't have another nightmare or an accident.

In most of my bad dreams, an animal chased me. Some nights a black bear got after me, even though I'd seen bears only in storybook pictures of "Goldilocks and the Three Bears." If it wasn't a bear chasing me, it was a blacksnake—the one Mama called a "corchwhip." Eventually, I learned it was spelled coachwhip, named after the horse-and-carriage whip, but we pronounced it with an *r*, the way some people say *Warshington* for Washington.

Sometimes we'd see a corchwhip slither across the sandy rutted road as we walked to our grandparents' house. In fact, we once saw one that was five-and-a-half-feet long, as long as Daddy was tall.

I'd heard that a corchwhip could outrun a man. And if a snake could outrun you, I figured it could outsmart you too. I was pretty sure the serpent our Baptist preacher talked about—the snake that tempted Adam and Eve and introduced sin to the world—was a corchwhip.

After I fell asleep that cold winter night, I dreamed it was summer. I was walking barefoot through the woods, between our house and the nearby Suwannee River, minding my own business, when I heard the rustle of leaves behind me. From the sound, I knew it was a snake, so I took off running. Faster and faster I ran. Branches, brambles, palmettos, and persimmons slapped me in the face as I flew through the woods, the soles of my feet barely touching the ground. Just when I thought—out of breath and panting—that I'd outrun the snake, I heard the rustle of leaves again and screamed into the darkness—

"*Sn-n-a-a-a-k-e!*"

Daddy flew out of bed like he'd been shot from a slingshot, and started yelling for us to wake up and get out of bed.

"My Lord, Ethel! It *is* a snake!" Daddy yelled as Mama jumped up and pulled a cord that turned on the overhead light.

Daddy threw quilts off the cot, and Mama shook them as my sisters and I jumped around, shivering. But after much shaking and re-shaking of the covers, no snake fell out.

"You must'a mistook the girls tangled-up legs for a snake," Mama said to Daddy.

"Crawl back in bed and go to sleep," Daddy finally said. "Susanette was just having another nightmare."

Just a nightmare? Go back to sleep? Daddy didn't understand. I could not go back to sleep.

Everybody else was soon breathing heavy while I lay staring into the dark room, unable to think of anything but the snake. I wanted to scream "Snake!" again so everybody would wake up and keep me company. But I'd heard the story of the little shepherd boy who cried "wolf" once too often.

How I wished I could quit having scary dreams. Just as I wished I didn't have that other nighttime problem, the one Mama called my "bad habit."

2

My Bad Habit

Around daylight, I jerked myself awake as I tried to catch hold of something—anything. I'd dreamed I'd fallen through the cut-out in the loft floor of our packhouse, the hole made for the wall ladder to reach the barn's loft. I woke up just before hitting the feed barrel—the steel-rimmed barrel Anetha once fell into for real.

Just another bad dream, I realized. I hadn't fallen. I was fine.

Well, no . . . I wasn't fine. I was wet. My flannel gown was sticking to my legs as if coated with sticky paste, the white stuff Mama made with flour and water for us to make paper chains for the Christmas tree. Why couldn't I wake up when I had to pee? I dreaded what Mama would say when she saw me. Not "Good morning, Sleepyhead," like Daddy sometimes did. No. Mama would ask what she always did. "Susanette, d'you wet the bed again?"

I always wanted to say, "No, ma'am," but lying was the same as stealing—wasn't it?—one of those "thou shalt nots" in the Bible. If I lied, I'd burn in Hell. But would I burn in Hell anyway for wetting the bed?

Mama used to call my wetting the bed an accident. Now she called it a bad habit. She had scolded and spanked me, trying to break my bad habit. Nothing worked. Not even Great-Granny

Dosia's remedy that Mama had started using. "Rub her nose in that wet spot," Granny told Mama. "And she'll soon learn to pee in the pot. Remember? That's how we cured your little brother, Harold."

I couldn't imagine handsome Uncle Harold wetting the bed. I knew him mostly from the framed picture of him in his Navy uniform that sat on my grandparents' cabinet radio. He now lived with his wife, Aunt Louise, way up in Indiana, wherever that was.

Now, every time I wet the bed, Mama used Granny's remedy. She would put her hand on the back of my neck, push my nose into the wet spot, and rub my nose back and forth, back and forth on the soggy, smelly sheet. I would hold my breath till I couldn't. The rubbing left my nose feeling raw, but what I hated most were the staring eyes of my big sisters. How I longed to be grown-up like them. *What was wrong with me? Why was I so different?* I knew I shouldn't pee while I slept. But after I fell asleep at night, I totally forgot what I knew while awake.

Every time it happened, Mama would strip off the wet sheet, and Daddy would hoist the mattress onto his shoulders, take it outside, and throw it onto the front corner of the wire fence that surrounded our yard. Mama said the fresh air helped get the stink out.

When that pee-stained mattress lay astraddle the fence, I felt glad we lived at the end of a long dirt road instead of a busy highway. But throughout the day, I worried. *What if company comes?*

3

Company

Daddy was always inviting people over, never bothering to run it by Mama. Like the day we were at Castleberry's Feed and Seed in Live Oak and he invited this stranger over. When the fellow asked where we lived, Daddy answered, "We live so far in the backwoods, we have to pump sunshine through hollow logs."

Daddy was always joking around like that. He eventually gave the man directions, saying, "From Live Oak, go south on 129. Take Highway 51 toward Mayo. Drive about nine miles and look for the Philadelphia Baptist Church sign. Turn left there, onto a dirt road. Go another nine miles until you come to a dead end, and then you'll see our house."

Live Oak

At the turn of the nineteenth century, when the railroad was king, Live Oak was the fifth largest city in Florida, after Jacksonville, Pensacola, Tampa, and Key West, in that order.

The town was ideally situated in North Florida at the intersection of an east-west railroad and a north-south railroad when phosphate and lumber industries were booming.

During this, its golden age, Live Oak grew rapidly. Hotels and large Victorian homes shot up almost overnight.

For a few years, it was the largest inland city in the state.

Suwannee Co. Clerk of Court website: *http://www.suwgov.org/index.php/history*

I thought Daddy's directions were pitiful. If he really wanted people to find us, he should tell them once they got on that dirt road to look on the left for a house with a green tile roof. That house wasn't ours—Mama's parents and grandparents lived there—but it served as the perfect landmark. Once they passed there, they'd need to veer into the woods onto a rutted lane.

Daddy also never mentioned that they'd come to a fork down that lane. If they went left, they'd end up at our stinky pigpen, next to the packhouse where we stored cured tobacco every summer. They should take the right fork, which led through a tunnel of oaks with low-hanging limbs dangling Spanish moss that might brush their windshields as they passed underneath. When the moss cleared, they'd see our house, its tin roof a rusty brown, and its clapboards a silvery gray, having never been slapped by a loaded paintbrush. A porch stretched all the way across the front, and the breezeway separated the two rooms on the east side from the two rooms on the west side.

Despite Daddy's pitiful directions, tons of visitors found their way to our house. The instant we sisters heard a car or truck coming down the lane, we ran to the front yard, jumped up and down, and waved our arms. "Y'all get out and come in!" we hollered as the vehicle rolled to a stop. If the pee-stained mattress lay across the fence, I hoped our enthusiastic waving would distract our visitors—and maybe it did because nobody ever asked about the mattress, thank goodness.

Some people came to visit for the first time. Others knew their way almost too well. Relatives on Daddy's side of the family—his two brothers and two sisters and their families from South Florida—spent all their summer vacations with us, arriving in sleek sedans and wood-paneled station wagons, cars with fancy add-ons: a roof rack, a beaded driver's seat, even a knob on the steering wheel for turning corners one-handed.

With their gussied-up cars, our relatives appeared to have

more money than they knew what to do with. For the life of me, I couldn't understand why they wanted to spend two weeks on our farm when they lived close to the beach and minutes from parks populated with parrots and palm trees.

If they longed for peace and quiet, our farm wasn't the place—what with roosters crowing, hens clucking, pigs oinking, cows lowing, and us yelling, "Whoop-piggy!" to the hogs, and "Coh-anch!" to the cows at feeding time.

"What does Coh-anch mean?" Cousin Garfield asked one day as I called to the cows.

"I don't know," I said, "But the cows know. See 'em coming?"

Often, our relatives' visits overlapped. Before one family left, another arrived. How Mama felt about all the cooking, cleaning, and washing she had to do with nonstop company, I don't know, but she never complained. As for Daddy, his dark eyes lit up the minute anybody arrived. He'd tell joke after joke to the adults and play tricks on all the kids—all the visiting kids, that is. And when Daddy concentrated his attention on my cousins, I resented them.

One night, adults occupied every comfortable seat in our house, so, as Daddy played tricks on our cousins, I backed up against the wall, slid my back down it, and plopped on the floor.

"That's a rooster, that's a pullet, and that's a hen," he said to Cousin Clarice—who was Anetha's age—as he pointed to her forehead, nose, and chin. Then, pointing back at her nose, he asked, "Now, what'd I call that?"

"Pullet!"

Daddy obliged, pulling her nose. She wriggled away, giggling.

"I got your nose again," Daddy said as he pinched her nose a second time and held up his fist so it looked as if he had her nose trapped between his fingers. Clarice got hold of Daddy's hand with both of hers and pried his fingers apart, only to find his thumb pretending to be her nose.

"If I lived up there and you lived down here," he said, pointing to

Garfield's forehead and then his chin, "would you come up to see me?" Garfield had started to nod his head when Daddy zipped his finger back up, bumping Garfield's nose hard on the way. Garfield grinned, but then backed away from his Uncle C.G. and sat on the floor right next to me. With that, Garfield became my favorite cousin. We compared the size of our feet and hands and found them to be the exact same size.

Outside, it was pitch dark, and I soon got sleepy, but with a house full of company, nobody went to bed until everybody did. Bedtime could be very, very late. As late as *ten o'clock*. I wished Mama would hurry and spread quilt pallets on the floor so I could go to sleep.

"If anybody else shows up tonight," Daddy said, "we'll have to hang 'em up on nails." I pictured people suspended by the backs of their collars, their bodies and limbs dangling, even though I was pretty sure Daddy was joking. After all, the four nails in our walls were taken. The two zinc washtubs hung on the two nails in the open hall. A picture calendar hung on the nail above my head. And the last nail held a portrait-like photograph of Daddy's family, all dressed up. Daddy's father looked especially dapper in a three-piece suit, his dark hair neatly parted.

I knew Grandfather Howell only from this picture. He ended up dead from heart trouble when Daddy was eight years old. But in my eyes, this mysterious man behind glass—dark hair, a faint smile, an intent gaze, all dressed up in a suit—was the handsomest man I'd ever seen. I liked the way he posed for the camera, one hand dangling casually off the arm of his chair.

"I'm gonna marry a man like Granddaddy Howell," I'd say to anybody who'd listen. Then I'd lower my chin and demonstrate the deep, hearty laugh I imagined my husband would have. But nobody paid me a bit of mind, especially when the house was full of company. Consequently, I sometimes felt just as happy to see our guests go as I did to see them drive up. Mama may have felt the same way. Yet no matter who visited, how long they stayed, how much food she cooked, and how much laundry she had to do, she always smiled and said as they packed up to leave, "I wish y'all could stay longer. My goodness, it seems like you just got here."

From Mama, I learned about Southern hospitality. Never once did I leap for joy when our summer company packed suitcases and loaded them onto roof racks or into the trunks of their fancy vehicles. I wouldn't do that—until the dust on the lane obscured the back ends of their cars.

4

Smarty Pants

Proud to be getting ready all by myself on washday Monday, I pulled my pink sundress over my head and down. Then I stepped out of my britches and tossed the homemade underwear into the dirty clothes pile in the closet. *Ahhh . . . better. Why wear those ol' stiff and scratchy britches? Who would know?* I was now ready to go to Grandma's.

Mama washed clothes every Monday, just as Grandma Rye did, yet Mama usually walked us kids to Grandma's on Monday so we could help there. I was glad Mama was generous that way because Grandma had three washtubs of cool water in which we could play—I mean—rinse clothes. She also had one of those newfangled wringer washers, a Speed Queen that Granddaddy Rye had bought for her. Grandma let him make all the big decisions like that, knowing he believed in buying only the top of the line. "You get what you pay for," he often said.

After breakfast, I walked with Mama, Patsy, Anetha, and our dog Tommy up the rutted road toward our grandparents' place, which Mama referred to as the *homestead*. As usual, Tommy scouted the path ahead for snakes.

Mama's grandparents, Granddaddy Tip and Granny Dosia, had

lived in a log house on that homestead, beginning in the 1800s. But in 1944, the year I was born, the log house was torn down, and in its place, Granddaddy and Grandma Rye built a new house the four of them now shared.

About halfway to their place, the red-orange sun nudged itself over the horizon of Granddaddy's corn-field and peeped through golden tassels of cornstalks.

"Susanette, don't stare at the sun," Mama scolded. "I've warned you about that. The sun can blind you."

I liked looking at the sun when it first appeared, a glow about the size of a nickel, a nickel that would buy a Co-Cola for somebody who

Granny Dosia and me on the porch of my grandparents' new house

liked it. As for me, I couldn't understand how anybody could drink that fizzy stuff, the way it burned your throat as it went down. Granddaddy Rye called it *Coke*. According to him, the drink con-tained a drug by that name. Yet Mama and Daddy let Patsy and Anetha order Co-Cola at the drugstore soda fountain nearly every time we went to Live Oak. Each time the lady behind the counter asked for my order, I'd say, "Water." Mama always followed up, say-ing, "She's finicky," as if ordering water needed some explanation.

The sun floated higher in the sky that washday morning and gradually shrank to the size of a dime, a dime that would buy a Sugar Daddy for anybody who liked caramel on a stick—and, boy, I did! Every time Granddaddy Tip gave me a dime, I bought a Sugar Daddy off the rolling store that came by our house.

As soon as the rolling-store man opened up the side of his truck, I looked for a yellow wrapper with red letters. He had other candies too—Mary Janes, Mounds bars, Almond Joys, and Baby Ruths. I'd tried and liked all of them except the Baby Ruth. Daddy offered me a bite of his once, but it looked like something that starts with a *T* and rhymes with *bird*, so I didn't even want a nibble.

If I licked a Sugar Daddy slowly, I could make it last all day. My sisters also liked Sugar Daddies, but they licked theirs too fast. After finishing theirs, they'd try to sweet talk me into letting them lick mine. If I refused, they called me *Stingy*.

As we neared our grandparents' house, I spotted Granddaddy Tip, his hair white as sugar. He sat in his high-backed cane rocker on the front porch, his crooked-stem pipe dangling from his lips.

Patsy reached the swinging wooden gate first and pushed it open. Tommy dodged through ahead of her, gave a single bark, as if to say *Hello* to Granddaddy Tip, and lay down in the shade of the porch. Tommy's pink tongue dripped slobber as he hassled (our word for panted). Tommy sounded like he was saying, "hass-uh, hass-uh, hass-uh." The rest of us bounded up the steps and hollered, "Hey, Granddaddy Tip!" He was hard of hearing.

I stood by his rocker long enough for him to pat the curls on top of my head. He liked me best. I knew that because he sang to me when I sat in his lap. He never sang to my sisters. Never mind that they considered themselves too grown up to sit in his lap.

Just as the screen door closed behind Anetha, I opened it again. We all greeted Granny Dosia, who sat in a small rocker in the living room, her thinning gray hair pulled back into a tiny bun. Her crutch leaned against the wall. Old, wrinkled, and crippled, Granny Dosia seldom moved except to place a pinch of snuff inside her lower lip. Or spit.

We heard Grandma Rye rattling dishes in the kitchen, so we traipsed on through the house to find her.

"Hey, Mama, I brought the girls," Mama said to Grandma, who had her hands in the kitchen sink and her back to us. "I'll head on back home and get my wash started before it gets real hot."

"Okay, honey," Grandma said as she wiped her hands on a

muslin towel and then turned to us, "Hey, young'uns. We'll go out to the washhouse in a jiffy. Let me put on another apron. I spattered bacon grease all over this one."

As Mama went back through the house and said bye to Granny Dosia and Granddaddy Tip, Grandma Rye took a fresh apron from a kitchen drawer and unfolded it. My sisters and I waited in the hall between her and the back door. Grandma pulled the apron sashes behind her back, cinching them tight. The waistband disappeared under her big bosom. I watched as she twisted and looped the sashes this way and that, but I got lost in the loops. I had not mastered a bow of any kind, much less tying one behind my back.

Grandma's apron was as essential to her as the dress she wore. Only once did I see her wearing pants—after she'd helped Granddaddy Rye hoe the tobacco patch. She returned from the field covered in dust. All other times, she wore dresses, and she always smelled sweet as talcum powder.

When people said I was the "spittin' image" of her, I swelled with pride. We both had naturally curly hair, though mine was brown and hers was salt and pepper. If you faced her, you might think her hair was short, like mine. But when she turned, you could see that its length had been twirled 'round and 'round and pinned to the back of her head. "Papa never let me have my hair cut," she said. At night, when she sat down and removed bobby pins, wavy strands pooled in her lap.

My sisters had long hair too, and theirs was straight as a board—except right after Mama took their braids out. How I coveted long hair, but Mama wouldn't hear of it. "Length pulls the natural curl out,"

Left to right: Me, Patsy, and Anetha

she said. That made no sense to me since Grandma had long hair and hers still had curl, or at least waves. But I knew better than to argue with Mama.

Before my hair grew long enough to even touch my shoulders, Mama would get one of Daddy's old razor blades and whack away. That dull blade pulled like crazy. I'd scrunch up my shoulders, which seemed to help until she started cutting near my temples. Then, I'd squint my eyelids shut to hold back tears. "Be still now, and sit up," she'd say, "or I'll mess up." Tears always popped from my eyes no matter how hard I tried to hold them back. "I'm sorry, honey," she said, then. "I know. You're tender-headed like your grandma."

"Okay, girls," Grandma said now as she tucked a hankie into her apron pocket. "You can go on ahead to the washhouse. I'll get the pan of starch from the refrigerator."

Patsy and Anetha pushed open the back screened door and jumped over the three board steps to the ground. I stayed behind and held Grandma's free hand as we took the far-apart steps, one at a time. My sisters raced around the corner of the house to the gate that led into a field of Bahia grass and the washhouse. After Grandma and I went through the open gate, she ducked to avoid running her face smack-dab into the clothesline. As the two of us waded through the tall grass, Patsy and Anetha tagged the washhouse as if to say "we beat y'all." They now ran in circles.

The exterior of the washhouse was covered with a green tar-paper-like material that felt rough, as if it had been coated with coarse sand or dry grits before it was painted. Granddaddy had built the square-shaped building. It had a peaked tin roof and two small windows on opposite sides.

Grandma pushed in the washhouse door and stepped up onto the slab floor. Sun lit up the raw wood walls.

I wanted to run and play with my sisters, but I hated the tall Bahia grass, wet with morning dew. Its tall stems, which reached my waist, sprouted *V*-shaped tassels of seeds with black, linty fibers that latched on like fleas to anything that came near. After the short walk to the washhouse, the fibers were making me itch.

"Give me a few minutes to get everything ready, girls," Grandma said. "Then you can stick the hose through the window and turn on the water."

"Yes, ma'am," we said, and I plopped down in the doorway on the slab floor, letting my legs dangle. The gray concrete felt cool against bare skin. My toes barely brushed the sand of the foot-worn path. Patsy and Anetha ran here and there, jumping in the grass, their pigtails flying. I envied them, their hair long enough to braid. And I envied their togetherness, their oldness, their lean-ness. The sun's rays bounced off their heads like angels' halos.

Anetha was on the skinny side, so Granddaddy Rye called her *Runt.* He nicknamed lots of people. He called Mama *Mutt*—why, I don't know—and me *Grunt* because he said I grunted like a pig when I squatted. It didn't hurt my feelings too much. After all, Grandma Rye—also on the plump side—grunted each time she picked me up, just before she said, "You're like a chunk of lead."

Mama said I'd always been chubby, and she often told people a story about how I loved sugar.

"Susanette was just a toddler, hardly walking," she said, "when I left her in the front room one day while I went to the kitchen for a couple of minutes. When I came back, I found her sitting in her little chair in the middle of the dining table with the sugar bowl in her lap, eating the sugar with the spoon I kept in the sugar bowl. How she got herself and that little chair up on top of that

The sugar bowl on our table. Grand-daddy Rye gave it to Grandma on their first wedding anniversary in 1917. Grandma gave it to Mama on her and Daddy's first anniversary in 1941. (Hand-painted Nippon)

20

table, I don't know, but she did love sugar."

Maybe I was eating sugar because people were always taking mine. My grandparents and even aunts and uncles who visited often grabbed me and kissed me on the neck, saying, "I'm gonna get all your sugar." I didn't care for all that kissy, kissy stuff. But I didn't mind when my sisters took my chubby hands in theirs, rubbed and patted them, and said, "Ain't her skin soft?" as they pointed to the dimples in the backs of my hands. I can't deny I enjoyed their attention, but what I wanted more was to be their buddy, not their baby.

The popping of the tin roof above the cobwebbed rafters of the washhouse announced the day was getting hot. I watched my sisters from the doorway as they leapt over one another like frogs. Then Patsy ran around in a figure eight and Anetha followed. From my low vantage point and with the sun behind them, they resembled the two silhouettes on Grandma's living-room wall of a lady with a ruffled bonnet and a top-hatted gentleman. Of course, Patsy and Anetha, being girls, wore nothing on their heads except braids. As the two of them cartwheeled closer, their unbleached muslin britches looked stark white next to their summer-tanned legs that were coated with Bahia grass fibers.

Meanwhile, my own legs itched like crazy. And the more I scratched, the more they itched. *Before we poke the garden hose through the window to fill the washtubs,* I thought, *I'll wash the itchy things off.* I would, of course, have to borrow the hose from Patsy. Being the oldest, Patsy always acted like she owned the hose. Actually, Patsy thought she owned everything.

I wished Grandma would hurry up and tell us, "Turn on the spigot." The water would feel cool on my legs—cold even, since the electric pump in the other room of the washhouse drew water directly from underground. Daddy said it came from "freshwater springs that flowed beneath beds of limestone." I liked the sound of that and wished I could see underground.

Hurry was evidently a word Grandma never learned in her eight years at Ladyland, the same school Mama attended, and the school Patsy would soon go to. I looked over my shoulder to check Grandma's progress. She raised a side window and propped it up with a stick. The other window already had a prop under it, but Grandma was far from ready. She still had to turn the three zinc washtubs upright from their drain-dry positions. They rested on wooden stands near the washer.

How could my sisters be so oblivious to the itchy Bahia grass fibers when I itched like I had poison ivy? I decided I couldn't wait for the water hose. The dew on my legs had dried, so I stood up to brush the fibers off with my hand. I brushed my legs, ankles—and was brushing my feet when I heard Anetha whisper to Patsy, "Susanette ain't wearin' britches."

I heard the words as if she'd shouted. Then Patsy sang out louder, "Susanette forgot her bri-i-i-itches!"

My sisters' fingers pointed at my bare bottom. I bolted upright and balled my hands into fists. But it would be two against one, and they were stronger. So I clamped my hands to the hem of my dress and yanked it down. When I looked back at my sisters, their halos had vanished. Embarrassed by my sisters, I was crying by the time I heard Grandma say, "Here, sweetie, put your foot in." She held a pair of underpants low enough for me to step into them. I poked one foot in, then the other.

I think I would have gotten away with my cool attire that day if I'd remembered not to bend over. Or if I didn't have such smarty-pants sisters.

5

Simple as That

How or why Grandma had such nice underpants for me to wear that washday, I didn't ask, but I wished all my britches felt like that, soft and kind of stretchy, with white elastic that went around my waist. And no safety pins.

My regular britches, muslin hand-me-downs Mama had made for my sisters, featured a front waistband that came to a point near my belly button, casing around the back that held a strip of black rubber, and two annoying safety pins on each side of my waist.

According to Mama, store-bought elastic couldn't be found during the war. So, Mama had made do by cutting rubber strips off an old tire's inner tube, leftover from Daddy's Model A, a car he no longer owned. He'd sold it for a hundred dollars when I was still a baby because he wanted to use the money to buy a tractor after his plow horse died.

Mama's make-do elastic was about as stretchy as store-bought white. But if she left the black rubber inside the casing of our britches when she boiled them in the washpot on washday, she said it stained the white muslin. Mama remedied that, though, by securing the rubber at each side, temporarily, with safety pins. On washday, she took the rubber out before washing the britches.

Before we wore the britches again, she rethreaded the rubber strip through the casing and re-pinned it at each side. Simple as that.

The steel safety pins and the black rubber that stuck out of the casing didn't seem to bother my sisters, but I constantly had to adjust my britches so the pins and rubber would chafe a different spot.

Happy to be wearing softer underpants, I helped Grandma turn the three washtubs upright on their wooden supports, pedestals Granddaddy had built to make washday easier on Grandma's scoliosis-curved back.

Granddaddy had Grandma on a pedestal too. Instead of calling her Delma, he called her *Shug*, short for Sugar. Although I never heard him tell Grandma he loved her, his sweet name for her and the things he built for her, plus the way his sky-blue eyes looked at her, gave his secret away.

"Okay, girls, turn the water on," Grandma called to Patsy and Anetha, who were still running around outside.

"Wait, 'Netha!" Patsy snapped, abbreviating Anetha's name. "Don't turn on the spigot till I tell you!"

Patsy stuck the nozzle end of the hose through the open window to me. I held it over the washing machine, and Patsy gave Anetha the go ahead, "Turn the water on."

As the water flowed, my sisters ran inside, and Patsy reached for the box of Cheer that sat on a shelf in the corner.

"It's my turn to pour the soap," Anetha protested.

"Patsy, why don't you sort the clothes today?" Grandma asked. "Remember, according to color—whites, lights, and darks."

As Anetha sprinkled the powder into the washer, clouds of suds formed. With the washer now about two-thirds full, Grandma told me to move the hose to the rinse tubs and fill them.

As soon as Patsy finished sorting the clothes, each of us jumped into a pile.

"Okay, let's put the whites in first," Grandma said, pulling a couple of white towels from under me. I rolled off the pile and jumped up to watch her push them into the suds.

With Grandma's help, Patsy poured a cup of Clorox into one of the rinse tubs and stood beside it. Anetha and I always had to look around for something to stand on next to our tubs. When Granddaddy built the platforms the proper height for his *Shug*, he didn't stop to think that they might be too high for his granddaughters. Anetha turned an enamel milk bucket upside down, and I dragged over the pale-green milking stool. We needed our shoulders to be at least level with the rim of the tub so we could *wrench*—our word for *rinse*—the soap out of the clothes. *Wrenching* was my favorite washday chore. Swirling my arms in the tubs of cool water felt nearly as refreshing as wading in Running Springs on the Suwannee River.

After the whites churned awhile, Grandma stopped the machine and pressed a lever to rotate the wringer arm into position to feed the whites through the rubber rollers and into Patsy's tub of bleach water. Starting with a dish towel, Grandma overlapped one item over the tail-end of another until she had a string of whites moving through the rollers and into Patsy's tub. As streams of soapy water ran back into the washing machine, a little splashed on the floor and formed rivulets toward the drain hole in the concrete floor.

"Can I feed some in?" Patsy asked.

"Remember that little girl Mary I told y'all about?" Grandma asked, but she continued feeding—handkerchiefs, washrags, towels, pillowcases—as she proceeded to tell us a story we'd heard many times.

"Little Mary was helping her mama wash clothes," Grandma said, "and when she fed a shirt into the rollers, she forgot to turn it a-loose quick enough. That wringer got hold of Mary's little fingers, and before her mama could stop that thing, the rollers pulled Mary's arm in all the way up to her armpit."

Every time Grandma repeated that story, I imagined little Mary's arm, black and blue, and flat and floppy like the long sleeves of Granddaddy's shirts as they emerged from the wringer rollers. The first time I heard Grandma's story, I pictured the little girl as Mary George, who lived nearby. She was just a few years older than Patsy. The next time I saw her, I checked out her arm, first thing. To my surprise, it appeared normal.

Grandma added another load to the washer, repositioned the wringer head, and transferred whites from Patsy's bleach tub through the wringer into Anetha's tub, and then into mine.

I reached down deep and swirled the cool water, sloshing it to my shoulders. *Wrench and slosh. Wrench and splash.* Waves surfed over the rim of the tub, wetting my dress and dripping to the floor. I looked up at Grandma, afraid she might scold me, but she didn't even raise an eyebrow.

After letting me rinse for a few minutes, she repositioned the wringer so each flattened piece fell into a bushel basket on the floor. Before long, my tub held no clothes and the basket overflowed.

"I got this side," Anetha said as she jumped from her bucket and grabbed one of the basket's wire handles.

"And I got the other," I said as I got down off my stool.

"Hold on just a minute," Grandma said. "Some of those things need starch."

She fished around in the basket and pulled out a few pieces, dipped them in the pan of homemade liquid starch, wrung them out with her hands, and tossed them back into the basket.

"That basket's too heavy for you," Patsy said, pushing me aside.

Off my big sisters went, out the door of the washhouse, half carrying, half dragging the basket of wet clothes. I waited for Grandma, who reached for her wide-brimmed straw hat that hung on a nail on the back wall. She tied the hat's string under her chin and leaned over and whispered, "Fair skin is the sign of a lady. We'll have to get you a hat."

Ha! Ha! Ha! I knew something my sisters didn't.

"Let's not hang the clothes on that end, sweetie." Grandma called to Anetha, who was hanging a pillowcase under the mulberry tree that towered over the east end of the clothesline. "Birds perch on the limbs up there and eat the berries," Grandma said. "We'd end up with purple drops on the clean clothes." Grandma meant purple poop, but such an unladylike word would never escape her lips.

"And don't forget," Grandma added. "Use one clothespin to attach two things together on the wire. We don't want to run out of clothespins or clothesline and have to drape clothes over the rail fence yonder."

The use of a fence for drying laundry was a common practice in our community, but Grandma frowned upon it. She never spelled out the reason, but I thought I knew: she didn't want passersby to get an up-close look at her underwear, just like I didn't like visitors seeing the cot mattress atop our fence.

I tried to help hang clothes, but the clothesline was above my head and Grandma's spring-type wooden clothespins would not cooperate. Squeezing and clipping them while I held the wet clothing was like rubbing the top of my head and patting my stomach at the same time—something Daddy could do, but I could not. So I handed clothes to Grandma to hang. When the basket was empty, the four of us crowded together, all hands on the pole (attached to the wire at the top with a bent nail), and hoisted the clothesline up so high the wet laundry no longer touched the Bahia grass.

Back in the washhouse, we continued with other loads, and by noon, all the laundry hung on the line. Grandma drained the washing machine and dipped water from the rinse tubs to clean the soap out of the washer, leaving the rest of the rinse water in the tubs. She knew Granddaddy would dump them when he came in from the field to eat dinner.

Sure enough, the tubs were in their drain-dry positions when we returned to the washhouse midafternoon, carrying armloads of sun-and-wind-dried laundry we'd taken off the line. Grandma set up her ironing board—one Granddaddy had built and attached to the washhouse wall with a giant hinge. Grandma simply twisted a small, whittled stick that released the board. Upon its padded surface, she set her electric iron, an appliance Mama didn't own.

"Can I iron?" Patsy asked.

"I'm afraid you'll get burned, honey." That's the way Grandma said no.

While Grandma ironed slowly and carefully—the same way she did most things—we sisters folded kitchen and bathroom towels and washrags. We also took turns with the sprinkling bottle to dampen handkerchiefs and embroidered pillowcases, as well as a few starched, crocheted doilies.

With Grandma still ironing and us with no job, we looked for something to do. The week before, we'd plundered through an old trunk that sat in one corner of the washhouse. All it contained were old papers and pictures of people we didn't know. So Patsy took the jar of buttons off the corner shelf and poured them on the floor.

"Grandma, we need some twine and scissors," Patsy said, after we'd chosen a big, heavy button.

Grandma stopped ironing long enough to get what we needed to make our button buzz, a trick Mama had taught us. We'd done it so many times we knew the directions by heart.

HOW TO MAKE A BUTTON BUZZ

Items needed
- Button—large; heavy; flat; with two holes; glass or pearl (plastic is too lightweight)
- Ball of twine
- Scissors

Instructions
1. Cut a piece of twine about a yard long.
2. Thread the ends of the twine through two holes of the button, and tie the ends in a knot.
3. Move the button along the twine to form equal loops on each side of the button.
4. Adjust so the knot is at the end of one loop.

5. Palms facing, slip your middle fingers through the loops on each side.
6. Pull hands apart enough that the string forms a *V*, thanks to the button's weight.
7. Now, wind the thing up. Pretend it's a jump rope, and make it go over and over.

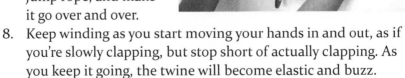

8. Keep winding as you start moving your hands in and out, as if you're slowly clapping, but stop short of actually clapping. As you keep it going, the twine will become elastic and buzz.
9. If you can't hear it buzzing, put your ear closer—but keep your hair clear, especially if it's long. (If you get it caught in the twisted twine, you'll never get it out by yanking it, so get the scissors and cut it loose.)

6

Red Devil Lye

My sisters and I occasionally stayed home on washday, but Mama never wanted our help, at least not until it was time to hang clothes on the line. I had no problem with that since, unlike Grandma's setup, ours included no washhouse, no hose, no wringer washer, and no rinse tubs on stands. Mama washed our clothes in an iron washpot in the backyard. Her other equipment included a scrub board and her two zinc washtubs, one for bleach water, one for plain water.

On washday, Mama set the tubs on the ground next to the iron washpot, which stayed put from one washday to the next. She filled the pot and tubs with buckets of water she toted from the hand pump near the back steps. Sometimes she got lucky, and rain partially filled the iron washpot before washday. If the weather turned really cold, the water in the pot might freeze, but the ice would melt as soon as Mama got a fire going under it. The fire was necessary, she said, to melt the lye soap—bars she made from lard once a year, after hog-killing day, using Granny Dosia's recipe.

In addition to melting the lye soap and any ice in the pot, the fire kept Mama warm when winter winds howled across the field behind our house. I guess the fire had the same warming effect, though, in the hot summertime when Mama was already sweating and didn't need any extra warmth.

After boiling the dirty clothes and linens in the pot, Mama took them out with a broomstick, one item at a time, to see if they had come clean. If not, she put them on the scrub board and rubbed and rubbed till the stain completely disappeared.

"Some women beat their clothes with a stick to get them clean," Mama said, "but that's just a good way to break buttons."

After washing and rinsing the clothes, Mama wrung them out with her hands. Like Grandma Rye, she also dipped a few pieces—Daddy's dress shirts, dresser scarves, and pillowcases—in starch, which she mixed up fresh each washday. While cooking breakfast, she added a handful of

> ### Lye Soap Recipe
> 1 gallon cracklins (saved from hog-killing day)
> 1 quart water
> 1 can lye (Red Devil brand)
>
> Put cracklins, water, and lye in heated washpot, with not too much fire under the pot. Start cooking it slow, and cook it until the lye eats all the cracklins. The lye will eat up every bit of fat, as well as the rind, but it won't eat a bit of the lean meat. So, if there's any lean meat left, scoop it out and throw it away. Then douse the fire under the pot and let the mixture cool. As it hardens, the soap will shrink away from the sides of the pot. Cut it into bars for body soap, or break it into chunks for washing clothes.

starch powder to a pot of cold water, boiled it, and then added more cold water to cool it. Grandma stored her starch from one washday to the next in her refrigerator, but Mama couldn't do that since we didn't own a refrigerator, and she said starch would spoil like fresh milk without refrigeration.

"Girls, y'all can come give me a hand, now," Mama called after she had a bucket of clothes ready for us to hang on the clothesline. This job at home was easier than at Grandma's, thanks to the design of our clothespins, made of shiny aluminum, stamped "Gillespie Engineering Company, Hadley, Texas." Just a gentle push attached them to the wire.

One problem arose at home that didn't occur at Grandma's, though. Her clothesline had grass growing underneath it, but nothing grew under ours since Mama always insisted that we pull up any grass or weed that sprouted in our sandy yard. As much as I hated the tall Bahia grass around Grandma's washhouse and clothesline, especially when it was wet with morning dew, the grass did keep sand off clothes when we accidentally dropped them.

Washday at home dragged on longer than it did at Grandma's. The day was usually shot by the time our laundry dried, so Mama waited until Tuesday to iron. She let us sprinkle the clothes, after which she'd set up her padded ironing board near the hearth or by the open window, depending on the season. If we had a fire going in the fireplace, she heated two flatirons there. Otherwise, she fired up the oil stove in the kitchen to heat them.

The iron handle of a flatiron got about as hot as the soleplate, so she gripped the handle with a pot holder. As she ironed, she put so much of her own weight on the iron that I half expected the board to crash to the floor. It would squeak and creak in protest, but it never collapsed. When one iron cooled to the point that no steam rose from the damp fabric, she returned the iron to the heat and grabbed the hotter one.

Mama evidently enjoyed ironing. I noticed that she always hummed church songs when she ironed. She did the same when she sat at her Singer sewing machine, which means she hummed a lot because she sewed everything my sisters and I wore. The minute she pinned tissue pattern to cloth, she began to hum. She stopped only when she needed to pin an outfit on one of us to see how deep to take in the seams.

"Can I go look in the mirror?" I asked each time she pinned a half-made dress on me. The only mirror in the house was in the bedroom above her vanity.

"Okay, but hurry back."

Mama didn't understand that it took quite awhile to look at a new outfit from every angle. "Come on back over here," she'd say when I took too long. "I want to stitch it up." But Mama didn't just "stitch up" anything. When sewing checks, stripes, and plaids, she pinned, basted, and machine stitched the cloth so every little line or check matched perfectly. Nearly everything she made had some special detail—lace, rickrack, piping, ruffles, a Peter Pan collar, puffy sleeves, a tiered skirt, a wide sash, or embroidery— like the small flowers she hand-stitched on the front

Anetha (left), Patsy (standing), and me

of the pastel dresses we wore for our one-and-only studio photograph.

I hoped to create pretty things the way Mama did when I grew up and got married. But I hoped to do laundry like Grandma, in a washhouse equipped with a wringer washing machine and an electric iron.

MAMA'S LAUNDRY ROUTINE (1940s)

1. Make starch: stir a handful of powdered starch into a pan of cold water; bring to a boil; stir until thickened.
2. Sort the clothes and linens: whites, light-colored items, and dark and dirtiest.
3. Tote water to the iron washpot in backyard; fill two-thirds full.
4. Build a fire under the washpot to bring the water to boiling.
5. Shave a cake of lye soap into the boiling water.
6. Set two zinc tubs on the ground; place them so smoke won't blow in your eyes when rinsing the clothes. Tote water to fill tubs.
7. Add whites to the boiling water. Stir with a broomstick handle.
8. For the really dirty items, take them out, one at a time, and scrub hard on a washboard. (Don't beat them though; you don't want to break any buttons.)
9. If they're still dirty, put them back into the pot to boil some more.
10. After the whites are clean, bleach them to whiten, then rinse and starch the ones that need it.
11. Add the next pile of clothes to the boiling water.
12. Wring the rinsed clothes with your hands, hang them on the clothes wire, and prop it up, high off the ground.
13. Go back and start scrubbing the next load.
14. When all the batches of clothes are on the line, snuff the fire, and wait for the washpot to cool before emptying. Empty the zinc tubs, and turn them upside down to drain.
15. Pray it doesn't rain before the clothes dry.

7

Electricity

Thunder rumbled in the distance and raindrops tapped the tin roof overhead as dusk turned to dark. Daddy tugged the string that turned on the dangling light bulb above the dining table, then closed the wooden shutter by the smutty fireplace. He didn't bother with the glass windows on the front of the house. They could stay open since the front porch roof would keep the rain out.

Mama stood at the stove, scrambling eggs to go with heated-up pork 'n' beans for supper, one of my favorites. As we sat down to eat, the wind picked up, cooling off the room.

"God is great, God is good, let us thank Him for this food. Amen," Anetha said. It was her turn.

Amen barely escaped her lips before Daddy said, "Man! We need this rain. I hope we get more than a sprinkle."

"Me too," Mama said as a bolt of lightning lit up the room like daylight. Then the room went pitch dark.

"I'm scared," I said.

"Nothing to be afraid of," Daddy said. "The wind probably blew a tree limb across a power line."

"I'll light the lamp," Mama said. Her chair creaked as she pushed it back. Rain pelted the roof, muffling the sound of her shoes as she slid them across the linoleum floor, feeling her way to the oil lamp that sat on the buffet. Finally, a match strike lit up her silhouette. She lifted the glass chimney, lit the wick, put the fragile chimney back in place, and turned the brass screw that shortened the wick and reduced the smoke and flame.

"We probably won't get the current back on till tomorrow," Daddy said, as Mama set the lamp in the middle of the table. "But I'd rather have a good rain than lights."

I'd rather have lights, I thought. I could hardly see the food on my plate by that dim oil lamp. Others in the family sometimes talked about the days before electricity. Even Patsy and Anetha said they remembered when that oil lamp was the only light we had in the whole house. I thought I remembered too.

Getting electricity wasn't easy, Daddy said—not as simple as paying a deposit and having the current turned on. Daddy and Granddaddy Rye first applied for electricity in 1943, the year before I came into the world.

"We went and talked with a man at the REA [Rural Electric Administration] office in Live Oak," he said. "The man told us the REA couldn't justify erecting poles and running wires as far out as we lived unless we could convince most of the people in our community to sign up for service and pay the required deposits. Plus, with the war going on, the REA man told us, 'any new-service customers must *qualify*.'"

To qualify, farms had to pass inspection. Each farmer had to earn a certain number of points, based on what crops and livestock their farms produced. Daddy said the rules were similar to those for a farmer getting a deferment from the military because of goods he produced.

The U.S. Government's Rural Electrification Act of 1936 provided federal funding for installation of electrical distribution systems to serve rural areas, but even in the mid-forties, only about half of those in rural areas had electricity because power lines still did not extend there.
http://www.livinghistoryfarm.org

According to Daddy, Granddaddy Rye especially wanted electricity for his new house. "We went door to door," he said, "encouraging neighbors to sign up for electric power, pay their deposits, and agree to have their farms inspected. Nearly everybody in the Ladyland Community got on board, and after inspections, all of us who'd paid deposits qualified."

But Daddy and Granddaddy faced one more obstacle: the land for the power line had to be cleared.

"We got together with neighbors," Daddy said, "and cleared a strip of land through the woods, all the way from Hawley Touchton's place, about three miles north of us, down past us and about a half-mile farther to the Saunders's place on the river. Afterward, the REA paid us a small amount for our work."

Daddy said that Granddaddy got an electrician, Mr. Morgan, to wire his new house before it was completed in early 1944, and Mr. Morgan also wired our house. But power didn't get turned on until 1947, when I was two years old.

"The entire process of getting electric power," Daddy said, "from application to having the current turned on took about four years. By then of course, the war had ended."

I didn't know or understand much about the big war the adults talked about. But I knew Daddy never had to go off and fight, as many fathers did.

According to him, he'd joined the Florida National Guard while in high school. "I learned how to fight in the Guard," he said, "but when the war broke out, I got deferments because I was farming." He said the government recognized that "food produced by farmers was as essential for our nation's survival as ammunition manufactured to kill the enemy."

During the war, Daddy also served under the Suwannee County Agricultural Agent as the War Foods Administrator, and helped with the Victory Gardens program, part of the Agricultural Stabilization Program; the government wanted people to learn how to grow their own fruits and vegetables.

"To classify as a Victory Garden, which warranted a small payment from the government," Daddy said, "the garden had to include seven varieties." Daddy's job required him to go around and check to see if the gardens people planted met the requirements.

After the war ended, he continued working for the County Agent, but he then measured the acreage of field crops, such as tobacco, to ensure that farmers didn't exceed their government-allotted acreage.

"It was all about price control," he said. "If a farmer planted too much, the excess had to be destroyed, a practice started during the Depression."

> **Government Quotas**
> During the Great Depression, under President Roosevelt's New Deal program, the government paid farmers to farm less. Millions of acres of planted crops were plowed under and millions of young pigs were slaughtered to meet the government's subsidy guidelines. With many people out of work and some starving, some saw this as wasteful carnage. The Supreme Court declared the AAA and these practices unconstitutional in 1936, but the agency that replaced the AAA continued to set quotas on certain crops in an effort to regulate prices.
> http://www.ushistory.org/us/49c.asp

At times, we saw very little of Daddy because he stayed so busy with his measuring job and with farming. He even rigged his red Farmall tractor with car headlights, so he could work into the night. Plus, neighbors often asked him to go help them with something—with a tractor or some other piece of farm equipment that needed repair. He was a good mechanic. He was always coming home with grease under his fingernails. He often got grease on his clothes too, and Mama fussed at him about that, saying she wished he would remember to change into raggedy clothes before working on machinery. "Washing grease out of your clothes takes a lot of scrubbin'," she said.

Despite his many jobs and helping neighbors repair equipment, Daddy kept trying to improve things around our place.

The improvement that changed our lives took place during the summer of 1947, while Aunt Laura (Daddy's baby sister) and her husband were visiting.

8

Summer Surprise

Aunt Laura called her husband *Etchie*, which sounded like "Itchy" to us kids, so that's what we called him. For many years, Aunt Laura and Uncle Itchy had no children for my sisters and me to play with when they visited. But I always looked forward to their visits because they always brought us a surprise.

Uncle Itchy might bring playground equipment like a ball and bat or a dozen colorful T-shirts from the lost-and-found of the Miami Parks and Recreation Department where he worked. Other times, he brought kitchen equipment for Mama—items he'd purchased from a going-out-of-business restaurant. He once brought her a set of heavy platters with "Joe's Old Fashioned BBQ" written on the side, and best of all, a cooking pot big enough to boil a peck of peanuts at once.

Uncle Itchy was a big man and he always wore sunglasses—shades, he called them—even inside the house. He had dark curly hair and a tan, either from his Miami parks job or his heritage. He was Jewish, a fact that concerned some of our Baptist friends and relatives. I overheard more than one of them say that Jews would "burn in hell for crucifying our Savior"—which didn't seem right to me. I thought generous Uncle Itchy would have a better chance of getting into Heaven than some of them.

I don't remember what gifts Uncle Itchy brought us the summer of 1947, but I well remember what he left behind.

The morning after he and Aunt Laura arrived, we had just finished our usual breakfast of grits, bacon, eggs, and biscuits when Uncle Itchy said to Mama, "C.G. and I are going to run to town this morning."

After the men left in Uncle Itchy's wood-trimmed station wagon, my sisters and I helped Mama and Aunt Laura pick several buckets of tomatoes for canning.

We kids were outside playing hopscotch in the shade of the big oak tree east of the house, later, when the men returned from town. The station wagon was full of lumber and sheets of tin sticking out the back end. Uncle Itchy parked near our hopscotch drawing.

"Let's build the thing here in the shade," Uncle Itchy said to Daddy as they got out of the car. Daddy agreed.

"Y'all play somewhere else," Daddy said to us as they began to unload the car. And later, when he headed to the packhouse, he told us to stay out of our uncle's way.

I wondered what Uncle Itchy was up to. But we sisters obediently moved to the other side of the tree trunk.

Daddy returned with a saw and hammer, which he handed to Uncle Itchy before going back to the packhouse. Soon, the bang of the hammer echoed through the woods as our uncle nailed two-by-fours together.

"Whatcha building?" I asked enthusiastically a little later, for the structure was beginning to look as if it might be a playhouse.

My older sisters rolled their eyes and snickered as if I'd asked a stupid question.

"It's a surprise," Uncle Itchy said.

Aunt Laura came out every now and then and took pictures with her Brownie camera. Surprisingly, she took nary a one of us kids, as she usually did. Instead, she focused all her attention and the camera on her husband, and then Daddy, who was using post-hole diggers and a shovel to dig a hole behind our house, near the tobacco barn.

Hours later, Uncle Itchy yelled, "Laura! Ethel! . . . Come out here! I need to measure your *bee*-hinds."

At that moment, I recognized we were not getting a playhouse.

After measuring Mama's and Aunt Laura's backsides, Uncle Itchy built a bench seat into which he sawed two circular holes to match their rather wide dimensions. Behind each hole, he attached a square lid with hinges so it could be lowered to cover the big hole. And in each lid, he cut a smaller circular hole that approximated the size of a kid's bottom—though if my bottom was ever measured, I don't remember it.

To the top of the out-house, he nailed tin; and to the front, he attached a door with big hinges. After he cut diamond-shaped holes in each side for windows, he stopped sawing and went to investigate the hole Daddy was digging. We sisters followed.

Uncle Itchy, shirtless, building our out-house. Our home, seen from the side, is in the background.

The hole looked like it could be my grave.

"I built the outhouse on skids like we talked about," he said to Daddy. "So, when you're ready, we can chain it to your Farmall and drag it over and set it over the pit."

Within minutes, our new outdoor toilet sat over the deep pit, and everybody crowded inside the new outhouse to check it out.

I'd always known that some people had outdoor toilets. I'd used a few of them when we visited neighbors. And other people, like our Miami relatives and our grandparents, had indoor bathrooms.

We'd never had either. We'd always used a slop jar at night, and during the daytime, we had the whole outdoors. Over the years, I'd learned to look for dog fennels to break off and take with me when I had to go into the woods. Their soft, somewhat-sticky new growth worked much better for cleanup than just about anything else you could find in the woods.

Dog Fennel

While everybody in the family seemed to think our new outhouse was the best thing to happen since we got electricity, I wasn't so sure. Its diamond-shaped windows, no bigger than a folded napkin, let in little light and were too high for me to see out. And those kid-sized holes?—way too big for my butt. *What if I fell into that deep dark pit? Or what if a black widow spider lived down there and sat in wait to bite me?* One had bitten our neighbor, Mr. Herring, as he sat in his outhouse. He nearly died, so Grandma Rye said.

In the days that followed, I was expected to use the new outhouse just like everybody else. So when I had to go, I'd beg my older sisters to join me, having faith that they'd catch me if I started to fall through the hole. And if a black widow bit me, they'd be there to see me die.

Surprisingly, I never fell in, and a spider never bit me, so I gradually overcame my fear. In fact, as time went on, I became quite proud of our "facility" because it had features that set it apart from other privies in the community. The pit supposedly made it more sanitary, and ours had a toilet-paper dispenser, something I'd never seen in a neighbor's outhouse. Not that our paper dispenser stayed filled. Only when we expected company did Mama lay out the money for toilet paper. We never called it toilet "tissue," though it did feel similar to the tissue paper used inside fancy gift boxes—crinkled like it too, but it was softer than pages from our old *Sears and Roebuck* catalog. Or corncobs.

"We used red and white corncobs when I was a boy," Daddy said one day. I figured Daddy was just joking since he joked a lot and I'd never seen red-and-white cobs; ours were cream-colored.

"Why would a person visiting the outhouse need a white corncob if he already had two red ones?" Daddy continued. Everybody shook their heads, as if to say they hadn't a clue.

"He'd use the red one first," Daddy said. "Then he'd use a white one to see if he needed the other red one."

Daddy's joking never ended.

Most of our neighbors still had regular old outhouses without pits. And now, when I visited one of them, I couldn't help but notice the sound of the flies buzzing beneath the bench seat. The buzzing sometimes compelled me to look down the hole. The collection on the ground consisted of all shapes, sizes, and colors. For a little while, I wouldn't be able to tear myself away from the yucky scene and stench. Sometimes maggots worked alive in the mustardy-colored stuff. Not a pretty sight. But the iridescent-green tumblebugs that worked around the dried-up outer edges fascinated me. The bugs could form perfectly round balls of poop, more than twice their size, and roll them off, pushing forward with their front feet, then turning upside down and pushing with their back feet—never stopping to rest—and never giving up as they rolled them off, out of sight. *Where did they take them?*

When I asked Mama, she said they stored them up for their babies to eat when they emerged from eggs. Surely Mama was joking. But then again, Mama didn't joke like Daddy.

Our outhouse with the deep dark pit, of course, didn't permit tumblebug watching. But if I wanted, I could lie on my stomach in the cow pasture behind our house, up close to a cow paddy, resting my chin on my hands for hours at a time, watching tumblebugs roll off cow dung. Not that I'm saying I ever did that.

9

Granddaddy Tip Rocked

"Be careful, young'uns," our great-grandfather said, as my sisters and I bounded up the concrete steps—one, two, three, four, five. Mama went inside to find Grandma Rye. Patsy and Anetha followed, letting the screen door slam behind them. I stayed on the porch with Granddaddy Tip, who stopped rocking long enough for me to climb up and straddle his bony knees.

The sweet aroma of pipe tobacco enveloped me as I settled on his lap, facing him. I unbuttoned and re-buttoned, unbuttoned and re-buttoned his sweater.

My great-grandfather's attire never changed, winter to summer—a long-sleeved khaki shirt and matching trousers. Cream-colored long johns peeked out at his wrists and ankles. Over all that, he wore a wool cardigan—the same navy sweater, year-round—and kept it buttoned up, even when the temperature reached ninety-five degrees in the shade.

"Uncle Tip, you'd be more comfortable if you'd take off that dad-blamed sweater," Daddy told him one hot summer day. But Granddaddy Tip quickly set Daddy straight.

"Aye, God, Buddy, what'll keep out cold will keep out heat."

Everybody who knew him and my great-grandmother called

them *Uncle Tip* and *Aunt Dosia*, whether related or not. "Out of respect," Mama said. Daddy knew them long before he knew Mama, so he'd always called them Uncle Tip and Aunt Dosia.

Sitting in my great-grandfather's lap, I unbuttoned his sweater again and reached for the red tin of Prince Albert, sticking out of his khaki shirt pocket.

"We'll pack more tobacco in my pipe later," he said as he patted the tin in his pocket and tilted his pipe for me to see it was full.

I spied a hole in his sweater that wasn't a buttonhole. I poked a finger in, then two, but jerked my fingers out when I heard a vehicle. Down the road, dust boiled behind a dark-colored truck. Patsy and Anetha came running out of the house.

Seldom did a vehicle pass without stopping. Surprisingly, this truck didn't, but the driver slowed as he passed and hollered out the open window. "Howdy, Uncle Tip! Whatcha doin' today?"

"Aye, God, Buddy, not much. Just watching the world go by."

Aye, God, Buddy prefaced almost anything Granddaddy Tip said.

"Who was that?" I asked.

"One of the George boys."

From an early age, I recognized that Granddaddy Tip and Granny knew everybody, and everybody knew my great-grandparents—pillars of the Ladyland Community. They'd lived there longer than anybody. Now, they were very, very, very old. Mama said Granddaddy Tip was born during the Civil War—whenever that was.

Standing upright, he towered over every member of our family. But he seldom stood. His cane-backed rocker provided the perfect spot to watch the world go by. Rabbits scampering across the road. Bushy-tailed squirrels nibbling acorns and chasing each other. Sparrows flitting from branch to branch. Quails sprinting over fallen leaves. Red-headed woodpeckers tapping tree trunks. Doves pecking at the ground. Crows, cardinals, and blue jays squawking.

Suddenly a bird lit on the lawn and spread its wings over the St. Augustine grass.

"Look at that bird!" I said to Granddaddy Tip, pointing.

"Yeah, that's a mockingbird. They do that to scare up bugs to eat," he said.

"I knew *that*!" Patsy said.

He wasn't talking to you! I wanted to say. Why did Patsy have to know everything before I did?

I scooted down in my great-grandfather's lap, close enough to his chest that I could see my curls reflected in his eyes. He wore no glasses—didn't own any—and had no teeth, real or false. His sunken cheeks accentuated his angular features and French ancestry. Some family members claimed he was related to the Southern poet Sidney Lanier, an accomplished flutist. But Granddaddy Tip never boasted that. Besides, Mama said he was a musician in his own right.

"He used to play the fiddle at square dances," she said.

I never got to go to one of the square dances Mama raved about, and I never heard Granddaddy Tip play his fiddle, but I knew he could sing.

"Sing that song about me," I begged as I patted his chest, then gripped the arms of the rocker, so I wouldn't fall off once he got started. He began to rock, then patted the top of my head and tapped his feet as he sang—

> *Prettiest little girl in the county o,*
> *Mammy and Pappy both said so—*

I had no reason to question the words of my great-grandfather, the patriarch of our family. So as Granddaddy sang "Prettiest Little Girl in the County O," my chest puffed out like a chameleon's throat, making me forget about what had happened earlier that morning. I'd had another accident and Mama had made me rub my nose in it again.

In the middle of the song, though, Granddaddy Tip stopped.

"Young'uns, get down from there before you fall," he said to my sisters.

They stood on one of the four plinths, or bases, at the front edge of the porch. Each base held a square column that supported the porch roof. The ledge around each column wasn't quite as wide as their feet. If they slipped and fell off on one side, they'd land on the concrete floor. If they slipped off the other side, they'd land on the dirt, five or six feet below. A softer landing to be sure, but they might get scraped by the jagged rocks as they fell. River rocks formed the base of the porch. But my sisters paid Granddaddy Tip no mind. They just kept stepping around the narrow ledge.

"Young'uns! I said, 'Get down before you fall and get hurt!'"

Each of my sisters held onto the column with one arm and leaned out into the sunshine as if to say, *We don't have to do what you say.* Granddaddy Tip had never laid a hand on any of us.

"Hardheaded young'uns, cain't tell 'em a thang!" he said, and resumed my song from the beginning—

> *Prettiest little girl in the county o,*
> *Mammy and Pappy both said so.*
> *All dressed up in calico,*
> *Gwine take you to the party o.*
> *Cornstalk fiddle and pea vine bow,*
> *Gwine take you to the party o.*
> *Prettiest little girl in the county o,*
> *Mammy and Pappy both said so.*

10

White Lightning and Moss-Teasing Day

After Granddaddy Tip sang my favorite, "Prettiest Little Girl in the County O," he launched into his favorite, "Little Brown Jug." I never paid much attention to the words of that one until he began the chorus, "Ha, ha, ha . . . ." Then I joined in and sang, "Ha, ha, ha, you and me, little brown jug, *down hollow deep*." While singing, I imagined a brown jug rolling around on the bottom of the Suwannee River. I didn't know that the real words to "Little Brown Jug" had to do with loving alcohol. If I'd known, I would have been shocked, for Daddy said alcohol was against our religion. Or

> **Little Brown Jug**
>
> Me and my wife live all alone,
> in a log house we call our own;
> She loves gin and I love rum,
> and don't we have a lot of fun!
>
> *Chorus:*
> *Ha, ha, ha, you and me,*
> *little brown jug, don't I love thee!*
> *Ha, ha, ha, you and me,*
> *little brown jug, don't I love thee!*
>
> 'Tis you that makes me friends and foes,
> 'tis you that makes me wear old clothes;
> But, seeing you're so near my nose,
> tip her up and down she goes.
>
> *(Repeat Chorus)*
>
> I got a dog, he's a hound,
> Me, my wife, and a bobtailed dog,
> crossed a creek on a hollow log,
> The log, it broke, and we fell in,
> and little brown jug got filled again.
>
> *(Repeat Chorus)*

was it the other way around?

I also didn't know that my great-grandfather used to make his own white lightning from sugarcane skimmings—back when Mama was a little girl. Nor did I know (or care) that the "toddy" he drank at night was actually alcohol.

The drink that interested me, he drank at breakfast.

Since he was the patriarch of the family, Grandma Rye always set her father's place at the head of the table—the dining table, which she kept covered with a starched-and-ironed tablecloth. At each place setting, she set a blue willow plate and a matching cup and saucer.

Just before breakfast, instead of pouring steaming coffee into Granddaddy Tip's cup, as she did all the other cups, she filled his with steaming water from a stout metal kettle she kept on a back stove burner. After the blessing was said, Granddaddy Tip added to his cup of hot water a spoonful of sugar and fresh cow cream until the drink resembled white shoe polish. He then poured the concoction into his saucer, lifted it to his lips, blew on it, and slurped it down.

"Uncle Tip, why don't you drink coffee like everybody else?" Daddy asked one morning.

"Aye, God, Buddy, I wouldn't kiss a pretty girl that drinks coffee. It'll turn you black."

"Papa!" Grandma Rye scolded her father, "Coffee won't turn you black, and you know it. Don't say that. The girls will believe you, like Ethel did when she was little."

Mama had told us that story. At a very young age, she believed her grandfather, and she could hardly wait to pass the information on. She knew just the person she wanted to enlighten. She passed her newfound knowledge along on moss-teasing day.

When Mama first told us the story, we didn't know what "moss-teasing day" meant, so she explained.

"When I was a little girl," she said, "our mattresses were not stuffed with soft cotton like they are today. Granny Dosia sewed up our mattress covers and stuffed them with Spanish moss. Eventually, of course, the moss needed to be fluffed up—a process we called *teasing*."

Moss? Mama had told us not to mess with Spanish moss because redbugs lived in it and they would eat you up—leave welts that itched for two weeks or more.

As if reading my mind, Mama said, "Granny Dosia knew how to get rid of redbugs in the moss. After the menfolk gathered the moss from the trees with pitchforks and laid it across the rail fence, Granny poured scalding water on it—water she heated in the washpot.

"The hot water not only killed the redbugs," Mama continued, "it also caused the outer covering of the moss to slough off, leaving black, hair-like fibers. A mattress stuffed with moss fiber felt spongy and made less noise when you turned over in bed than a mattress stuffed with corn shucks. Lots of people back then slept on corn-shuck mattresses."

Knowing how corn shucks made a rustling sound when my sisters and I peeled them back to shell corn for the chickens, I could imagine the noise they made when you rolled over at night.

"After a few months, of course, our nice moss mattresses would flatten out," Mama said, "and then it was time to take the stuffing out of the ticking and tease it—fluff it up. Granny Dosia seldom had to do that herself, though. A group of colored women in the community would go around from time to time and offer to tease your beds. They didn't ask for cash. They'd do the job for whatever people could give them—lard, cracklins, a piece of meat, turnip greens or collards, sweet potatoes, cane syrup—anything."

After all the explaining, Mama got to the story.

"The women who'd come to help Granny sat in a circle in the shade of the oaks, talking and laughing as they teased

the moss—pulling it apart with their fingers. Late that afternoon, Granny Dosia went to the kitchen, a separate building from their log house. I followed and watched as she built a fire in the wood stove, ground some roasted coffee beans in her grinder, and poured the grounds into a pot of water she set on the stove. After the coffee boiled, she called to the moss teasers, telling them they could come to the kitchen and get themselves a cup of coffee.

"One of the colored women was Mandy Caldwell. She often helped Granny with other chores, and I had been taught to call her Aunt Mandy. She came to the kitchen first, and I was waiting.

"'Aunt Mandy,' I said the instant she stepped inside, 'that coffee is what turns you black.'

"Aunt Mandy doubled over in laughter as she slapped her thighs and said, 'Do, Jesus! Miss Dosia, listen at that child.'"

"Then what happened?" I asked.

"Aunt Mandy went right ahead and poured herself a full cup of that black coffee!"

I loved the stories Mama told about her childhood when she lived with Granddaddy Tip and Granny Dosia. Sometimes, I wished I lived with them too.

11

Dippin' Cows and Dippin' Snuff

Another story Mama told and retold always tickled me. Not because Mama got into trouble with her Daddy, but because of what Granny Dosia did. Mama said it happened on cow-dippin' day.

"I was playing outside with my little brother Harold, when I noticed blackberries getting ripe around Ladyland School, which had let out for the summer. At the time, we weren't living with my grandparents. We lived across the field from them, on the old Peak place, right next to Ladyland School. I thought we should pick the blackberries. So I went and got two buckets, one for me and one for my little brother.

"We had dropped quite a few berries into our buckets when I said to Harold, 'We should take these to Granny. Go to the house and ask Mama if we can.' We had never walked to our grandparents' house from the Peak place by ourselves, but from the front of the school, we could see their log house across the field. Harold set his bucket down and went back to the house. When he came back out, Harold said, 'Yeah, we can go.' But after we got about halfway across the field, Harold up and changed his mind. 'I want to go back home,' he said.

"'Come on and go with me,' I said. 'It ain't that far.' But Harold refused. So I poured his berries into my bucket, went partway back with him, and watched him go inside. Then I headed out again across the field. When I got close to my grandparents' yard, I heard popping. I looked back and saw my daddy on his horse, popping his braided cow whip in the air to drive the cows.

"Daddy was herding them toward Granny and Granddaddy Tip's house because it was cow-dippin' day, which meant "get rid of ticks" day.

"Back then, it was open range—cows roamed the woods where they picked up ticks. Ticks were a big problem. Now that cows are fenced in, we don't have that problem, so the government did away with the vats long ago."

The End of "Open Range"
In 1949, Florida Governor Fuller Warren approved Senate Bill No. 34, which required owners of livestock to prevent their animals from "running at large or straying upon public roads." Under its provisions, ranchers and farmers could be held liable for damage done to property or persons by free-roaming livestock.
http://floridamemory.com

"But back then on cow-dippin' day, Daddy always rounded up his cows, as well as Granddaddy Tip's herd, and drove them through the hammock, to and through the dippin' vat over near the Drew Railroad Bridge on the Suwannee River. The vat, a long runway of concrete, tapered down, then back up. The low area held treated water that stunk like creosote. When cows went through it, the chemicals in the water killed any ticks on them.

"Anyway, as I said, Daddy was headed across the field, herding the cows. He got to Granny and Granddaddy's house about the same time I got there with the blackberries. But instead of going ahead and rounding up Granddaddy's herd as he usually did, he got down off his horse and yelled at me, 'Come here, Mutt!'—he always called me Mutt.

"'Your mama told Harold that y'all couldn't come over here to your Granny's by yourselves, and you did anyway.' Daddy sounded real mad, so I tried to explain, telling him that Harold said Mama gave us permission, but Harold up and changed his mind—said he didn't want to go.

"'No, Mutt,' Daddy butted in, 'your mama said you couldn't come, and you did it anyway, and I'm gonna wear you out!'

"Daddy pulled his leather cow whip off the saddle and started to climb over the fence to where I stood when Granny came out of the house and said, 'Milton, you ain't gonna whip that child.'

"'Yes, I am, Dosia,' Daddy said. 'She's my young'un. She didn't mind her mama, and she's gonna get a whippin'.'

"Granny walked over and stood between me and Daddy and said, 'Milton Rye, you ain't gonna whip this child. Ethel has never, ever told me a lie. If she said her mama said she could come here, then that's the way she understood it. Ethel did not tell you a lie. You ain't gonna beat this young'un unless you beat me first.'

"To my surprise, my daddy turned around and climbed back over the fence, got up on his saddle, and headed off to gather up the rest of the cows."

The ending to Mama's story made me giggle. I saw Granny Dosia as spunky and strong enough to stand up to a man holding a cow whip instead of crippled and unable to do much but sit and shell peas, peanuts, and pecans—and spit when she dipped snuff.

Mama also told us stories about

Cattle Ticks

Cattle ticks caused red-water fever, also known as Texas fever. An official tick eradication program, begun in 1906, called for coordination between county, state, and federal officials. At one time, Suwannee County had 64 dipping vats, some made of concrete, some of wood.

The dipping solution actually contained arsenic. Forty years later, most of the cattle ticks had been eradicated, but the arsenic that ended up in soil and groundwater was still being cleaned up.

http://www.fs.usda.gov
http://www.floridahealth.gov

how Granny could square dance—up until she broke her leg. The story about Granny's accident was sad. Mama said it all happened one Halloween night.

"Harold and I were much older then, old enough to attend school. By then, we'd moved from the Peak place and back into the house with Granny Dosia and Granddaddy Tip. We'd all gone to the Halloween party at the school that night. As we walked back home, we started cutting up, singing and skipping along the dirt road—Granny too—when all of a sudden she got her feet crisscrossed and tripped. She fell hard. It was pitch dark—no moon—we could hardly see. Granny said she couldn't get up—said she was hurt. We were all in a panic, not knowing what to do since we could not see our hands in front of our faces. And we knew she was hurt bad if she said so because Granny never complained.

"After we finally got her home, somebody went for Dr. Green in Mayo. He came and examined her—as best he could. Modest Granny didn't want him to pull up her dress to take a look. When he finally examined her, he said she had a badly broken leg. He told Mama what she needed to do. 'Delma, sew up a couple of cloth bags the length of Dosia's leg and fill 'em with sand.'

"After Mama got the sandbags ready, Dr. Green put one on each side of Granny's broken leg, placed a board next to each bag, and tied all that up to form a brace. Then he attached a pulley at the foot end of it with a flatiron for weight to keep her leg stretched out. Poor Granny stayed like that, flat on her back, for weeks and weeks. Even so, her leg didn't heal properly, so when she could eventually stand, she had to use a crutch to get around."

Mama's story made me feel bad for Granny Dosia, who now spent most of her time sitting in my grandparents' living room, her crutch propped against the wall and her spit can on the floor next to her chair. Sometimes Patsy, Anetha, and I sat on the floor next to her and watched as she took her hair down and brushed it. She combed it away from her thin face, caught a handful at the back of her neck, and pulled it tight—so tight I thought the many wrinkles on her face would disappear, but they never did. After twisting the hair around her fingers, she secured it in a knot with U-shaped hairpins—a few tortoiseshell ones, others gray like her hair—wiggling each one back and forth as she pushed it in. I marveled that the hairpins stayed put. When I tried sticking them into my own hair, they fell to the floor the instant I turned them loose.

Like Granddaddy Tip, Granny Dosia had no teeth and no plans to get any, and like him, she wore warm clothes winter and summer. She buttoned her long-sleeved floral print dresses up to her chin. The hem of her gathered skirts brushed her clunky black leather shoes that laced up over flesh-colored cotton stockings. Though she was no longer able to do any work around the house, she wore an apron, perhaps from habit, or because its pocket held her snuff can. Periodically, she would slip her hand into her apron pocket, open the can, pinch a bit of brown powder, and drop it between her lower lip and gum.

"Granny," Patsy said one day as our great-grandmother dipped, "can I have some?"

"No, sweetie, you can't have any of my snuff, but I bet we can fix you up some." She looked over at Grandma Rye, who had already risen from her chair.

"Come on, young'uns," Grandma Rye said to us, "I'll make you some."

We followed her to the kitchen. From behind a glass-paned cabinet door, Grandma retrieved a can of Hershey's cocoa powder. She dipped out a heaping spoonful and dumped it into a bowl. She reached under her biscuit-making table—one Granddaddy Rye had built for her—grabbed the bail of a big clear glass jar, and swung the five-gallon jar of white sugar onto the table. The red lid on the jar was so big her fingers could hardly reach across it, but she managed to unscrew it. She took out a scoop of sugar, added it to the cocoa, stirred it together, and doled out equal portions into three blue-willow tea cups.

"Take it outside, now," she said, after handing each of us a cup.

We hurried through the house and into the front yard.

Having watched Granny Dosia dip snuff, we knew exactly how it was done. I set my cup on the edge of the front porch took a pinch, and dropped it into the pocket between my lower lip and gums. My mouth watered. It tasted so good I didn't want to spit it out. I let the sugar melt, and swallowed. *Um-m-m.*

"Susanette's eating hers!" Patsy said to Anetha with a smirk.

"I was just tasting it!" I said as I put in another pinch. This time, I spit like my sisters.

"Let's see who can spit to the orange tree?" Anetha said.

I was no match for my older sisters, of course. Like all contests, they won, hands down. What we needed was a contest for the most drool on our chins or cocoa stains on our dresses. That was a contest I could win.

Part II
Born in the Front Bedroom

12

The Unwanted Baby

The truth is, I was an unexpected and unwanted baby. But Mama put a good spin on it when she told me the story, saying, "You surprised us."

"After we had Patsy in '42 and Anetha in '43," she said, "we didn't think we needed more young'uns. Your daddy worked two jobs to make ends meet, and I had my hands full. Patsy had just turned two, and I was still nursing Anetha when we found out another baby was on the way.

"We worried at first, but then your daddy began to get excited, considering the odds of having a boy after two girls—a boy who'd enjoy hunting and fishing and could help with the farming. He picked out the name Clarence Alton—Clarence after his daddy, and Alton after a man he worked with in the agricultural office."

"I started going to Dr. Price for monthly checkups, and on one visit, your daddy paid the doctor's delivery fee in advance. He was to deliver you here at home, with your Grandma Rye's help, like when Patsy and Anetha were born."

"As it turned out, though, when I woke up your daddy in the middle of that October night, telling him to 'go get the

doctor,' your grandma was busy taking care of Granny Do-
sia—she was sick. So on the way to get the doctor, he dropped
us off there. You were born in their front bedroom."

As Mama finished telling me the story, Daddy, who had been outside, walked in and began adding details Mama had left out.

"Yep, when I realized your mama had gone into labor, I jumped
out of bed, threw on some clothes, and took her, Patsy, and Anetha
down to your grandparents'. At the time, I had that car I'd built
from Buddy Rye's old car, a rusty relic he'd abandoned. It had the
body of a Model-A-Ford coupe, but not the engine. I drove it to
Live Oak as fast as it would go—fifty-five miles an hour. I knew it
was eighteen miles to town, and no shorter back.

"I got to Dr. Price's house at the same time as a man named
Fink," Daddy said. "Mr. Fink wanted the doctor to go to his house
to deliver his wife's baby. But Dr. Price said he'd go with me first
because I'd already paid his fee. He followed me in his car, and we
got back to your mama in no time flat!"

"It seemed longer than that to me." Mama said, frowning.

"Your grandma helped Dr. Price deliver you," Daddy said, "while
I paced the floor in the next room and looked after your sisters."

"Dr. Price laid you on a muslin diaper," Mama said, "drew its
corners together and tied 'em in a knot. He hung the bundle from
his drop scales and announced—so your daddy heard—"an eight-
and-a-half-pound baby girl."

"I heard you screaming your head off," Daddy said. "When I
went in, I told your mama she could pick out your name, and she
chose Susie Jeannette."

"What made you choose that?" I asked, for I knew that Patsy,
named Laura Patricia, had Aunt Laura's name, and Anetha had the
name of one of Daddy's high school classmates (just a smart girl he
admired, he *said*).

"Why'd I pick Susie Jeannette?" Mama asked herself. "I just liked that name. But every time Patsy—two years old when you were born—tried to say Susie Jeannette, it sounded like 'Susanette,' and that stuck."

"Good thing I'd paid Dr. Price in advance," Daddy said. "Otherwise, he might have followed Mr. Fink home. Forty-five dollars he charged me!—when he had charged just $35 for delivering Patsy and Anetha!"

Daddy added something else about Dr. Price's leaving in a rush—not staying for breakfast after delivering me, to rush over to the Finks' house—but my mind stayed focused on what he'd said about me, the unwanted baby. I had cost him $45 and my sisters had each cost him only $35. What was it Granddaddy Rye often said? "You get what you pay for!"

13

Tommy, the Babysitter

In November of 1944, when I was a month old, Daddy's boss in the agricultural office gave Daddy a puppy. Male. Nobody ever said so, but I'm pretty sure the boy dog was a consolation gift for my being born a girl. You'd think Daddy would have given the dog one of the names he'd picked out for me—Clarence or Alton—but no, instead, he chose *Tommy*.

"Why Tommy?" I asked Daddy when I was older.

"Well, my boss got the puppy from his neighbor Bob Miller in Live Oak," Daddy said. "Miller's dog had puppies and his wife had a baby boy on the same day you were born. They named their son *Tommy*, so I thought the name Tommy sounded like a good name for the puppy—a Heinz 57 mutt—part hound, maybe some bull-dog, with a blaze up his face."

Blaze sounded like a perfect dog's name, but what did I know?

"I think my boss intended for Tommy to be my dog," Daddy said, "but Tommy soon got attached to you young'uns."

"Yeah," Mama said, "Tommy often stood guard over y'all, even in the field. When I had to go out to hoe weeds, I'd set up the play-pen in the shade of a tree at the end of the row and put y'all in it. Tommy would lie there, right next to the playpen, keeping watch over y'all.

"One time, Tommy kept barking and I couldn't figure out why. You were just a few months old and you kept crying. I checked but couldn't find any problem, so I figured you were just tired and would soon go to sleep."

Having heard this story before, I knew what happened next, but I itched to hear it again.

"I told Tommy to hush his barking," Mama said, "and I went back to work, but he started up again after I walked off. So when I finished hoeing the next row, I went back to the playpen again.

"The day was a scorcher. Thinking you might be too hot, I took off your booties, a pair I'd made for you. Then I found the reason you kept crying and Tommy kept barking. Ants had gotten inside one of your booties and big red welts covered your little foot. When I saw all those ant bites, I wanted to cry too." Mama shook her head and looked as if she might cry. Her sad face gave me a warm feeling.

"At the house, whenever I'd put y'all down on a pallet for a nap," Mama continued, "Tommy would get right up beside you and fall asleep. You seemed fascinated by his eyes and would try to touch them. He never snapped at any of you girls, though, not even when you poked him in the eye. He'd just change positions so you couldn't reach his eyes."

"Did you punish me for sticking my finger in his eye?"

"No, you were just a baby, hardly crawling."

With that, Mama got up and found a photograph she'd taken of Tommy and me in the front yard, watching a

Tommy, watching over me

mother hen and her yellow biddies.

"Mother hens can be very protective," she said, looking at the picture. "I think Tommy was just waiting for you to go after one of the biddies. If you had, that mother hen would've gone after you, and Tommy would've attacked her. Feathers would have flown.

"Tommy served as my second set of eyes, helping keep y'all out of trouble—like the day I told y'all to play in the yard while I scrubbed the floor. Before long, Tommy came bounding up into the open hall, barking his head off. I yelled at him to get, and he took off, but he soon came charging back, barking without stopping. I knew then that something was wrong.

"I put down my scrubber and went to the front porch to check on y'all. I saw you sitting in the sand beyond the front gate, crying. I didn't see your sisters anywhere, and knew right away they'd decided to walk down to visit Mama and Granny, and you'd tried to follow them."

"How old was I?"

"Just a little older than you were in that picture with the hen and biddies," Mama said. "Thirteen months, maybe. Hardly walking. I figured you couldn't keep up with your sisters, so they had run off and left you in the dust. I picked you up, brushed the sand off your legs and hands, and took you back to the playpen on the porch. Tommy followed me up the steps, and I told him to stay there beside you."

"I headed down the road after Patsy and Anetha, but stopped long enough to break me off a switch. I didn't go far before I met your sisters and Mama. Your Grandma Rye was bringing them back, figuring they didn't have permission to go there. As soon as she saw my switch, she started beggin' me, 'Honey, please don't whip 'em. They just wanted to come see me.' But I had to teach them they couldn't take off like that without permission. Of course, they started running toward home and stayed so far ahead of me that they didn't catch but a couple of licks of the switch.

"When we got to the house, Tommy had not budged from where I'd told him to stay. I don't think we could have ever found a better babysitter."

14

Close Your Eyes

Mama held my hand and led me, and only me, to the back bedroom. "But I ain't sleepy!" I protested. I resented having to stay inside and sleep while my older sisters got to go outside and play.

At night, we still shared the cot in Mama and Daddy's bedroom, but for some unknown reason, Mama made me take naps in the back bedroom, a room that gave me an unsettling feeling the instant I walked in there because of a memory I had of that room, something that happened when I was really little.

Mama had led me into that room one Saturday for a nap and had asked me when I'd last had a *bowel movement*. Thinking that meant a *stomach growl*, I wracked my brain to remember the last time I'd heard my stomach growl because I was hungry. Finally I answered, "About two weeks ago."

My answer evidently shocked Mama because, before I knew what had happened, she'd filled up a red rubber thing she called a "hot-water bottle"—it had a long tube attached—and had me stretched out on a quilt on the floor and was pumping water into me from the wrong end. I thought I might pop like a balloon—and then wouldn't Mama have a mess? I'd never experienced anything so uncomfortable. Finally, she let me get up to sit on the slop jar.

I wished I could forget that memory but I couldn't no matter how hard I tried.

A few weeks after that, following a yucky supper that I didn't want to eat because Mama had cooked liver with onions, mustard greens, and rutabagas, she asked me the same question. Remembering the uncomfortable experience in that back bedroom, I stood looking at Mama, not answering for fear I would say the wrong thing. "Tell your mama when you last *binexcused*," Daddy demanded. How I knew what Daddy meant by that nasty-sounding word he used, I don't know, but I did. He wanted me to tell Mama when I had been to the toilet. "This morning!" I said. Evidently, I gave the right answer because Mama didn't go looking for that red hot-water bottle. Thank goodness.

In years to come, I would figure out that Daddy was not saying one word, but two: been excused.

Mama eventually figured out something too. She learned that a piece of her chocolate—she called it ex-lax—would work for us kids like it did for her. The chocolate tasted kind of like a Hershey's candy bar, so I always wanted another bite. But Mama was stingy with her squares of chocolate and stored them out of our reach.

"I ain't sleepy!" I protested this day, but like every other time Mama told me to climb up on the bed in that back room and close my eyes, my protests did no good.

The bed was twice as high as the cot, so it took climbing to get up there. Mama threw open the wooden shutter on the back wall, then turned and stared at me as she said, "Lay down now, and close your eyes."

Knowing from experience that Mama wouldn't leave that room until I closed my eyes, I squeezed them shut. But the moment she stepped out, they sprang open and I looked around the room.

According to Daddy, this room and the kitchen across the open hall were originally part of the back porch, but the Ward family, who owned the house before us, enclosed the back porch on each side of the open hall, which turned their small two-room house into our big four-room house.

I lay staring up at the rafters and tin roof overhead and at the walls, full of cracks and crevices that, according to Daddy and Mama, had once been a hiding place for little critters.

Daddy said that soon after he and Mama bought the place, they invited a traveling Baptist revival preacher to spend the night. The church didn't pay the traveling preachers much, but the congregation provided room and board for them.

Mama said the preacher acted real friendly and everything seemed fine when they turned in for the night. But the next morning, that preacher was dressed and ready to leave before daylight—wouldn't even stay for ham and eggs. "We couldn't figure out why the rush," Mama said, "until after he left and I went into that back room to change the linens. I found tiny blood spots all over the sheets and realized bedbugs had about eaten that preacher alive.

"To get rid of the bedbugs, we had to sun the mattress for days, and I scrubbed down every inch of wood in that whole room— walls, floors, rafters—with lye soap. The bugs had evidently been hiding in the cracks and crevices of the walls in the daytime, and we didn't know about them until the preacher brought 'em out."

Mama's last comment made me wonder if preachers gave off a different scent from regular people.

Mama had lots of real life stories, which I thought were better than the stories she read from our big storybook. Another one had to do with that back bedroom.

"One spring night, I thought it time you girls had your own room," she said, "so I put y'all to bed in the back bedroom. I put Susanette in the middle where she couldn't roll off, and put a towel under her, since she was apt to wet the bed."

I wished Mama would leave out that part of the story. I hated being reminded.

"I made y'all go to bed earlier than usual that night," she said, "because I'd been ironing all day, and your daddy had spent the day tilling the fields surrounding the house in preparation for planting. After I got y'all bedded down, I went back across the hall to relax and do some embroidery.

"Before long, the wind started howling," Mama said. "Your daddy and I thought nothing of it, since March usually brings wind. But after a while, I heard y'all coughing. I thought all of you might be coming down with bad colds, and after the hacking got more persistent, I told your daddy I should go get the jar of Vick's salve. I grabbed the flashlight to go find it."

Mama thought Vick's salve on our necks would cure anything that ailed us. Anytime she smeared it on, she always added one of Daddy's white handkerchiefs, as if a handkerchief could keep the oily salve off nightclothes or bedcovers. I don't know which annoyed me the most—the smell of Vick's salve, the greasy feel of it, or the knot in that handkerchief.

"In the hall that night," Mama said, "I could smell dust in the air. I found the Vick's in our bedroom, then walked over to the heavy curtain that stood in for a door to separate the two bedrooms. When I pulled back that curtain and aimed the flashlight at y'all, I could not believe my eyes. The sheet and y'all were covered in a thick layer of brown dust and dirt."

Mama said the night we almost choked to death in that back bedroom, she had to drag each of us out of bed for a second bath before putting us back to bed on the cot in her and Daddy's room.

Patsy and Anetha said they remembered the night we almost choked to death on dust and had to have a second bath. I thought I did too, but Mama said that was impossible. "You weren't even two years old yet, and you didn't wake up through the whole ordeal, even during your bath. You could sleep through a tornado."

I sniffed the air in the room now where I was supposed to be napping. It no longer smelled of dust; it smelled like tobacco. Daddy had stored cured tobacco in the room before he built the packhouse. I actually liked the tobacco scent—the only thing I *did* like about that room—because the familiar smell reminded me of Granddaddy Tip's open can of Prince Albert.

I'd been tossing and tumbling in the bed for what seemed like forever when I heard my sisters talking. It sounded like their voices came from the backyard. But then Mama's rattling of dishes and banging of pots and pans drowned out their voices.

One side of the bed hugged the wall, so I crawled over to take a look. I was leaning out the unshuttered window looking for my sisters when I heard footsteps in the hall. I flopped back into the middle of the bed and squeezed my eyes shut. When I thought Mama was in the room, looking down at me, I rubbed my eyes with my fists, yawned real big, and stretched my arms way up over my head, hoping Mama would think I was just waking up. That had worked one time—she had let me get up. But today I heard the creak of the door, her footsteps in the hall, and more dishes rattling.

I sat up again and suddenly remembered I'd stowed away a half-eaten caramel Sugar Daddy the day before—candy I'd bought off the rolling store, the big black truck that came by every couple of weeks. Mama didn't like the high prices of items on the truck, but with Live Oak eighteen miles away and us with no transportation, the rolling store sometimes saved the day. She'd buy items such as sugar, flour, or baking powder from the driver, Mr. O. C. Jones. (He had taken over the route after Mr. Grover Fort retired from the job.) Both men accepted cash—or trade, like a live chicken or fresh eggs. The day before, Mama paid Mr. O.C. with a chicken. She grabbed a Rhode Island Red from the yard, held it upside down by its legs, and handed it over to Mr. O.C., who threw it into a slatted wooden cage attached to the back of his "store." Then Mama picked out the stuff she needed without having to pay cash for it.

Over time, Patsy, Anetha, and I had tried just about every candy and gum Mr. O.C. carried, thanks to the dimes Granddaddy Tip gave us. I don't think I ever tried a sweet I didn't like—Milky Way, Mounds, Hershey's—but I liked Sugar Daddies best because the hard caramel would last a lot longer than a regular candy bar.

The day before, we sisters unwrapped our candy as Mr. O.C. drove away, chicken feathers swirling and mixing with clouds of dust. The rolling store was hardly out of sight before Patsy and Anetha took the last bite of their Milky Ways. Then they wanted to lick my Sugar Daddy. I'd refused, and later I'd gone inside, wrapped my candy back up, and hidden it under the cot.

Remembering where I hid it, I now slid quietly off the bed in the back bedroom, went into the other bedroom, and found my candy right where I'd left it. I scurried back and climbed up on the bed. I tugged at the wrapper stuck to the candy. Finally, I got it loose, but I'd hardly started licking when a bumblebee flew in through the unshuttered window and tried to light on my candy. I flailed my arms to keep that black-and-yellow fuzzy bee off my caramel. As I tried to knock it away, I suddenly felt a stabbing pain on the chubby part of my leg. I screamed.

Mama came running into the room to see what the problem was and caught me sitting in the middle of the bed holding my leg up with one hand and my half-eaten Sugar Daddy in the other. As the bee flew up, she knocked it to the floor, and I heard a crunch as the sole of her shoe came down on it.

I half expected Mama to take off that killer shoe and use it on my bottom for eating candy in bed. Instead, she took the candy from my hand and walked out. I sat there squeezing my leg and sobbing. Patsy and Anetha came running through the hall and stuck their heads in through the doorway, but Mama shooed them out when she came back with two wet washrags. She folded one rag and laid it over the red welt forming on my leg, then used the other rag to wipe tears and caramel off my face.

Mama said I was lucky, that a bumblebee's stinger is not barbed like a honeybee, so the bee hadn't left its stinger in me. And I was lucky, she said, that the bee didn't sting me more than once, because—unlike a honeybee that loses its stinger when it stings—a bumblebee can sting again and again.

I didn't feel lucky. I felt pain. But as Mama wiped caramel off my hands, I got my hopes up that she would let me get up and go play outside with my sisters. Instead, she told me to lie back down.

Mama hung the dirty washcloth on the iron bedstead above my head and lay down next to me. She began stroking my hair and humming a familiar song. I gave up and closed my eyes. The last thing I remember of that afternoon is wondering what Mama did with my Sugar Daddy.

15

Billy Shade

Daddy returned from town one day with a stranger. He introduced the sandy-haired young fellow and said Billy would be staying with us and helping with the farming.

Daddy had met Billy for the first time that very day. Billy had walked into the agricultural office where Daddy worked, looking for a job—said he was hitchhiking from town to town hoping to find something to do. Daddy told Billy the agricultural office had no jobs to offer, but Daddy identified with the young fellow, having done his share of hitchhiking as a teenager. As they talked, Daddy learned that Billy had been living in an orphanage, just as Daddy had, as a boy, after his father died and his mother got sick. Daddy wanted to help the young man, so he told him, "If you want to work on my farm, I'll give you room and board and pay you thirty dollars a month."

Billy was carrying all his belongings in a paper sack when he arrived with Daddy at our house. I thought Mama would let him sleep in the back bedroom where she made me take naps, but instead, she told him he could sleep in the front room on the couch, which would fold out to make a bed. (Daddy said he'd bought that couch from his Aunt Daisy and Uncle Clarence, the relatives who took him in at the age of fourteen, just before the orphanage was to kick him out for being too old to stay there any longer.)

Patsy, Anetha, and I soon became attached to Billy, whose last name was Shade—it fit him perfectly. He was like the shade of a big oak tree on a hot, sunny day: nice to have around.

Daddy occasionally entertained us with tricks, and Mama read stories to us and taught us how to do things, like make windmills with construction paper and a stick. But they didn't play with us like Billy did. Every chance he got off from work—on breaks at noon and late in the afternoon after he'd finished whatever Daddy had asked him to do—Billy would do anything we asked. Sometimes he threw a ball back and forth over the house to us. But most of all, we liked for him to play catch. He'd stand on the ground at one end of the porch and catch us as we jumped off the high porch into his strong, outstretched arms.

One day, Billy kept catching us, one after the other. As soon as he set one of us on the ground, he reached out to catch the next one who sailed off the porch. With the three of us, he was steadily playing catch.

"Okay kiddos, let's quit for now," Billy said late one afternoon as he turned away, no doubt exhausted from working in the field in the hot sun. But as he said "let's quit," Anetha had already started running across the porch. She flew off the edge, expecting Billy to be there. Realizing she'd sailed off into the air, Billy whirled around and tried to grab her, but missed. Anetha hit the ground hard. The impact knocked the breath out of her and left her with grains of sand embedded in her knees and nose.

Billy obviously felt bad about it; he apologized over and over.

He must have enjoyed his time at our place—maybe it was the warm climate—because he wrote to his friend, James Earl somebody, and suggested that he move down to Suwannee County and work for Granddaddy Rye. As far as I know, though, James Earl never showed up.

I don't remember how many months Billy stayed with us or the day he left. But after he moved on, we got postcards he'd mailed from different places across the country. He was evidently still hitchhiking from job to job. Then one year at Christmas, he sent us a picture of himself with his new wife and baby. They looked like a happy little family. After that, we lost touch with him.

I wonder sometimes where Billy Shade is and if he still remembers the Howell family.

16

A Cold, Wet Bed

One cold winter morning, I awoke with a start, as I had many times before. Again, my flannel nightgown, fresh and clean the night before, was soaked with pee. *Heck!* I said to myself, though I knew I shouldn't even think that word. Daddy said it was shorthand for *Hell*, the same as *darn* was short for *damn*—the worst word of all.

How I dreaded telling Mama I'd had another accident. She had punished me for my bad habit more times than I could count—if I knew how to count. Patsy had been trying to teach me. She could count all the way to a hundred. She also knew all her ABCs, thanks to Granddaddy Rye, who had paid her a penny for every number and letter she learned. Evidently, that put him in the poorhouse, though, because he'd never offered me a cent. Anetha neither.

Still asleep, Anetha lay next to me on her side of the cot. I pulled the heavy quilts up around my neck. Patsy, sleeping on the opposite end of the cot, tugged back.

A rooster crowed.

I shivered as I struggled to turn on my side to see if Mama and Daddy were up. Their bedcovers lay crumpled in a wad. Daddy probably had a big fire going in the fireplace. I wanted to go join them—warmth from the fireplace didn't travel across the open hallway—but I dreaded seeing the look on Mama's face when she saw me wet again. She'd bring me back to the bed and rub my nose on the wet spot. I lay still, moving only my eyes around the room. I stared at the cardboard closet in the corner that was missing its door, then at the white enamel slop jar under the crib, the bed with bars that Mama kept threatening to put me back into if I didn't stop wetting the bed like a baby.

I hated that Anetha and Patsy would see Mama rub my nose on the wet mattress. They had snickered once. Mama scolded them. So now they always just moved away from me when I was wet, as if I had some dreaded disease like leprosy that they might catch. My embarrassment didn't stop in the bedroom either since Daddy would drag the smelly mattress outside where it would spend the day teetering atop the front corner of the wire fence for God and the world to see.

Clutching the edge of the top quilt, I yanked it up again to my chin. I could feel cotton batting at its frayed seams. Mama had hand-stitched various scraps together—unbleached muslin, flour-sacks, leftover fabric from her and Grandma Rye's print dresses, silky rayons from my Miami grandmother's fancy ones. Mama used any fabric she could get her hands on, and it didn't seem to matter what scraps and colors she put together, the quilts turned out pretty. Mama's scrub board hadn't been kind to some of the fabrics in the top quilt, though. Loose cotton batting tickled my nose. I sneezed. The cold air fogged. I watched it fade away, then sucked in a breath, blew it out, "Hah-h-h-h-h," and watched my breath disappear again.

I wished the nose rubbing was already behind me and I was dressed in dry clothes by the big fire in the other room.

When Mama built a fire, she used fat-lighter'd splinters chopped off a pine stump. The tar in the lighter'd sizzled and crackled when she stuck a match to it.

For his fire starter, Daddy preferred kerosene, the stuff he put in our oil lamps and the kitchen stove—or better yet, gasoline. Every time he used gasoline though, Mama pitched a hissy fit.

"C.G., you gonna burn the house down and us in it! You ought not to use that stuff! It's dangerous, and you know it!"

"Stand back," Daddy would always say as he tossed a lit match onto the logs.

"WHOOF!"

As I lay in bed procrastinating, I got an idea. Since I knew the nose rubbing was coming, why not get it over with before my sisters woke up?

Quietly, I lifted the covers, slid my legs over the side of the cot, and eased my wet self over the edge. After my feet touched the rough wood floor, I stood on tiptoe, bent over the bed, and pressed my nose against the soggy sheet, exactly as Mama had done dozens of times. Back and forth, back and forth I rubbed my nose in the stench until my nose felt sufficiently raw and I thought I would surely remember this punishment when I fell asleep that night.

I put the cover back in place, slipped out of the room, and hugged myself for warmth as I crossed the open hall. The white ceramic knob on the living-room door felt cold as ice. I twisted and pushed. A gust of wind propelled me into the room.

Mama stood near the fire, her dark hair already neatly combed and pinned back. She was tying the sash of her apron. Daddy wore a long-sleeved dress shirt as if he planned to go to town. Perched on the edge of a straight-backed chair by the hearth, he pulled a sock onto one foot.

The door slammed shut, and he and Mama looked in my direction. As I rounded the dining table in the center of the room, their eyes zeroed in on my nightgown. It clung to my legs, making it difficult to walk. Mama's brow furrowed and I knew her question before she asked it. Actually, it was more of a statement for she already knew the answer.

"Susanette, you wet the bed again?"

"Yes, ma'am," I answered, looking down at my bare feet. "But I already rubbed my nose in it."

"You awh-weady wubbed your nose in it?" Daddy repeated as a question, mocking me. I had trouble with my *R*s, and Daddy was pointing that out. Again.

"Yes, sir."

Will Mama escort me back to the bedroom and rub my nose on the mattress again?

She twisted her mouth to one side and looked over at Daddy. As they stared at one another, they shook their heads.

"Come here, honey," Mama said as she reached out, put her arm around me, and pulled me in close to her. "Stay here by the fire with Daddy and warm up. I'll go get you some dry clothes."

Mama ain't gonna rub my nose in it? My idea worked?

I felt proud—almost giddy—that I'd thought to punish myself. I vowed to keep punishing myself if I wet the bed again, so Mama wouldn't.

Daddy put on his other sock and laced his shoes as I stood by the fire.

"Are you getting ready to go to town?" I asked.

"Yeah, I've gotta go to the bank."

Daddy never went into detail with us kids about his business affairs, but from hearing him and Mama talk, I knew he borrowed money from the bank each year to plant various crops and paid the money back when he sold the harvest.

Patsy and Anetha came into the room, brushing hair out of their faces. Mama returned soon after, with dry clothes for me on one arm, dirty linens on the other.

"I stripped the cot," she said to Daddy, his cue to take the mattress outside and sling it over the fence to dry. I wished the mattress wasn't so heavy; I'd take it out myself and sling it on the back corner of the fence, instead of the front corner.

Will anybody see it today? I wondered. Seldom did a vehicle *pass by* our house. Most came to a dead stop at our fence, either because the driver had gotten lost and needed directions, or because the occupants had come to stay a while.

17

The House Uncle Harold's Money Built

About the only person who drove on past our house without stopping was the O'Brien mail carrier. Daddy had never bothered to erect a mailbox because he didn't like the O'Brien post office's three-day-a-week mail delivery. Instead, we shared our grandparents' Live Oak address: Rural Route 4, Box 245.

Six days a week, Mr. Dave McNeil stuffed letters and packages addressed to the Laniers, Ryes, and Howells into my grandparents' oversized mailbox. I liked this arrangement, since this meant we saw our grandparents daily. And seldom did we pick up the mail and head straight home. We spent so much time at our grandparents' place that their house felt as much like home as ours.

Granddaddy Rye called their house "shotgun-style" because, he said, if you took a notion, you could "shoot a bullet through it, front to back, without hitting a thing." That was, of course, if the front and back doors were open.

The house was painted white, inside and out, and all its windows had glass panes, plus screens that kept out most gnats, flies, and mosquitoes. It also had an indoor bathroom. It even had light switches on the walls—low enough that I could reach them.

Mama said that carpenters built my grandparents' new house

according to a Sears and Roebuck plan and finished construction just months before my October 1944 birth. Otherwise, I might have been born in my great-grandparents' log house, the house where Mama and her family spent a lot of time when she was growing up. They moved away only for short periods when her daddy found work elsewhere. They lived for a while in Punta Gorda, then on an island in the Gulf of Mexico, and finally at the Peak place next to Ladyland School, but Mama said they always ended up back at Granddaddy Tip and Granny's log house.

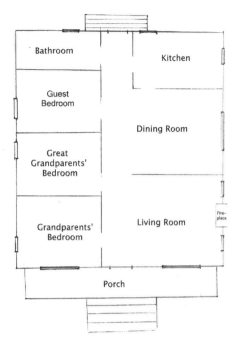

The layout of my grandparents' Sears and Roebuck home
www.antiquehome.org/

Uncle Harold's money made the new house possible, she said. Her younger brother was just fifteen when he heard from Granddaddy Rye's brothers that the War Department was paying big bucks to men willing to go where the work was. So he dropped out of school and fibbed about his age to sign up. He ended up building roads and bridges on faraway islands and in South America. For over two years, his family didn't know his exact address for he was forbidden to tell them. But he wrote often, telling his family about gigantic snakes, monkeys, and parrots in the trees. In most of his letters, like the one below, he sent checks and told them to put the money toward a new house.

85

9/26/42   *Nassau, Bahamas*

Hello, Mother, and Dad,

How are you getting along now, and did you get my last letter I wrote you? Well at last I am sending you a check. You probably thought I had forgotten about it. The money that I send home is for you all to use, and there is plenty more where this came from. I want you all to have anything you want. If I come home, and find you all trying to save any of this . . . I am going to spank both of you.

Listen Daddy when you find out about the lumber [for the new house], and how much it will cost, let me know how much it will be, and I will mail you a check for it. Don't get any old bad lumber, no matter how much good one costs. We want a good looking house. Get someone who knows about a circulating heater, and if you want that we will get one instead of a fireplace . . . .

Well I guess I had better close for this time. Answer real soon and let me know all the news.

Your son,
Harold Rye

P.S. Enclosed is a check for $50.00.

Grandma Rye held on to every letter Uncle Harold wrote home. Forty-eight are included in *C.G. and Ethel: A Family History* (2008).

"When Harold finally returned home," Mama said, "he didn't get to enjoy the house his money had built because draft papers were waiting. He enlisted in the Navy and left again."

Now, Uncle Harold had a family of his own and lived in Indiana, so I knew him only from letters, pictures, and stories Mama told of their childhood.

"Harold was just a toddler, cutting teeth," she said, when he began to bite me. I couldn't put a stop to it—at least not until the day he bit my arm through my sweater. "I jerked back, not knowing one of his teeth had caught in my knitted sweater—and out came that tooth. That put a stop to him biting me."

I laughed every time Mama told that story. But I didn't laugh when she told the one about Granddaddy Tip's teasing her little brother because he wet the bed. Mama said he'd tell Harold, "Let me get one of my shoelaces, and I'll tie it around that thing there, so you won't wet the bed tonight."

I wondered if Granddaddy Tip knew I often had nighttime accidents. He had never teased me. For months now, I had punished myself, rubbing my nose on the wet mattress while praying and wishing I could stop. At twilight every night, I said, "Star light, star bright, first star I've seen tonight. Wish I may. Wish I might. Have the wish I wish tonight." And at bedtime every night, after finishing with "if I should die before I wake, I pray the Lord my soul to take," I'd pray under my breath for what I wanted more than anything else in the world.

An 8x10, hand-tinted photograph of Uncle Harold in his Navy uniform sat on top of the radio cabinet in my grandparents' living room. When my sisters and I huddled near the radio on weekday afternoons, listening to *Uncle Remus* stories, Uncle Harold's blue eyes stared at me—though Patsy swore he looked straight at her, and her only. She claimed to be his favorite niece.

Each time Grandma Rye alerted us that it was time for *Uncle Remus,* one of us dragged over a cane-bottomed chair and positioned it close to the radio cabinet while Grandma twisted the knobs to reduce static and adjust the volume. The three of us would perch on the edge of the chair and lean in to get our ears closer to the radio's fabric-covered speakers.

Listening to the story of Brer Rabbit and Tar Baby in the briar patch—and how that crazy rabbit got stuck tighter and tighter—I became absorbed in the tale—imagining that I stood in the briar patch too. Only when the tale ended and I looked up and saw Uncle Harold's eyes staring at me did I realize where I was, still sitting in the house Uncle Harold's money built.

During late 1947 and early 1948, Grandma Rye didn't call us in to listen to *Uncle Remus* any more. "The noise of the radio might disturb Granny Dosia," she said. Granny Dosia was very sick—so sick she could not get out of bed, even to go to their nice indoor bathroom. She never wet the bed, though, that I knew of. When she needed to go, Grandma Rye would fetch the white enamel bedpan.

18

Sh-h-h, Granny's Sleeping
1948

My sisters and I bounded into my grandparents' living room one cool January morning. The screen door slammed shut behind us.

"Sh-h-h. Your Granny Dosia's sleeping," Grandma Rye whispered. I wanted to explain that the taut spring made the screen door slam shut and the paneled door was awfully heavy, but I just tiptoed behind my sisters across the living room and peered into our great-grandparents' bedroom. A plain roller shade blocked the light of day.

In the dim light, Granny lay motionless. A black iron bedstead sat catty-cornered in the room, a setup Mama never liked—said catty-cornered furniture made any room feel smaller. But Grandma Rye said this arrangement made it easier for her to get around the bed to tend to Granny.

The room had no closet. A tin-covered, hump-backed trunk held all of Granny's belongings, including handmade sunbonnets she no longer wore for she no longer went outside. A four-drawer chest, painted black as tar, held Granddaddy Tip's clothes. The furnishings in the room had come from their old log house that had been torn down to make room for the new one.

Mama said when the new house was built, Granddaddy Tip didn't want it wired for electric lights, saying, "Electricity's dangerous! The hot wires might catch the house on fire." Granddaddy Rye didn't listen. He had the whole house wired for electricity anyway. He wasted money putting lights in my great-grandparents' room, though; they never flipped the switch to turn on the lights.

Their dark, sparsely-furnished bedroom contrasted starkly with the rest of the house where scalloped shades and sheer ruffled curtains set off windows; where mirrors, pictures, and calendars decorated walls; where colorfully embroidered scarves shielded wood tables and cabinets from dust and scratches; where fancy crocheted doilies protected the arms of upholstered furniture.

Grandma Rye, who had been sitting on the living room sofa, stood, put aside a crocheted piece she'd been working on, and went to the kitchen to start cooking the noon dinner. After we heard her banging pots and pans in the kitchen, we tiptoed into our great-grandparents' bedroom. The door always stayed wide open since the fireplace in the living room served as the heater for the whole house.

We stood beside the bed, looking at Granny's wrinkled face, the only thing that wasn't covered. She slept soundly, so we had nothing to do but stand and stare at her, stare at each other, or stare at the medicine cabinet, high on the wall, out of reach of children. Well, not entirely. Granny's hump-backed trunk sat directly under that medicine cabinet.

Anetha climbed up on the trunk, stood on tiptoe, and turned the whittled piece of wood that held the door shut. She didn't even touch the tiny knob on the cabinet door, but the door swung open like magic, to reveal an assortment of remedies and rubbing potions: a green tin of Mentholatum ointment, a blue jar of Vick's salve, bottles of liniment, camphor, some white lotion, and I don't know what else. Escaped vapors permeated the air, giving the room a heavy, medicinal odor.

Patsy unscrewed the tin cap on the bottle of white lotion. We poured a dab into our palms, smoothed it on our grimy hands, and rubbed them together. Dead skin and dirt peeled off and fell to the floor like eraser dust. We uncapped and recapped a number of bottles and tins, being careful not to awaken Granny. And by the time Grandma Rye appeared in the doorway, the medicine cabinet was securely closed.

"We was just checking on Granny," I whispered to Grandma Rye as she curled her finger at us.

Unfortunately, all the potions in that alluring cabinet—even the medicines prescribed by Dr. Green in Mayo—did not make Granny Dosia well. In the days that followed, Mama spent more and more time helping Grandma Rye feed Granny and helping to bathe her frail body.

"I need to write Bud," Grandma Rye said one morning while Mama gave Granny a sponge bath with a rag.

Later, at the dining table, Grandma dipped the pen's nib into the upper chamber of a Scripto ink bottle, and wrote on a ruled tablet. I couldn't read the words, but from what Grandma said, I think it went something like . . .

Dear Bud,
I hope this finds you and your family well. I am sorry to have to tell you that Mama is getting weaker day by day . . .

Bud was her brother, Alonzo, who lived in Baltimore. (He called her Sis.) Grandma had told us stories about walking through the woods to Ladyland School with Alonzo when they were kids, swinging their lunch pails as they walked, carrying their blueback spellers. She said Alonzo looked out for her. Both graduated from eighth grade at Ladyland, which was as far as the grades went.

"Alonzo worked on the farm with Papa for a few years after he finished school," she said. "But when World War I broke out, he joined the Army."

After enlisting, he was stationed in Baltimore. Mama said that's where he met his future wife, Ethel Severn. When he took her to Florida to meet his folks, her fine manners impressed them so much that when Mama was born, they gave her the name Ethel.

Uncle Alonzo married Ethel Severn in Baltimore, with his family's blessing, but not their presence. To them, Baltimore was a world away.

I had never met Uncle Alonzo, his wife Ethel, or their children, Buck and Wilbur. But Grandma had many handsome photographs of Buck and Wilbur as babies—sepia-toned portraits in heavy portfolios, embossed and stamped in gold: *Studio of Vincent-Mitchell*. I adored one photograph, labeled on the back, "Buck Lanier—eight months, ten days," in which he sat on a bearskin rug that looked soft as rabbit's fur.

After Grandma Rye wrote Uncle Alonzo and told him about Granny Dosia's condition, Grandma said she felt sure her brother would answer right away—that he might even come down to visit. But the answer Grandma Rye received came, not from her brother but, from his wife. I never saw the letter, but Mama told me later that it went something like—

Dear Delma,
I wish you wouldn't send letters like that to your brother.
They upset him so.

Mama told Grandma Rye that she would answer her namesake's letter, and did.

"I wrote Aunt Ethel," she said, "and told her she needn't worry about us upsetting Uncle Alonzo anymore by giving him updates on Granny. And, the next time he heard from us was when we wired him—sent him a telegram—telling him Granny was dead."

Granny died the night Grandma Rye went home with us to take a rest, while Mama stayed behind to care for Granny.

"I feel so bad not being there with Mama when she died," Grandma Rye said over and over to everybody she talked to. The adults put their arms around her and assured her she had done all she could for her mother for a long, long time.

Men from the funeral home in Live Oak came and took Granny Dosia away. They brought her back the next day in a casket. They set it on a stand in the bedroom she'd shared with Granddaddy Tip. Granny looked like she was just taking a nap. I wanted to say, "Sh-h-h-h, Granny's sleeping," to those who talked loudly in the living room. She looked comfy in her satiny casket bed so I didn't cry. I didn't understand that Granny was gone forever.

Neighbors stayed through the night. "It's an old custom, left over from the time when bodies were not embalmed and none of the houses had screens on windows," Mama explained later. "A dead body served as an open invitation to panthers and wildcats that roamed the woods. In real hot weather, we used to lay the body out on a pine board—a cooling board—and watch over it."

Everyone who came to pay their respects brought food. The surface of Grandma's dining room table, buffet, kitchen table, and stove soon disappeared under bowls, platters, pots, and pans filled with ham, fried chicken, beef stew, chicken pirleau, yams, potato salad, acre peas, butter beans, creamed corn, macaroni and cheese, biscuits, cornbread, pies, cobblers, layer cakes—every food you could think of. Friends and neighbors continued the vigil, sitting through the nights, up to the day of the funeral, three days later.

Uncle Alonzo arrived just in time, alone. He came on the train, and since I had heard Grandma Rye say her brother worked for the railroad, I assumed he steered the train all the way from Baltimore to Live Oak.

Uncle Harold, who still lived in Indiana, didn't make it, but he sent his regrets.

I remember standing with my sisters the day of the funeral, dressed in our Sunday best, next to Granddaddy Rye's truck. We watched as men loaded Granny Dosia's casket into a sleek black hearse for transport to Philadelphia Baptist Church. There, my memory ends. I don't remember any prayers said or songs sung during the funeral service, either in the church or at graveside. I don't remember seeing Anetha become hysterical when men shoveled dirt on Granny's casket, as she told me, years later, that she did. Nor do I remember watching Patsy, back at home that night, make a wish and blow out all six candles on her birthday cake. But I'm sure I saw and ate some of her cake because Mama never failed to bake and decorate a birthday cake for us, complete with a candle for each year.

19

Young and Old

"Alonzo took his mother's death hard—sobbed like a baby," a cousin said after Granny Dosia's funeral. But that same day, back at my grandparents' house, my great uncle seemed quite jolly. His laugh reminded me of Grandma Rye's. And since I was crazy about her, I couldn't help but like her brother, even if we had just met, even if Mama didn't like his wife, and even if he did keep asking me the same question over and over.

"Susanette, how old are you?"

I held up three fingers and told him, but it came out "Pee."

"How old?" he asked again, as if he didn't understand.

"Pee!"

Again and again he asked. Again and again I answered, putting more and more emphasis on the *ee*.

Daddy had trouble understanding me too. Again and again, he'd tell the story about me trying to say "rabbit."

Uncle Raleigh, Granddaddy Rye's brother who lived in Macclenny, had given my sisters and me a white rabbit and a brown one. Normally, all of Uncle Raleigh's rabbits ended up at the meat market and eventually on somebody's table. We kept our saved-from-the-table rabbits in a hutch Daddy built under an oak tree east of our house. The white bunny was so pretty, she *had* to be a girl. She'd wiggle her pink nose as she sniffed and ate the cabbage leaves that I stuck through the chicken wire.

When I tried to tell Daddy about feeding the rabbit, it came out "abbit."

"What's an *abbit*?" he asked, cutting me off before I finished the sentence.

"I didn't say *abbit*, Daddy, I said *abbit*!"

"I know what a rabbit is," Daddy said. "But I have no earthly idea what an *abbit* is.

I slammed my arms down by my sides. "Daddy! If you *know* what's a abbit, then you *know* what's a *abbit*!"

Daddy told the story so often that even our Baptist preacher now greeted me, not with my name but, with, "If you know what's a abbit, then you know what's a abbit."

"How old are you?" Uncle Alonzo asked me again, as if my age had changed in the last minute.

"Peeeeee!" I repeated for the umpteenth time.

"Let's go slide," I said to Patsy and Anetha.

We put on our coats and headed out where autumn leaves still covered the ground. They provided a soft cushion for our bottoms as we slid down the railroad ditch that ran through the woods in front of our grandparents' house.

"One, two, three, go!" Patsy shouted. The three of us pushed off from the top edge of the ditch. At the bottom, we lay on our backs, inhaling the crisp winter air and making angel wings in the leaves as we stared up at Heaven, where Mama said Granny lived now. Oak branches appeared black against the blue sky. Come spring, the few dead leaves clinging to limbs and twigs would be nudged off by new growth.

We tunneled under layer upon layer of curling leaves, then hopped up, shook the leaves off, and scrambled back up the incline for another slide. The ditch, which looked like a giant *V* plowed through the woods, extended out of sight in opposite directions. It looked as if it had been there forever. Mama said she played in it when she was a little girl.

Daddy's father had helped build the railroad. "The dirt they dug from the ditch was used to build the grade for the ties and rails to rest on," Daddy said. "And the ditch then provided drainage for the tracks." Of course, the railroad was long gone.

After sliding down the steep embankment dozens of times, we went back inside.

"Where've you kids been?" Uncle Alonzo asked.

What? He wasn't asking my age?

"Sliding down the railroad ditch," Patsy said.

"Ah-h-h," Uncle Alonzo said. "When your grandma and I were kids, trains used to blow their whistles when they passed here."

The room seemed stuffier and hotter than when we'd left, yet Granddaddy Rye was stoking the logs in the fireplace.

"Yep," Granddaddy Rye said as he set the poker down and turned to Uncle Alonzo. "The S&SP! I used to hop aboard that train in Live Oak when I courted your sister. I probably looked like a hobo catching a free ride. When it slowed for the Wilmarth stop, I'd jump off out front there."

I couldn't imagine Granddaddy Rye looking like a ragged hobo. He usually wore jodhpurs, along with leather boots, tightly laced to his knees.

> **S&SP Railroad**
> The Suwannee and San Pedro (S&SP), a short logging railroad, later merged with the LOP&G (Live Oak, Perry, and Gulf), another logging railroad, known locally as the Lopin' Gopher.
> *http://www.suwclerk.org*

"Does the Drew Bridge still span the river?" Uncle Alonzo asked Granddaddy Rye.

Granddaddy Tip, who was not quite eighty-five years old, sat in the room too, but he didn't say much. Maybe he was thinking about Granny Dosia and how comfy she'd looked in her casket.

The Drew Railroad Bridge was named after the sons of George F. Drew, governor of Florida from 1877-1881. They owned the S&SP railroad, the bridge, and The Drew Lumber Company. The bridge could be turned by two men, using its manual crank system, to let large steamboats pass.

"What's left of it," Granddaddy Rye said. "They took up the tracks leading to it after the trains quit running, soon after you joined the service after World War I broke out. They reused the track but left the bridge. I used to fish off it."

"You know, my daddy helped build that bridge," Daddy said.

"Yes, Alonzo and I remember him well, don't we Alonzo?" Grandma Rye said. "We got to know him when he boarded with Mama and Papa—before he married your mama. Yep, I loved that gold watch he gave Papa, in trade for his room and board. Daddy let me wear it. I pinned it to the front of my dress. I've got a picture somewhere of me wearing that watch. But I wanted you to have it after you and Ethel married."

"Yeah, I was tickled to get that watch," Daddy said.

"I knew you'd like a keepsake of your father's," Grandma said, "since you were only about eight years old when he died."

"Yeah, I was proud to have that watch and carried it with me for quite a while—kept it in my pocket. But it was really too dainty and fragile for me. The crystal broke and one of its hands got bent, so I put it away."

I knew the watch they were talking about. It was stored in a small satin-lined box in a drawer in Mama and Daddy's bedroom at home. My sisters and I found it one day while plundering, our word for exploring. Patsy picked the watch up and pressed a tiny button at the top. Its cover flipped open to reveal a white face with black Roman numerals and thin black hands. We put it to our ears but couldn't hear it ticking, so we took turns trying to wind the thing, the way Granddaddy Tip wound his pocket watch. But no matter how much we twisted its little knob—or nudged its thin hands, or banged it against something—it never would tick.

Grandma Rye, as a teenager, wearing Grandfather Howell's watch.

I knew the old rusty bridge they were talking about too, though I'd never fished from the bridge, as Granddaddy had. When he took us fishing, we usually fished from the riverbank.

All the adult talk about the olden days soon became boring, so my sisters and I headed back outside to play.

Uncle Alonzo stayed for about a week after Granny's funeral before he headed back to Baltimore, never to be seen again by his father.

Map shows the route of the S&SP railroad,
which crossed the Suwannee River near Wilmarth.
http://www.taplines.net/floridarailway

20

The Suwannee River

Water began seeping up through the ground in early '48, the year Great-Granny Dosia died, just as the onion sets were sending up healthy-looking green spikes. Daddy had seen this happen before. He said it had to do with the "water table."

Some years, the river rose high enough in the spring-time that it backed up into our favorite swimming hole, turning Running Springs the color of black coffee. But by summer, when the weather turned warm enough for us to swim, the river always dropped back to its nomal level. By then, the water in

> **Suwannee River**
>
> Some say that "Suwannee" is a Timucua Indian word for crooked black water. The river gets its dark color from tannin leached from vegetation in Georgia's Okefenokee Swamp, where it originates.
>
> Stephen Foster made the river famous when he inserted its name into his song, "Old Folks at Home," though legend has it that Foster never set eyes on the stream.
>
> The river twists and turns for over two-hundred miles through North Florida before it empties into the Gulf of Mexico. Along the way, it is fed by fifty-five freshwater springs and three smaller rivers: Alapaha, Santa Fe, and Withlacoochee.
>
> On its circuitous route to the Gulf, the river meanders around three sides of the county that bears its name.
>
> For more history of Suwannee County, read *Echoes of the Past, A History of Suwannee County, 2000*.

the springs would be clear aqua, through which we could see the springs' white sandy floor.

Since we'd become accustomed to seeing the river rise and fall like that, a little water around the onions didn't seem like a big deal. After all, Daddy had planted the crop at the right time. He relied on the *Farmers' Almanac*, which told him when the moon and stars were in the right positions for planting.

The almanac didn't tell him *where* to plant, though, and that year, he'd planted the onions—five acres of them—on the lowest spot of ground on our property, an area we called "the bottom." He liked to plant vegetables there because the bottom had dark, fertile soil, unlike the dirt elsewhere on the place, which was similar to the white sand along Florida's beaches.

Next, Daddy turned his attention to the tobacco crop. I knew from listening to conversations between him and Mama that tobacco was our most important crop. It brought in more money than other crops he planted—corn, oats, peanuts, watermelons, and vegetables. (We didn't know then that smoking, dipping, and chewing tobacco could cause cancer.)

Daddy rotated the crops every year to prevent disease, and that year, he decided to plant tobacco next to the onions, but on higher ground. He'd already prepared the soil—turned it over with the plow, run the cultivator over it, and marked off rows about two feet apart. Late that February (other years, it was early March), our whole family got involved, transferring seedlings from the seedbeds to the field.

While Daddy loaded the drum, a fifty-five-gallon barrel, into the trailer behind the tractor and filled the drum with water, Mama, my sisters, and I pulled tobacco plants from the seedbed. The seeds had been sown in raised beds soon after Christmas. We pulled plants about five to seven inches tall and laid them in rectangular peach crates, which Daddy loaded into a trailer that he'd hooked to his Farmall. When we had enough plants for a day's planting,

Daddy hopped up on the tractor, and the rest of us climbed into the trailer.

In the field, Mama and Daddy led the way along each row. Mama walked backward, facing Daddy, and we girls followed. Mama carried the plants in a cloth bag slung over one shoulder. She dropped the plants, one at a time, into the metal "tobacco setter," the planter Daddy toted.

About three feet high, it had a small cone attached to a bigger cone. The small one held a tobacco plant, and the other would hold about two gallons of water. This mechanical contraption tapered to a sharp point at the bottom, so each time Daddy dropped the heavy setter into the dry sand, it made a cone-shaped hole for the plant's roots. Daddy squeezed a lever

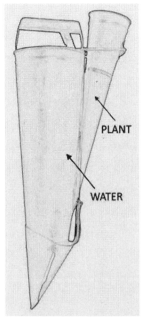

Tobacco setter

on the handle, kind of like a trigger on a gun, and that released the seedling, along with a gush of water. He then lifted the planter and took a step forward as Mama stepped backward and dropped in another plant. Following behind them, my sisters and I pushed squishy dirt back in place around the roots of each plant with our bare feet. As needed, Daddy walked back to the water barrel and refilled the big cone of the planter, giving us a short rest.

Some farmers in the area owned modern mechanical planters, pulled by tractors. For us, the planting process was entirely manual, but the five of us moved together like a machine: *Drop* plant. *Drop* setter. *Squeeze* lever. *Drop* plant/water. *Step* forward. *Pack* dirt.

Drop, drop, squeeze. Drop, step, pack . . .

Drop, drop, squeeze. Drop, step, pack . . .

Though it took just a few seconds to put each plant into the ground, hand planting Daddy's entire government allotment of three acres took days.

By the time we finished planting that year's tobacco crop, water that was seeping up out of the ground in the bottom covered most of the nearby onion crop. Daddy said the onions might not make it, but then joked that we now owned "lake front" property.

Mama didn't crack a smile at Daddy's joke. I didn't know then what Mama knew: she had never told us that when she was seven years old, she'd seen the Suwannee River flood. "I spotted the very first sign of the 1928 flood," she told us later. "I noticed water seeping up from insect and gopher holes in the railroad ditch where I played." But that was all Mama ever told us about the '28 flood.

"Looks like we might have to replant the tobacco on higher ground," Daddy said early one morning, about a week after we'd finished planting.

Uggh!

We spent several more days replanting. We needn't have bothered. The water kept rising.

We awoke one morning, after we'd replanted, and looked out. Water covered the fields. All of them.

"There's probably no hope for the onions or tobacco now," Daddy said. "The river is obviously coming over the banks."

Daddy got dressed and told Mama he was taking the tractor (we still didn't own a car) to see what her parents' place up the road looked like. Although water had flooded our fields, our house still sat on dry ground. Funny, because we'd never realized our house was on any kind of hill.

"As I made my way to the Ryes' place," Daddy said later, "water began to run across the road in several low places. I found Mr. Rye out by the corn crib, milking one of his cows. River water started running in around our feet. Before Mr. Rye finished milking, he had to move his stool and the cow's feed bucket three times to keep from getting his shoes wet.

"After his enamel bucket was about half full of milk," Daddy continued, "Mr. Rye took it to the house, and we walked over to the washhouse to check his electric pump. Water was shooting up around it, eight or ten inches. His pump was a closed-top cylinder. When he sank the cylinder down, it just hung there, and the water would come up around it."

I didn't understand a word Daddy said about that pump.

He said they stood there staring at the water shooting up around the pump, wondering what they should do, when Cary Neely drove up in his truck. Mr. Neely was Great-Granddaddy Tip and Great-Granny Dosia's foster son. They had taken care of him, after his mother died, until he became a grown man. He now had a wife and children of his own.

Mr. Neely had stopped to ask if Daddy and Granddaddy wanted to go with him to help move Mr. B. B. Saunders out of the clubhouse because it was about to be flooded.

Mr. Saunders's property joined ours on the south side, and his home was called "the clubhouse." Why? I don't know. I'd never been inside it, but we had walked there several times. From our house we had to cross a cattle gap. I was always afraid one of my feet would slip down into the hole below the bars of the gap. I also thought if cows and pigs tried to cross it, their hooves would slip through the bars and trap them. I wondered if it would cause them to break their legs as they struggled to get out. But someone told me later that a cow or pig would never step onto a cattle gap because they were afraid of it. I was certainly afraid of it and always stepped carefully across those slippery bars.

The dark-stained frame clubhouse had a wide-screened porch that overlooked the river and Hewitt Springs, also called Bathtub Springs. Lacy-looking cypress trees and tall oaks shaded the water that rippled over mossy green rocks.

Mr. Saunders not only owned this clubhouse, he owned a house in Georgia, several tobacco warehouses in Live Oak, and hundreds—maybe thousands—of acres along the Suwannee River. His wife, who always looked as if she'd just stepped out of a beauty shop—every hair in place and red-painted fingernails—didn't hang around much. She spent most of her time in their big home up in Valdosta.

Since the river was threatening the clubhouse, Daddy and Granddaddy went with Mr. Neely. Daddy said they used several boats and spent most of the morning moving things out. He never mentioned whether or not Mr. Saunders was there to help with the move, or if they just used his boats and went in and moved his furniture out in his absence. Nobody we knew locked doors, whether they were at home or away. Daddy didn't say, either, where they stored Mr. Saunders's belongings. Perhaps they put everything in one of his vacant tenant houses, one on higher ground.

When they got the last load moved and unloaded, Daddy said Mr. Neely, thinking they could go home, turned to leave. But Daddy reminded him about Kenny, a colored man who worked for Mr. Saunders. "Kenny didn't have much," Daddy said, "but I knew what he had wouldn't be as easy for him to replace as it would be for a wealthy man like Mr. Saunders. So, we went and moved Kenny out before going back to the Ryes' place."

While Daddy and Granddaddy helped our neighbors, Mama and our dog Tommy walked with my sisters and me to our grandparents' house. We'd been there quite a while before Daddy and Granddaddy showed up. By then, water had crept all the way to the steps of my grandparents' house.

Granddaddy and Daddy quickly decided they should take Granddaddy Tip over to the home of their closest neighbors to the north, Lot and Frieda Herring.

Just as they got back, Daddy's cousin Joe Hingson drove up in his truck. News had traveled fast. Mr. Hingson said that Hattie Ross, his neighbor, said we could all move into her vacant tenant house. Daddy told him, "I think our house is gonna be okay, but we need to move the Ryes out."

Mr. Hingson helped them load furniture and belongings into the two trucks—his and Granddaddy's. They took several loads up to Mrs. Ross's vacant tenant house.

"We really hurried with the last load," Daddy said later. "By then, it seemed like the water was coming in faster. We wondered if some dam broke upriver, although we heard later there was no dam on the river to break. We had to leave a few things behind, including the Ryes' new electric washer, stove, and refrigerator, but we took time to jack them up off the floor."

Daddy and the rest of the family would always remember more of the details of the '48 flood than I would, since I wasn't yet four. What sticks in my mind most is how frightened I was as I ran with my sisters toward Mr. Hingson's truck. It was well after sunset, nearly dark, when Mama told us she wanted us to go with Mr. Hingson. I didn't understand since I thought Mama and Daddy planned to go back home. But Mama said, "Run! Run with Joe to his truck!" He'd left it parked quite a distance down the road, on dry ground.

The ruts on the road had already filled with water so we sprinted along the edge. As the rising water moved in, floating leaves and debris, strange noises echoed through the darkening woods. I ran as fast as I could, not thinking that the noises I heard probably came from rabbits, squirrels, 'possums, polecats and other wildlife running for dear life—like me. I didn't give a thought, either, to Granddaddy Rye's helpless, fenced-in livestock, our dog Tommy, or even Mama, Daddy, Grandma, and Granddaddy, back at their house. I thought only of saving myself from that rising water.

21

Aftermath

Mr. Hingson held his truck door open wide as Patsy, Anetha, and I—all of us breathing hard—scrambled into the cab. After slamming the door, he ran to the driver's side, slid in, and started the truck. As we sped away, I looked back to see river water filling our footprints.

"Your cousins will be surprised to see y'all," Mr. Hingson said. "Maybe Ruby will have supper cooked when we get there."

Mmm . . . like Mama, Mrs. Hingson was a good cook. The two of them were second cousins. Mrs. Hingson's grandfather, Porch Lanier, and Granddaddy Tip were brothers.

Also, Daddy's and Mr. Hingson's mothers were sisters, so that made them first cousins, but Daddy said they were actually more like brothers. "I lived with Joe before Joe married Ruby," he said, "and even for a short while after the wedding because I was helping him farm."

The Hingsons lived about five miles from us, north of the church we all attended. Their house resembled my grandparents' house, as if built from the same Sears and Roebuck plan.

When we arrived around dark, the whole family met us on their front porch: Mrs. Hingson, Mary Frances, who was Patsy's age,

Duane, my age, and the older two, Yvonne and Theron.

I guess we looked a mess because Mrs. Hingson told us we could "go wash up" and that Yvonne and Frances could "set the table."

After washing our hands, we went back to help, but the dining table was already set with silverware, plates, glasses of iced tea, platters of pork chops and biscuits, and bowls of rice and peas—all things I liked.

I felt comfortable at the Hingsons' big table and perfectly secure in their home that night. There was no rushing water to be seen or heard—except at bath time. Then, the water was crystal clear and gushed only from the shiny faucet into a white bathtub. I wished we had a smooth tub like that at home instead of an old rusty washtub.

After we dried off, Mrs. Hingson told Mary Frances to loan us some clean clothes. The shirt she gave me reached my knees, and its short sleeves hung below my elbows. But the panties, made of stretchy cotton, fit better than my own britches.

Meanwhile, Mrs. Hingson spread quilts on the floor. When it was time for bed, Patsy and Mary Frances took one pallet. Anetha and I lay down on the other, but then I jumped up and ran back to the bathroom for one last pee.

When the lights went out, the house grew quiet, and I drifted off to sleep, blissfully unaware that river water was creeping up the steps of my grandparents' house like the intruder it was.

At daylight the next morning, Granddaddy Rye came for us.

Rubbing sleep from my eyes, I realized I had not peed while I slept. I wanted to shout to the world that I was dry, but I bragged only to Anetha. Mrs. Hingson said we could give Mary Frances her clothes back later, so we left wearing borrowed clothes.

"Where we going?" Patsy asked after we got into the truck.

"You girls are gonna stay with me and your grandma for a while," Granddaddy said.

"Where's Mama and Daddy?" I asked.

"They went home last night after we moved the animals."

"Where'd you move 'em to?" Anetha asked.

"Well, we rounded up the cows and herded them over to the Herring place."

"Is that where Granddaddy Tip is staying?" I asked.

"Yep. Him and all the animals. After we got back from moving the cows, the water was too high to run the pigs out, so we loaded 'em into boats and rowed 'em out."

Pigs in boats? I was sorry I missed that.

"Here we are," Granddaddy said a couple of minutes later.

The tenant house that Grandma and Granddaddy had moved into was just down the road and around the corner from the Hingson's place. The old tenant house had never seen a lick of paint, so from the outside, it looked kind of like home. But it had no electricity, so its two rooms, jam-packed with my grandparents' belongings, were almost dark as night. It had a woodstove, though, and Grandma was already putting it to use. I smelled bacon frying.

After breakfast, Granddaddy said, "Shug, I'm going down to our house and check on things."

"Can we go?" Anetha asked.

I considered staying with Grandma, but decided to go, afraid I might miss seeing something as funny as pigs in boats.

Anetha hopped into the truck first. She always wanted to be as close to Granddaddy as paint on a board. I sat next to her since Patsy thought she owned the spot by the door. Granddaddy slid in on the driver's side, ducking his head to keep from knocking off his hat, which he never left the house without. He also had a habit of tucking his khaki pants legs into his tight leather boots—dark brown, laced to his knees. He looked as if he was ready to jump into a saddle, but he no longer owned a horse.

When we got within sight of our grandparents' house that morning, I could not believe my eyes. Their house sat in the middle of a giant lake. Its black, glass-like surface stretched out of sight.

"We'll take the boat from here," Granddaddy said as he stopped at the edge of the water. He'd left his boat half in and half out of the water, tied to a fence post that marked the edge of his land. He untied it and we jumped into the familiar wooden boat we'd ridden in many times. The three of us disagreed about who should sit where, and after a bit of squabbling and shoving, I again ended up squashed between my older sisters.

"Sit still now and don't rock the boat," Granddaddy reminded us as he stepped into the boat. "I don't want to have to fish one of you outta the water today." Granddaddy's boat contained no life-saving equipment, except the rope, the paddle, and Granddaddy.

He pushed off with the paddle, then dipped it into the water on one side, then the other, as he guided us along the fence, which gradually disappeared underwater.

"Look over there." Granddaddy pointed his dripping paddle.

"Is that a water moccasin?" Anetha asked, stretching her eyes so big I saw whites all around. I stiffened and gripped the edge of the bench seat. The snake, about ten feet away, was gliding along parallel with us.

Not one to waste words, Granddaddy said, "Might be."

For once, I was happy to be bracketed by my sisters. Thankfully, Granddaddy rowed away from the snake and over the wire fence, toward the house. I turned and watched to make sure that snake didn't follow. It finally disappeared near the tops of tall bushes sticking out of the water.

At the house, the boat glided right over the porch. Granddaddy tied up to one of its columns and stood in the boat, his hat nearly brushing the ceiling. When he stepped over the side of the boat onto the porch, his knee-high leather boots disappeared under the dark water.

"You girls wait here," he said, as he eased open the screen door, then the heavy wooden door. "I'm going inside to check on the appliances."

My grandparents' new house, Suwannee River flood of '48

When he came back out, he was smiling. "We jacked 'em up high enough. That'll make your Grandma happy."

Back in the boat, he pointed the boat toward our house, which was now on an island, not quite as big as our yard. Daddy, Mama, our dog Tommy, and Betty, Mama's milk cow, weren't hard to find. We didn't stay long. But before we left, Mama packed a paper sack of clothes for us to take back to our temporary home.

In the days that followed, folks stopped by the Ross tenant house to say hello and sympathize with Granddaddy and Grandma about their flooded home. They also talked about the loss of crops. A number of farmers had been affected.

"What'd you lose?" they asked Granddaddy.

"Several acres of cabbage and all my tobacco crop."

"How about C.G.?"

"Onions and tobacco," Granddaddy said. "And even if the river goes back down, the ground's gonna be too boggy to replant right away. Then, of course, it'll be too hot. It's a bad situation."

Even *I* knew that losing the tobacco crop was a big deal.

Within a few days, though, Granddaddy and Daddy got surprising news. The agricultural agent in Live Oak sent word that the federal government would allow a flooded-out farmer to plant his tobacco allotment on land other than his own. And folks in the community stepped up to help one another. Mr. Hingson said Granddaddy Rye could plant tobacco on his farm, and his brother, Oliver, offered land to Daddy.

"We'll pay you rent," Daddy and Granddaddy told them, but the Hingson brothers wouldn't hear of it. Daddy found out later that Oliver, to make room for Daddy's crop, had plowed up several acres of his own corn crop. And some other nice farmer loaned Daddy and Granddaddy one of those modern tobacco planters that not only plowed a trench for the seedlings, but covered the roots. When the tobacco was planted this time, my sisters and I didn't have to help.

As neighbors continued to stop by our temporary address to ask how things were going, they expressed surprise that our house was still on dry ground. One man smiled and raised his eyebrows as he said, "Hm-m-m—C.G. and Ethel, all alone on a secluded island, huh?"

Living on that island was no picnic, though, Mama claimed later.

"When the river first moved in," she said, "our well water was crystal clear, as it always had been. But long before the flood water peaked, we started seeing sediment in our water glasses. We put a cloth sugar sack over the mouth of the pump, and every so often we had to take that sack off and wash the sand and mud out of it."

"We got a good scare one night too," Daddy said. "We woke up to an eerie sound—a high, piercing squeal, but a lot louder than any pig I ever heard. We eventually figured out that it was metal grinding against metal. It was the Drew Railroad Bridge. Evidently, logs floating out of the swamp into the river's swift current were slamming against the bridge and causing it to turn—just as some people said happened during the flood of '28. Every time one of them logs hit that bridge, it let out another *ee-e-e-e-e-e.*"

As for me, after the initial scare of the rising water and that water moccasin next to the boat, the flood and its aftermath turned out to be nothing but fun. I was happy to be living with our grandparents. My sisters and I had their undivided attention, and they never scolded. In fact, Grandma acted like she didn't even notice when I had a nighttime accident on the quilt pallet. She just hung the quilt to dry on the clothesline in the backyard where people passing by would never see it.

I liked living with my grandparents in the cozy tenant house so much that I was in no rush for the flood to end at all.

When we made a second trip to my grandparents' house, Grand-ma Rye went too, and I felt more comfortable in the boat. The water had gone down so much that Grand-daddy was unable to row his boat across the porch. *Shucks!*

On the third trip, we didn't get to ride in the boat at all. Granddaddy drove his truck right through the muddy puddles and all the way past their house to ours. There, we picked up Mama and Daddy and went back to our grandparents' house, with Daddy and us kids in the back of the truck.

As soon as we stopped at my grandparents' gate, the adults noticed a line about a foot and a half above the porch floor. They said it showed just how high the water had risen. Inside, Daddy pointed to the sheetrock walls, swollen below the water line. The house had a strange smell, and throughout the house, the floor's pine planks had buckled.

As the adults surveyed the damage, we sisters played a game we made up. We attempted to walk the length of the buckled boards without falling over. But we stopped our game after we noticed that Grandma was dabbing her eyes with a hankie.

"We've got a lot of work to do before we can move back in," Granddaddy said, putting his arm around her, his voice hoarse. "Course, we'll have to wait until it all dries out."

"Maybe we can start as soon as we finish gathering tobacco," Daddy said.

"Yep," Granddaddy agreed. "Guess we should open all the doors and windows and leave it to dry out."

As the windows were raised and propped up, a breeze began to blow through.

Satisfied they'd done all they could that day, Granddaddy and Grandma took Mama, Daddy, my sisters, and me home to stay, and the two of them returned to the Ross house.

Low spots on our farm still held water—ponds that had never been there before—so in the days that followed, my sisters and I had fun wading and pretending to swim.

One morning we saw the Hingson's truck coming down the road. I figured they were coming to fetch Mary Frances's clothes. But no, they just came to visit. They were still there when the George  family, our neighbors to the northwest, showed up. Their son Billy was my age. The day turned into a big party. All of us kids spent the afternoon catching minnows in the ponds, using lightweight aluminum pots Mama loaned us. We carried the water-filled pots back to the yard, poured the river water out, placed the flopping minnows on boards, and cut their heads off. No adult interfered as we pretended to scale, gut, and filet our "fishes" the way we'd seen them do.

A few days later, several men, who claimed they were state officials, showed up. They'd come "to seine fish from the ponds and return them to the river," they said. It didn't seem right that they could come on our land and take our fish. Daddy let them, but they missed a

> ### Suwannee River's Crest, 1948
> Natural levees along the Suwannee River, which reduce the risk of flooding, range from 20-40 feet. At nearby Luraville, where flood stage is reached at 37 feet, the river's crest on April 12, 1948, reached 53.50 feet. *http://water.weather.gov/*

few. One small pond near our house still had several perch in it long after they left. Later, as the water began drying up, the fishes had so little room to swim that Daddy was able to catch them with his bare hands. Instead of transferring them to the river as the "officials" had supposedly done, though, Daddy scaled and gutted them so Mama could put them in the frying pan.

In early June, Daddy caught another mess of fish from the only pond left, the one in the bottom land where the onions had rotted. That water eventually disappeared too, leaving behind thick mud that dried, cracked, and peeled up like old paint.

In mid-June, we found one more fish, a big one—with our noses. We followed the odor that led us to a catfish stuck in the wire fence. Daddy said it was the biggest catfish he'd ever seen in his life. It was way too far gone for Mama to fry, but it gave a bunch of buzzards a meal.

We found no more fish on our land, after that. Not even smelly ones. But the odor that came from the rotted cabbages in Granddaddy's field was enough to make a polecat puke.

22

All Dried Out

Late that summer, Daddy and Granddaddy Rye began work on my grandparents' water-damaged house, beginning with the floor.

"The pine planks have finally dried out," Daddy told Mama one night, "but they're still so warped, it's taking forty penny nails to force 'em back into place."

What? Unbelievable. Nails were expensive. *Forty pennies* would buy me *four* caramel Sugar Daddies. When I eventually learned that "40 penny" meant the nails were five inches long, I found that equally hard to believe.

When every board had been hammered back in place, Daddy and Granddaddy sanded and varnished the floor, and repaired and repainted the walls, inside and out. The house then looked almost like new. Even Grandma's Boston ferns on the front porch, growing in wooden boxes Granddaddy had built for her, were recovering from their near-drowning experience, and Grandma Rye could hardly wait to move home.

As Daddy and Granddaddy discussed moving day one afternoon at our house, Granddaddy said, "I offered again to pay Hattie rent for her tenant house, but she won't take a dime."

"That Hattie Ross is a fine woman," Daddy said.

I didn't know Mrs. Ross well, but I knew she lived in a fine house—painted the whitest white, with window shutters that perfectly matched the red geraniums in her front yard (red was my favorite color), and a windmill in the backyard. A white picket fence surrounded everything. From the tenant house, which Granddaddy and Grandma were still living in, we'd had a good view of her place, across the road and through the pines. I never got to go inside Mrs. Ross's house, but I'd vowed to one day live with my future husband in a house just like hers with red shutters, red geraniums, a picket fence, and a windmill.

"Yep, Hattie's a fine woman," Daddy repeated, as if to himself, after Granddaddy left. "I never will forget her husband Green."

I was thinking how the color green was a funny name for a man and almost didn't hear what Daddy said next, "Green was always pestering Hattie to wash his neck."

What? When I marry and live in a pretty red-and-white house, I don't plan to wash my husband's neck. I'd never seen Mama wash Daddy's. I'd never seen Grandma Rye wash Granddaddy Rye's. And I'd never seen Granny Dosia wash Granddaddy Tip's neck.

"Yeah," Daddy said as he looked over at Mama and winked. "Some wives used to do things like that for their husbands." Mama shook her head slowly and looked back down at the pillowcase she was embroidering with yellow flowers. (Yellow was my *second* favorite color. Buttery yellow. Not egg-yolk yellow.)

"That Green Ross was a mess!" Daddy continued. "He'd say to his wife, 'Hat'—that's what he called her—'I want you to wash my neck.' And that Green—he'd be stretched back in his big easy chair resting—doing absolutely nothing! 'Okay, Green, I'll be there in a minute,' Hattie would say. She was busy in the kitchen. 'Hat,' Green would call her again after a few minutes passed, 'I want you to wash my *neck*!' 'Okay, Green. I told you I'd be there in a minute.' 'Hat,' Green would say in another little while, 'I said I want—' 'Green!' Hattie interrupted, 'Have a little patience! I told you I'd be there in a minute!' 'Don't you worry, Hat,' Green said, 'My patience ain't near 'bout wore out yet.'"

Daddy was always full of stories and none of us ever bothered to ask where he heard them. I figured this one had been passed on to him by his old high school buddy, the one he called George Frederick, whose family lived in the Rosses' tenant house when Daddy was in high school. Back then, Daddy and George Frederick rode the same school bus and visited back and forth with one another.

That was back when Daddy was living with his cousin, Joe Hingson. Like I mentioned before, Daddy lived in an orphanage after his daddy died and his mama got sick. His mother's twin brother, Clarence, agreed to take Daddy in just before he turned fourteen, the orphanage's upper age limit. Daddy lived with him and Aunt Daisy for several years. But after Daddy and his uncle had a falling out because his uncle insisted that Daddy stay home from school to work on the farm, Daddy moved in with his cousin, Joe. Daddy completed his high school education at the age of twenty-one; then he stayed on with Joe, helping him on the farm while he waited for Mama to graduate high school, so they could marry and buy a farm.

Daddy continued telling stories about the Rosses.

"I remember hearing too," Daddy said, "how the Rosses' little girl asked her mother one day, 'Mama, how many birds do you think flew over the house today?' But before Hattie could even think of an answer, Green piped up, 'And what color were they?' Yep, that Green Ross was a mess. But when he died, I think he left Hattie in pretty good shape."

I thought that was a corny story Daddy told, but I agreed with Daddy that Mr. Green Ross had left his widow living in the prettiest house in the whole community, maybe in the world.

A few days after Granddaddy and Grandma Rye moved home, they went to the Herrings, got Granddaddy Tip, and brought him home. But my great-grandfather seemed different somehow. He often had a faraway look in his eyes.

Although our house had not flooded, Daddy and Mama's experience with sand in the water persuaded Daddy that we needed a deeper well. The one we had, which connected to the hand pump, was sunk to a depth of only thirty-four feet, Daddy said. He wanted to take it deeper. When Joe Hingson offered him an old electric pump he no longer needed, Daddy took it.

"I added a valve to prevent water from returning to the bottom of the well," Daddy said. That kept the water up in the pipe until more was needed."

At the same time Daddy installed Joe's pump, he installed a metal pipe that brought water right up to a spigot above the water shelf at the back of our open hall. The shelf, a foot-wide board about four feet off the floor, held a water bucket with a dipper, plus a portable basin for washing hands. Just as always, we continued to toss dirty water into the yard, onto the four-o'clock bushes. But with Joe's pump installed and the new pipe in place, Mama didn't have to go out into the yard to pump water when she needed it for cooking, for making iced tea or Kool-Aid, or even for washing dishes. And when anybody needed to wash up for a meal, we simply turned on the spigot. The shelf was only eye level for me, though, and the spigot was a foot above that, so I had to drag over a chair to stand on.

Daddy's next improvement involved the farm animals. He tore down the rusty gutter, one he'd cleverly constructed years before to deliver water from the hand pump to the animal trough. Where the gutter had crossed the yard, he ran a metal pipe and added a spigot at the end. (Years later, Daddy would even install a toilet-tank float in the animal trough, so when the cows drank the water down below a certain level, the float caused the water to trip on and automatically refill the trough.)

As fall approached that year, Daddy turned his attention to the land. The flood, he said, had washed away most of the topsoil. So, he planted the whole farm in blue lupin. Granddaddy did the same with his acreage. Weeks later, when the fields began to turn from lush green to a beautiful purple-y blue, Daddy and Granddaddy would plow the blooming plants under. The rotting foliage, Daddy said, would enrich the soil for the next year's crops.

23

The Road to Grandma's

"Mama, can we go get the mail?" I asked early one morning, just a few days before Patsy was to start going to school.

"It's too early." Mama said. "Wait a little while."

I don't remember how old I was when Mama first let us walk to Grandma's by ourselves, but the path was now as familiar to me as the creases in the palms of my hands, creases that resembled Granddaddy Rye's initials: M. M., which stood for Milton Mahone.

My sisters and I sometimes called Granddaddy Rye by his first name, Milton. We did the same with Grandma, often calling her Grandma Delma instead of Grandma Rye. It avoided confusion since Mama called her father's parents Grandma and Granddaddy Rye. She said her family lived with them on Pine Island in the Gulf of Mexico for a short time when she was a little girl. While she knew them well, they were almost like strangers to me. I doubted I would recognize them if they drove up. Mama said they now lived down in Punta Gorda, wherever that was.

"Can we go get the mail *now*?" I asked a few minutes later.

"Yeah," Patsy added, "Why can't we go now?"

"Please," Anetha chimed in.

Mama looked up at us—all of us standing on ready.

"I thought I might go too," she said, "and shave Granddaddy Tip today. But I want to finish this sewing first."

Sewing? It looked as if Mama was ripping, not sewing.

As we turned to walk away, shoulders drooping, Mama changed her mind. "Alright. Y'all can go ahead. Tell Mama I'll be along later to shave Granddaddy Tip."

We perked up and rushed out the door before Mama could change her mind back. Tommy joined us as we bounded out the swinging gate and down the crooked rutted path through the woods. Few cars traveled this way, and Mama said nature kept trying to heal the ruts, just as nature healed cuts and scrapes on our knees.

As we passed under the large oaks that formed a canopy over the road, I looked around at the shaded, leaf-covered ground, searching for lavender wood violets that sprouted in the spring. I wanted to find some to pick for Grandma but saw none.

Me, Tommy, Anetha and Patsy

This wooded area, like most of the land between our house and the river, was owned by the Drew family, descendants of Florida's twelfth Governor, George Franklin Drew.[1] Daddy hoped to buy the twenty-acre parcel in front of our house or trade it to the Drews for the twenty acres Daddy owned near the river, but so far, he hadn't

[1] George Franklin Drew, the first Democratic governor of Florida after the Civil War, served from 1877 to 1881. *https://www.floridamemory.com/collections/governors/drew.php*

sealed a deal with Mr. Herbert Drew, the one in charge of the Drew estate.

Beyond the oaks, we passed the area where we tossed trash— things like glass bottles and tin cans, stuff we couldn't feed to the chickens, the pigs, or to Tommy, and couldn't burn in the barrel in the backyard.

Smoke lingered in the air from the fire Mama had set in the barrel that morning. But this smokiness was nothing compared to other times. During the winter, the air sometimes became hazy with smoke from fires escaping from chimneys and fires in fields and woods. Farmers commonly set fire to the grasslands and the hammock before trees and grass budded out each spring.

Daddy explained once that burning things off cleared out the underbrush, killed diseases, and helped nature start over. Every year, he burned off his pastureland as well as the Drew woods in front of our house. As soon as the ground cooled, my sisters and I would stomp on every charred clump of wire grass we could find. The wire grass grew about a foot tall and had strong green needles like longleaf pines, but when burnt, the needles became tender and crisp.

Scrub oaks, pines, palmetto, persimmons, and a few Chickasaw plums lived together in these woods. In summer, the woods became dotted with black-eyed Susans. A few bloomed until the early fall. Now, beautyberry bushes showed off purple berries clinging to dark stems. On occasion, we picked the flowers and berries, and Mama stuck the stems into a water-filled quart jar and set it on our dining table. I thought she should take one of those pretty bouquets to church and set it on the squatty table in front of the preacher's pulpit, as Mrs. Edith Knight and other women in the church did with their roses and camellias. But any bouquet we picked always stayed put on our dining table until the water began to turn cloudy, at which time Mama tossed the water out and the shedding bouquet into the backyard burn barrel.

We made our way to the bend in the road where mud puddles formed after heavy rains. With no rain for days, the mud had cracked and peeled. We smoothed the cracks with our feet, making the charcoal-colored ground silky smooth.

Once or twice, Daddy had used his tractor and a chain to pull a stuck car from the mud in this low spot. Thankfully, Granddaddy's truck never got bogged down there, though muddy water sometimes splattered up through cracks in his truck's floorboards.

After smoothing the peeled mud, we trekked on. The road veered right, and from that point on, ran alongside Granddaddy's wire fence. As we approached the fence, a quail took flight, startling us. It reminded me of the day Mama walked the road with us and we spotted a quail in the road ahead, limping and dragging one of its wings.

"That bird's hurt," Anetha had said as she'd started toward it. "Let's catch it and help it."

"No. No." Mama said. "It's a mother quail. Let her be."

"But, Mama, she's hurt," Anetha protested, as if she might cry.

"No, I told you, she's not hurt. She's just pretending to have a broken wing. Watch. She'll try to lead us away from her nest of babies. Let's just ease along behind her."

We did as Mama said and kept following as the quail limped several yards down the road. Suddenly her wings fluttered, and up and off she went. I don't know how Mama knew all she did. Did she learn it at Ladyland? I would be so glad when I was old enough to go to school.

We passed the ramshackle house, left of the road, where Mama said she went to school when she was about nine. She said it served as the school while the one-room Ladyland School was being replaced with a new building with three classrooms. Soon, Patsy would begin first grade, the third generation to go to Ladyland.

Rotting boards and fallen chimney bricks littered the ground around the former temporary school. A few of the bricks from the crumbling chimney supported our jump board, back at home.

"Look at all the salamander hills," Anetha yelled and pointed at Granddaddy's pasture. Each mound of fresh dirt stood about a foot high. I learned later that these were actually *pocket gophers*, furry critters that store sand in pockets in their cheeks to carry it to the surface. But our word for the animal also had basis. Daddy said the word came from "sand mounder."

Blackberry vines grew alongside Granddaddy's fence. In summer, the berries turned from green to red to black. My mouth watered as I thought of blackberry cobbler. Mama made it with whole berries, whereas Grandma made it with juice squeezed from the berries. That's because neither Granddaddy Rye nor Granddaddy Tip had any teeth.

"Look out for snakes," Mama and Grandma cautioned every time we picked blackberries for cobbler, jam, or jelly. Their warnings were unnecessary, of course. We knew to look for snakes. We'd seen our share along this sunny stretch of the road where the ruts were wider and the sand softer.

We skipped along now, our bare feet making brz-z-z-t sounds as the soles of our feet skidded across loose sand.

"There's a snake track," Anetha said, stopping. "He's a big one."

She'd skipped a few feet ahead of Patsy and me, so we ran to inspect the snake track, curious to see its width.

"That ain't very big," Patsy said. I've seen way bigger than that."

Anytime we spotted a live snake, we knew to keep our distance; we weren't sure which ones were harmless and which ones could kill you. Adults often talked about deadly coral snakes, rattlers, and moccasins.

Once, when Mama walked with us, we came upon a snake she called a *spreading adder*. She said it was harmless, and to prove it, she picked up a stick from the edge of the woods and got close enough to poke it. The snake backed its head up, crooking its neck backwards, and in seconds, its head doubled in size.

"He wants us to think he's a poisonous puff adder or cobra," Mama said. "But he won't hurt you. And he eats mice, so we don't kill adders."

As we walked on now, Patsy pointed to a white streak across the blue sky. Seeing an airplane was unusual, but it didn't scare us, unlike the time we saw something we couldn't identify and ran home to describe it to Mama. "Probably just a blimp," she said, "nothing to be afraid of."

By the time we passed the pond in Granddaddy's field, a sinkhole that held water, we could see our grandparents' house in the distance. Mama said she used to swim in that sinkhole, the same spot where, long ago, Granddaddy Tip set up a still for making white lightning. He never went there anymore, but we did. Every Christmas, we went to the sinkhole to gather holly to make a wreath for the front-room door.

Mama was always making something pretty from what seemed like nothing. Once, she cut two or three bare branches from a thorny tree along that road, a tree she called a Hawthorn. What she wanted with those ugly branches, I could not imagine. But back at home, she stuck them into a large tinfoil-wrapped can filled with wet sand, and set it on the table. To our surprise, she handed us a bag of sugar-coated gumdrops we didn't know she had and told us to stick a gumdrop on each thorn. The candies transformed the ugly Hawthorn branches into a colorful sugarplum tree. Too pretty to eat. Almost.

In the Drew woods, not far from the Hawthorn tree, grew a spindly persimmon tree. The fruit would turn from green, to yellow, to orange. The summer before, we'd begged Mama to let us pick the persimmons when they were yellow. She refused, saying they were not fully ripe.

"But, Mama," Patsy protested, "they're already yellow."

"Yeah, but they're not yet soft. Let's wait a few days till they turn orange. Have a little patience."

We kept begging until Mama gave in. "Okay. Sure. Go ahead." She stood waiting on the road while we each picked one and sank our teeth into it.

"Aaaagh!" We gasped as we spit acrid persimmon bits onto the ground. The inside of my mouth felt as if it had dried and shriveled up like a prune. "Ptoo! Ptoo!"

"See?" Mama said. "You didn't believe me. You girls need to have a little patience."

At the time, I wasn't even sure what patience was, but I wanted some right then and there if it would get rid of the wrinkles and dry bitter taste in my mouth.

"There's a gopher track," Anetha said as we approached the graded section of the road. The critter we called a gopher, others called a gopher tortoise. One had evidently recently pulled itself across the road, clawing the sand and leaving a smooth track where its shell slid along. We followed the track, and off the side of the road, found its home, a sloping hole surrounded by piles of yellow sand. The yellow sand indicated the hole went deep. When Daddy and Granddaddy dug holes for fence posts using post-hole diggers, they always brought up yellow sand when they dug below a foot or two.

Anytime we came upon a gopher, its head disappeared into its shell. It wouldn't stick its head out again until we walked away. But that never stopped us from tapping its shell and nudging it with bare feet, hoping the gopher might change its mind.

Daddy accidentally ran over one once, but he never killed one on purpose, not even for food, as some people did. They said it tasted similar to turtle meat. But Mama said she'd never cooked or tasted gopher and didn't intend to.

As we approached our grandparents' house, the sun was warming the sand, but it wasn't hot enough to burn the soles of our feet as it did in summer months. Then, we had to slide our feet under the top layer to reach cooler sand, or jump off the road onto grass, being careful to avoid sandspurs, stinging nettle, prickly pears, and touch-me-nots.

The touch-me-nots bloomed only in summer. Once I'd picked some for Grandma and learned why they had the name *touch-me-not*. I ended up with tiny thorns in my fingers that proved impossible to remove, even with Grandma's tweezers. But you could stroke its leaves without getting hurt. I liked to do that, so I could watch its tiny leaves fold together like hands in prayer. [2]

"Let's race," Patsy said after we reached the straight, smooth part of the road near our grandparents' house. Thanks to the huge yellow road scraper that came by periodically, the fresh-packed dirt crunched under our feet. I wished the man who drove that yellow contraption, with a blade as tall as I was, would keep going down the narrow road to our house, but he always stayed on the main road, which turned west and led to the Holiness Church. We'd been to that church a time or two for revival services, during which people got "filled with the Holy Ghost"—that's what Daddy called it. He said they were "speaking in tongues." To me, it sounded like babble.

Racing with my sisters, I got tired, so when we reached the oaks with limbs reaching across the road like outstretched fingers, I slowed down. Spanish moss hung from low branches, resembling long beards—beards like I imagined grew on the chins of Santa Claus and God. High up, olive green mistletoe clung to branches, but it was hard to spot, except during winter months, when the branches were bare. Then, the mistletoe stood out as black lacy balls against the blue sky. Each year before Christmas, Granddaddy Rye used his rifle to shoot down clumps so we could hang green sprigs over doorways to invite kisses.

Ahead, I saw Granddaddy Tip, sitting in his porch rocker, his

---

[2] In the book, *Summer of the Dragon*, environmentalist and horticulture expert Don Goodman, who lost his arm to a Florida alligator at Kanapaha Botanical Gardens in Gainesville, calls this plant the bashful brier and *Mimosa pudica*.

crooked-stem pipe dangled from his lips.

"Hey, young-uns," he called out when he saw us coming.

After saying hey to him, we went inside to tell Grandma what Mama had said about shaving Granddaddy.

"Okay," Grandma said, "I'll finish this letter to Harold so she can set up shop here at the dining table."

24

Waiting for the Mail

My sisters shoved one another as they wrangled over the rocker on one side of my grandparents' front porch. On the opposite side, I sat on Granddaddy Tip's knees.

Patsy won the shoving match, plopped in the rocking chair, and rocked back, barely missing Anetha's bare toes splayed on the concrete floor. After rocking only three times, Patsy jumped from the chair she'd fought to win and said, "Let's play follow the leader," which actually meant "Follow me."

Anetha followed as Patsy marched down the steps through the grass to the front gate, around a clump of lilies, then back up the steps, and across the porch. She stepped onto the forest green bench next to the living room windows and jumped off, with Anetha right behind her, then shook the coral vine that shaded the south end of the porch. A few tiny, pinkish blossoms left from summer rained down, littering the floor. Arms outstretched like airplanes, my sisters traipsed around, waving their hands across fronds of boxed Boston ferns and around the chair where I sat with Granddaddy Tip. They bumped his chair and my head as if they owned the air we breathed and the porch itself.

They probably thought they did own the porch, since the

concrete floor held their footprints, frozen in time from when they were one and two years old. Good thing nobody tried to add my footprint, given that the floor was rock solid by the time I was born. Still, I felt jealous every time one of my sisters placed a foot over her print to show how much her foot had grown since she stepped in wet cement.

Patsy's footprint

As Granddaddy sang, "Froggy Went a Courtin'" to me, my sisters climbed up on one of the concrete plinths at the front edge of the porch and began their march, still one of their favorite activities, but it always bothered Granddaddy Tip.

"Girls, you'd better get down from there before you fall and get hurt," he warned.

Over and over, Granddaddy started and stopped singing as he warned my sisters. Each time, he'd begin in a nice tone of voice, saying, "You'd better get down before you get hurt." He would end up swearing, but he hadn't gotten there yet that day. He had just warned them nicely again when they stopped, and hopped down. *Huh? They minded him?* Then I saw why they got down. Mama was coming up the road.

"I came to give you a shave and haircut," Mama said to Granddaddy Tip as she came up the steps, "but we'll wait until after we eat dinner." She went inside to join Grandma.

I had seen Mama shave Granddaddy Tip many times. She would assemble a basin of water, a mug of hard soap, a soft shaving brush, a safety razor, and a towel. After she got Granddaddy Tip settled in a chair by the dining table, she would wet the brush in water, lather it up in the cup, and smear the lather over his face until he looked like Santa Claus.

I rubbed the palms of my hands against Granddaddy's white whiskers, so long they felt soft. From his porch rocker, we had a direct line of sight to the big mailbox, nailed to a post by the road.

The roomy mailbox held anything sent to us—the Howells, Laniers, or Ryes. Letters, duns (that's what Daddy called bills that needed paying), magazines like *Progressive Farmer* and *Farm & Ranch, Sears and Roebuck* catalogs, even small packages.

About the only parcel too big to fit inside the mailbox was one that came once or twice a year, a wide, square corrugated box, nearly a yard across and about six-inches deep. It had circular cutouts about the size of pennies. And boy, was it noisy, for it held a hundred fluffy little biddies. Their peeps overlapped to create one continuous sound. Since the box of biddies was too wide to fit inside the mailbox, the postman always got out of his car and set the box on the porch, along with the letters and other mail.

Whoever cut the penny-sized circles in the cardboard never bothered to punch them all the way out, so my sisters and I always took up the task. We sat on the concrete floor, punching out the circles to give the yellow biddies more fresh air. As we poked, biddy beaks nibbled at our fingers, making us giggle. Even so, when Mama cut the string and opened the box, we usually discovered three or four lifeless ones. "The hot transit was just too much for the weaker ones," she said.

Seeing the dead biddies being trampled by the others made me sad, but I never cried, perhaps because I knew that all of the tiny chicks would eventually end up in Mama's frying pan.

Although we were not expecting a box of biddies that day, the mail carrier, Mr. Dave McNeil, seldom passed without dropping something off.

"'Bout time for the postman," Granddaddy Tip said as he tugged on the gold-link chain dangling from a belt loop, and pulled his watch from a slit pocket in his khaki trousers. Holding the watch at arm's length, he stared at its filigreed hands that pointed to Roman numerals. "Quarter past the hour," he said, as he slid the watch back into its pocket.

He repeated that ritual every few minutes. In each instance, before putting the timepiece away, he raised it to his ear, tapped its edge against his palm, and twisted its winding stem, as if he thought it had stopped running.

I thought it strange that he checked his watch so often. But I knew nothing about a condition called dementia that can eat away at a person's memory until they eventually forget the faces of watches, and the faces of those they love. I also knew nothing about a place, in the panhandle of Florida, called Chattahoochee, where people could be "treated" for mental disorders or "put away." I didn't know then that Granddaddy Tip had already spent time there for a "mental condition."

Grandma pushed open the screen door and came out of the house holding the letter she'd addressed to Uncle Harold. I got down off Granddaddy's knees and followed her to the mailbox. She placed the letter inside, dropped three pennies on top of it, and let me raise the red flag to signal Mr. McNeill to stop, even if he had no mail for us. The instant he found Grandma's unstamped letter and three pennies, he would stamp the letter for her.

When he finally arrived to deliver our mail, I was back on Granddaddy's knees.

"Okay, sweetie," Granddaddy Tip said after all of us waved to Mr. McNeil and he drove off, "Hop down so we can go fetch the mail."

I scrambled to the floor and watched Granddaddy's lanky frame unfold. Though stooped with age, my great-grandfather still towered over every member of the family. He was, in my eyes, a giant of a man.

Part III
Living and Learning

25
Getting Educated
1948-49

Patsy had all the luck. Now that she'd turned six, she could go to school. Not only that, she was getting new dresses.

I watched as Mama folded a piece of gingham, making a double thickness. She flicked her hands up and down, popping the fabric the way she did bedsheets when folding them. The checked gingham waved in the air and settled on the dining table. After smoothing it flat with her palms, she laid down pattern pieces, arranging them this way and that until they fit like a jigsaw puzzle. She straight-pinned the pattern in place and tailor tacked darts through the tissue-thin paper. Finally, she guided scissor blades along the pattern's dark lines, cutting out the bodice, yoke, skirt, sleeves, and facings.

Hour after hour, the sound of Granny's treadle Singer (a gift to Mama) echoed through our house. By the end of the week, Patsy had three new dresses—all with full skirts and puffy sleeves—and the prettiest red coat I'd ever seen.

Patsy would go to the same school Mama and Grandma Rye attended. Grandma's schooling took place when Ladyland was a one-room log schoolhouse. After graduating from the eighth grade there, a student could go to Suwannee High School in Live Oak.

Unfortunately, Grandma didn't go to high school because she had no way to get to town except in her father's horse and buggy, and travel time would have consumed half the day.

While Mama was in the lower grades, the new three-room school was completed, and after she graduated there, she was able to go on to high school because, by then,

3-room Ladyland School
Drawing by student Donald Ray Avery

the state provided buses for rural students.

The state now even provided transportation to Ladyland, but only if you lived more than a mile from the school. We didn't. If we stood on our front porch, we could see the school, painted white, across Granddaddy's farm. I assumed Patsy would be walking to school since the bus wouldn't pick her up and we had no car. But Mama decided Patsy shouldn't have to walk a mile, carrying her lunch pail; never mind that Daddy said he used to walk five. Mama arranged transportation with Mrs. Annie Lou Johnson, who taught first and second grades.

One morning a week, when Patsy's teacher picked her up, she dropped off a basket of clothes for Mama to iron. They'd agreed that Mama would iron all Mr. and Mrs. Johnson's clothes each week in exchange for Patsy's ride to and from school all week.

Although Mama still washed clothes the way she always had, us- ing the fired-up washpot in the backyard, she had a new gas iron. She said it made ironing much easier than the old flatirons she used to heat on the stove or hearth. Plus, she said, the gas iron kept a steady, even temperature. Mama never seemed to mind ironing; in fact, she hummed gospel songs the whole time. Two of her fa- vorites were "In the Garden" and "Whispering Hope."

At school, Patsy became a star pupil, perhaps because she

already knew her ABCs and how to count all the way to 100. After Mrs. Johnson began to teach Patsy how to read, by sounding out the letters, Patsy decided she could teach Anetha. I don't actually remember Anetha's first lesson, but I heard Mama tell the story so many times that I had it memorized.

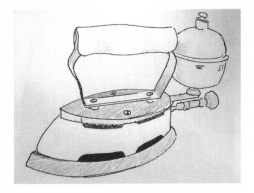

The gas iron operated similarly to a gas lantern. The small tank attached to the back of the iron provided pressurized gas and could be refilled. When hot, the iron rested on a trivet (not shown).

After school one day, Patsy pretended she was Mrs. Johnson, and Anetha was her pupil. With Anetha seated in a chair, Patsy got a copy of the *Farm Journal* that Daddy subscribed to, and opened the magazine to an advertisement that showed a can of motor oil that had the word OIL in capital letters.

"Now look, Anetha," Patsy said, using a teacher-like voice, as she pressed her finger hard on each individual letter in the picture, "Look! . . . O . . . I . . . L . . . now, don't that sound like *can*?"

Though Patsy's phonics and grammar might have been lacking, the report card she brought home showed nothing but *O*s (*O* stood for outstanding, *S* for Satisfactory, and *U* for Unsatisfactory). By the end of the year she had completed not only the first-grade reader, but the second-grade reader and speller as well, so Mrs. Johnson promoted her from first to third grade.

The following year, when Anetha was about to start school, she got Patsy's hand-me-downs, plus one new dress, and Patsy got all new clothes again. As for transportation that year, Mama didn't make any arrangements. She decided my sisters could walk to school. Maybe Mama didn't enjoy ironing as much as I thought.

In third grade, Patsy had Daddy's first cousin, Winifred Boatright, as her teacher. She substituted for Mrs. Merine Hunter, who was expecting a baby. (Women expecting babies were not allowed in the classroom.) Patsy, accustomed to calling Daddy's cousin by her first name, was also allowed to call her *Winifred* in class.

Winifred fawned over Patsy, I learned, years later.

"She loved to comb my hair," Patsy said. "She'd call me up to her desk and comb and weave it into braids and tell me how pretty it was."

Winifred was not the only one who thought Patsy was pretty. One of Patsy's classmates, Buddy Allen, told me he had a huge crush on Patsy in third grade, but he said Patsy wouldn't give him the time of day.

While my sisters attended school every weekday, I remained home alone with Mama. One early afternoon while she washed dishes, I sat in a chair in the front room, playing with my doll. The doll's eyes fascinated me; they would close each time I laid her on her back and open when I sat or stood her up. As her eyes popped open for the umpteenth time, the wooden shutter by the fireplace banged against the house.

"Looks like we're in for a good thunderstorm," Mama said, as she came into the room and pulled the shutter closed, making the room go dark. I couldn't see if my doll's eyes were open or shut until Mama yanked the string that turned on the overhead lightbulb. As she returned to the kitchen, acorns hitting the tin roof sounded like gunshots. A few minutes later, muffled thunder rumbled in the distance, and the pitter-patter of rain on the tin roof grew to a roar. Thunderstorms were common, so I was less afraid of them than I used to be. Until boom! Lightning lit the room. Everything looked white, then went dark. I felt as if needles stabbed my eyeballs, and my skin tingled all over.

"Ma-a-a-ma!" I screamed as I threw my doll to the floor and jumped from the chair. Suddenly Mama was by my side. "I've got sand in my eyes!" I cried.

"You got a shock of lightning," Mama said as she dried her hands with a dishtowel. "I felt it too. But we're okay. The lightning evidently hit the power line coming to the house. I'll light the lamp."

When my sisters came home from school, I began telling them about the lightning bolt that nearly killed Mama and me, but Patsy interrupted to say she had an important role in a school play.

The weather was cold the night we went out for Patsy's acting debut. All of us left home wearing coats, Patsy in her red one.

The inside of the school had been set up for the occasion. Folding doors, which normally separated one classroom from another, stood open, creating an auditorium. All of us hung our coats on hooks in the cloakroom. While we spectators looked for desks to sit at, Patsy headed to a dressing room next to the stage to get into costume and makeup.

"They burned a cork," she told me later, "and smeared smut on my face."

At the front of the auditorium, wine-colored velvet curtains hid the stage. The Ladyland Home Demonstration Club bought those curtains, Mama said. She and her friends raised the money by holding community-wide suppers, cake walks, and quilt raffles.

I don't remember exactly what the skit was about that night or any words Patsy uttered on stage. I just remember how much everyone laughed each time she opened her mouth.

After all the laughter and applause ended, the adults mingled as they laughed, talked, and congratulated one another on each child's performance. Finally, ready to go, Mama looked around for Patsy.

"Honey," she said to a girl with a smutty face, who was wearing Patsy's red wool coat, "You need to find Patsy and give her back her coat. We need to go home."

"Mama!" Patsy cried out, her hands on her hips, "It's me! I'm

Patsy!"

Mama said later she was just teasing Patsy, but I'm not so sure.

Back at home, Mama smeared Pond's cold cream (the only beauty product Mama owned besides face powder and Tangee lipstick) on Patsy's face to get the smut off.

Patsy's great performance and the other events I've mentioned might have been my only memories of the first few months I stayed home while my sisters went to school—if not for Daddy's friend, who dropped by early one morning to borrow a tool from Daddy.

Daddy had known the man for a long time. They laughed and joked around for quite a while. When the fellow got ready to leave, he asked if I wanted to go home with him and spend the day with his daughter, who was not in school either. You bet I did, and Mama and Daddy said okay.

Outside our front gate, the man opened the passenger door of his pickup truck. I jumped onto the running board and into the seat. He got in on the driver's side, and off we went. I was thrilled to be on my first outing without my parents or sisters to boss me. As we drove past my grandparents' house, I gave a big wave to Granddaddy Tip, sitting in his porch rocker, and he waved back.

A few miles down the road, Daddy's friend reached over, cupped his arm around me and scooted me closer to him. *He's afraid the door will come open and I'll fall out,* I thought. But then, his right hand slowly brushed across my bare leg and slipped through a leg hole of my loose-fitting muslin britches. *What is he doing?* His fingers felt rough on my tender skin. I squirmed away until I was hugging the passenger door, after which he clamped both his hands on the steering wheel and sped on down the bumpy road. I don't remember a word spoken after that. In fact, my mind is blank about the rest of that day. I don't remember if he told me not to tell, but I didn't.

On a couple of occasions, later on, Anetha and I found ourselves alone with this man, and it seemed he wanted to teach us a few facts we didn't know. He said that some words, like "Peter" and "come," had other meanings than those we knew. He tried to explain the meaning of those words and a few others. We thought he was wacky, and after each lesson, we found a hideout and giggled about what he'd told us.

We didn't realize we should have told Mama about him. Or how lucky we were that his attempt at "educating" us never went any farther than it did. But that might be because we got so we avoided him.

26

A Hot Brick

When it was freezing cold outside, it wasn't much warmer in our bedroom, which had no heat. So Mama would place a brick in the fireplace to heat it. Then she'd wrap it up with towels and put it in the bed with my sisters and me at bedtime. While it heated, we played games. Sometimes we played bread and butter come to supper, similar to hide and seek. One of us started out as the *It*, the one who closed her eyes and counted while the other two hid. Before opening her eyes, *It* yelled, "Bread and butter, come to supper." Nobody came, of course. We'd already eaten supper. So *It* went in search of the others.

Mama and Daddy helped by giving clues. If *It* went in the wrong direction, they said, "You're gettin' colder." If *It* headed in the right direction, they said, "You're gettin' warmer . . . warmer . . . ." And when *It* got really close to someone's hiding spot, Mama or Daddy said, "You're burnin' up! You're burnin' up!" The first person found had to become the next *It*.

Some nights, we asked Daddy to show us tricks, but if he had reading or figuring to do, we'd asked Mama to tell us a story. If we got lucky, she might even tell us two.

"Tonight, I'll tell you the one about the little girl who went to get kerosene," Mama said one night as she took my hand in hers and turned it over so my palm faced up. We had heard the kerosene story a zillion times, but never tired of it.

"There was a little girl who lived right here," Mama said as she poked the fleshy pad next to my thumb. I imagined our house sitting in that very spot. "One day the little girl's mother gave her a bucket and sent her to the store to buy some kerosene, so the little girl started walking . . . ."

As Mama told the story she traced a path down one finger and back up, down another and back up. I pictured myself as the little girl going to buy kerosene. I imagined walking along the rutted road to Wilmarth, a tiny settlement where Mama said trains used to stop before crossing the Suwannee River. I figured the O'Neals, the only family who still lived there, would have kerosene to sell in their old general store.

"The little girl got her bucket filled with kerosene and headed back home," Mama said, tracing the circuitous route home, down one finger and back up, down another and back up. "And when she got right here,"—Mama pressed hard on my palm—"she spilled it!"

I looked up at Mama, waiting.

"If you don't believe me, smell right there," Mama said with a serious face as she tapped my palm.

I raised my hand to my nose to sniff, expecting to smell the kerosene—sometimes when I sniffed, I thought I really did—but when I sniffed my palm, Mama bumped my hand and made me smack my own nose.

"Tell us the story about the little red hen," Anetha said. That was her favorite.

"One day, as the Little Red Hen was scratching in the field," Mama said, "she found a grain of wheat. 'This wheat should be planted,' the Little Red Hen said. 'Who will help me plant this grain of wheat?' 'Not I,' said the Duck. 'Not I,' said the Cat. 'Not I,' said the Dog. 'Then I will do it myself,' said the Little Red Hen.

And she did it!"

Anetha had this story memorized, so when Mama got to the last line of each part, Anetha jumped in with much emphasis—"And, *she* did it!"

"Now read 'Little Red Riding Hood' to us." I begged. Every time Mama read that one, I pictured my sisters and me walking through the woods to Grandma's house and finding that big ugly wolf in Grandma Rye's bed, wearing one of Granny Dosia's old poufy homemade bonnets.

"Another night. It's time for bed now," Mama said and stood up. "I'll get the brick ready."

That night, Mama nudged the hot brick away from the red-hot coals and onto the flat brick hearth with the poker, as usual, before realizing she'd forgotten to get anything to wrap the brick in. She left the brick on the hearth and went across the hall to the bedroom to find a towel or something thick to wrap it in.

Even though we sisters knew it was bedtime, we still had energy to spare, so we began to dance around the room, and in our rowdiness, Patsy accidentally stepped back onto the hot brick.

"Owwooohhh!" She screamed as she fell to the floor, holding her foot in her hands. Daddy jumped up from his chair and kicked the brick back into the fireplace as Mama rushed back to find Patsy on the floor, holding the bottom of her foot up and screaming "Owwoooeee."

"Oh, no!" Mama said as she looked at Patsy's foot and then ran into the kitchen. She came back with a glob of butter in her hand. As she smeared it on Patsy's burn, she kept saying over and over, "Oh, honey, I'm so sorry. I'm so sorry."

"Mama covered the bottom of my foot with butter," Patsy said later when recalling that night, "but it didn't stop the burning. I cried nearly all night long and kept my foot sticking out from under the cover. Even though the bedroom felt like a cold storage locker that night, my foot never cooled off."

By the next morning, Patsy's whole instep had puffed up into a giant blister, so she had to hop around on one foot. A day or two later, Mama got a needle, sterilized its point with the flame from a match, and popped the blister. For the next few weeks, she made Patsy wear two thick socks on that foot to keep it from getting dirty and infected.

Patsy's foot healed up without having to go to a doctor.

27

Making Biscuits and Butter

When Patsy and Anetha left for school one morning, Mama let me walk with them as far as Grandma's house and spend the day. I stayed on the porch with Granddaddy Tip for quite a while, but around midmorning I smelled food and went to the kitchen to see what Grandma was cooking for dinner.

"Just in time to help me make biscuits," Grandma said. "Which mixing bowl do we want to use?"

"Blue," I said, pointing to a bowl behind a glass-paned cabinet door. She took the chosen bowl from the shelf and set it on the wooden table Granddaddy Rye had built for mixing up biscuit dough and rolling out pie crusts. Colored folks also ate at that kitchen table when they helped with farmwork and Grandma cooked dinner for them—if, that is, she could get them to set foot inside the house. Some would say, "Thank you, ma'am. I'll just sit here on the steps." Grandma said some colored people didn't feel comfortable eating with white people.

Speaking of white, almost everything in Grandma's kitchen was white—the walls, the cabinets, the modern electric stove, the kitchen sink. Even the swivel towel rack attached to a window facing was white, except the half-inch of red on the tips of its dowels, as if somebody had dipped them into a can of bright red paint.

In the white kitchen, the little dabs of color stood out: the blue mixing bowl, the yellow oilcloth covering the dough table, a set of red rose glasses, the blue willow dishes behind glass-paned cabinet doors, and the blue-and-white, polka-dotted potholder that I loved. It looked like a chicken and sat in a small basket on a corner table, like a mother hen setting on eggs, her wings fluffed out to keep her eggs warm until they hatched. Grandma had made that potholder herself, using cotton stuffing, red rickrack for the chicken's comb, and bead buttons for eyes.

When I grew up, I hoped to have a white kitchen with dabs of bright color like Grandma's, instead of a dark kitchen like Mama's.

"I'll get the milk out of the refrigerator, and we can get started on the biscuits," Grandma said as she left the kitchen. Her brand-new Kelvinator stood in the corner of the dining room where Granny's pie safe sat before Grandma passed it on to Mama. (The pie safe now sat in a corner of Mama's kitchen; is was the perfect place for leftover food since gnats and flies couldn't get through its screens to the food. Mama said she might own a refrigerator one day. Maybe even a fancy stove like Grandma's, which had a deep well for cooking two foods at once, a clock for telling time, and a long, blue-white light that lit up the stove's entire cooktop.

With Grandma temporarily out of the kitchen, I squeezed between the stove and a cabinet and mashed—my word for pressed—the red and black buttons that controlled the stove light. On . . . Off . . . On . . . Off . . . On . . . .

"Honey?"

I straightened up like a soldier, with my arms at my sides. Grandma stood in the doorway, a jar of milk in her hands. How long had she watched me?

"We don't need that light in the daytime, do we?"

Sunshine streamed through the east window and cast sunny rectangles on the patterned linoleum floor. "No, ma'am," I said, and mashed the black button once more to turn the light off for the last time. That day.

"I don't feel good about you being that close to the stove, either," Grandma said. "How about if you go wash your hands so you can help me roll the biscuits?"

"They're clean," I said, holding them up, fingers apart, but when Grandma didn't say okay, I hurried across the hall to the bathroom and turned the knob marked *C*. I didn't bother with the *H* knob since my grandparents' house, like ours, had no hot water. In a flash, I was back in the kitchen.

Grandma dumped flour into a tin sifter, then held the sifter steady over the bowl and let me turn the knob. A mound of flour grew higher and higher until its peak rose above the bowl's rim.

"That's good," Grandma said, "and we don't have to add baking powder and salt today."

"Why not?"

"I bought a new kind of flour—self-rising, it's called. It's already got baking powder and salt in it."

With the sifter empty, I let go of the knob, and Grandma banged the sifter against her open hand to shake off any lingering flour dust before putting the sifter away. With a fist, she punched a well in the center of the peak of flour, and into that hole she poured lard from a can she kept on the corner table, then milk. She mixed the milk and lard together with her fingers and raked in flour, a little at a time, being careful not to let the liquid run over the edge of the well in the flour. Gradually, a soft ball of dough formed where the liquid had been.

"Okay, flour your hands," Grandma said.

With clean, floured hands, we each pinched off a glob of dough and rolled it around in our palms, tucking under loose edges before setting the ball of dough into a greased pan and flattening it with the backs of our fingers. The clump of dough in the bowl became smaller and smaller as we filled the pan with biscuit dough, sides touching. Finally, Grandma dipped her fingers in the can of lard and patted the top of each biscuit—some smooth and perfectly shaped, others rough and raggedy.

"Why do you grease 'em?" I asked, as she dabbed the biscuits.

"They brown better," she said.

"Now then," she said, washing her hands at the kitchen sink, "the roast should be done, so you can go to the bathroom and wash the flour off your hands and set the table."

I wanted to wash my hands at the kitchen sink like Grandma, but I knew from experience that when I reached up, the water would trickle to my armpits and wet my dress. In the bathroom, I turned the cold water on, rubbed my hands together, and watched bits of dough swirl down the drain.

The kitchen felt warm when I returned to see Grandma bent over the open oven door, a folded dishtowel in one hand, the cotton-stuffed chicken in the other. She pulled the iron skillet that held a pork roast toward herself, supported its weight with her towel-protected hand, and set it on the stove's big burner. After placing the pan of biscuits on the oven's top shelf, she closed the door and turned two dials, one to raise the oven's temperature for the biscuits, and another that controlled the big burner under the skillet. By the time the burner's coils turned red, she'd already transferred the roast to a platter. Soon, fat and juice in the skillet began to pop, and Grandma added a handful of flour she scooped from the blue bowl.

"You have to keep stirring when you make gravy," Grandma said as she stirred the juices with a spoon and added water with the other hand. "Otherwise, the gravy gets lumpy."

After pouring the brown gravy into a blue willow gravy boat, she lifted the lid of the deep well, and I got a whiff of the acre peas she was cooking (photo and recipe, p. 428).

"The rice and peas should be about done," she said as she reached in and picked up a grain of rice. She pinched it between her thumb and finger.

"It's done," she said, replacing the lid.

From a cabinet, she took a big glass pitcher and four blue willow plates. Carefully, I carried the plates to the dining table that was covered with a starched-and-ironed tablecloth. The wood table-top showed only when Grandma replaced a stained cloth with a fresh one. She owned a tall stack of tablecloths. Most had colored borders. Others looked solid white until the light hit them just right. Then you could see a design—*damask*, Grandma called the fabric. I longed to have a dress made of damask, even if the word did sound more like a cuss word than one describing fabric that shimmered in the light.

I placed Granddaddy Tip's plate where I knew he sat, at the head of the table, near the buffet. Granddaddy Rye sat on Granddaddy Tip's left, with Grandma next to him. I could take my pick of the spots left, since nobody else was coming to eat dinner with us, so I set mine at the foot of the table, opposite Granddaddy Tip, but next to Grandma, the refrigerator, and the three windows that were raised high and held up with props. Maybe I'd get some breeze there. Grandma's house always seemed hotter than ours, perhaps because no trees shaded any part of it.

I took knives, forks, and spoons from the top buffet drawer and was placing the last ones by my plate when Grandma came in, opened the refrigerator door and the inside freezer door to take out an ice tray. *Ah-h-h, cold air.* I stood next to her, inhaling the fog coming from the freezer, which stretched across the entire top of the fridge. Ice tray in hand, Grandma returned to the kitchen, where she ran water over the tray, then pulled a lever to release the cubes.

"You can put the ice in glasses while I sweeten the tea," Grandma said, taking down four tall glasses ringed with red roses. While I dropped cubes into the glasses, Grandma dragged the glass sugar barrel from under the wooden dough table and swung the heavy container onto the tabletop. That sugar barrel was about as big and about the same shape as the chair Mama made for me using a pot-bellied nail keg she upholstered with pink floral sateen fabric. Sitting on that tufted chair made me feel like a princess.

Anetha and Patsy stand beside my nail-keg chair in our front yard.

After unscrewing the lid of the sugar barrel, Grandma dumped two scoopfuls of sugar into the pitcher of tea and stirred.

"While I pour the tea and take up the food," Grandma said, "you can go tell your granddaddy and papa that dinner's ready."

I found Granddaddy Rye mending the chicken-yard fence and Granddaddy Tip in his usual spot on the front porch. Once seated, Granddaddy Rye said his usual speedy blessing, "Make us thankful for this food. Amen." Everybody except me picked up a bowl or platter. Grandma heaped a spoonful of rice onto my plate.

"I don't want gravy," I said, shaking my head hard when the gravy boat came around. I hated gravy of any kind, whether greasy red-eye gravy, milky-white country gravy, or smooth brown gravy.

"Oh, that's right," she said, pushing her chair back. "You want cream on yours."

From the refrigerator, she took a shallow bowl of milk with thick cream on top. Using my spoon, she drizzled the satiny cream over my rice.

By the time she sat back down, the men had helped their plates, but they stopped eating long enough to pass the meat, peas, biscuits, and butter our way.

"I don't want any," I said when Grandma started to spoon peas onto my plate. In my opinion, rice with fresh cow cream made a near-perfect meal, second only to grits with butter. My plan was to finish off my rice and cream and, for dessert, enjoy a big fluffy biscuit with cane syrup. Unlike Mama, who always insisted I taste everything on the table, especially if I wanted dessert, Grandma let me eat what I wanted.

After everybody cleaned their plates, I helped Grandma take bowls of leftover food and the dirty dishes, including my syrup-sticky plate, to the kitchen.

We'd finished cleaning the kitchen by the time Patsy and Anetha came home from school. They came in with red, sweaty faces, wanting something cold to drink.

"Grandma, the ice in here's an inch thick!" Patsy said, upon opening the freezer door to take out an ice tray. "You want us to help you *dee*frost it?"

"We'll do that chore another day," Grandma said.

Chore? It wasn't a chore. It was fun. My shoulders slumped in disappointment. I remembered helping once and how the refrigerator and freezer, with doors wide open, cooled the room, and how we'd rubbed chunks of melting ice on our faces, arms, and legs.

"But y'all can help me make butter," Grandma said.

So, while we drank our sweet iced tea at the dining table, Grandma took three bowls of milk from the refrigerator, set them on the table, and skimmed and scooped the cream into a quart jar. The skimmed milk left in the bowl would later be fed to the pigs.

Grandma screwed a lid on the quart jar, and we took turns shaking it. Anetha bumped it against her leg the way she'd seen Granddaddy do. After a while, bits of butter formed inside the jar. We continued shaking and bumping as more and more yellow clumped together. Eventually, Grandma said it was done and took over. She emptied the blue-tinted whey from the jar into an enamel bucket, scraped the butter out, and with her hands, patted it into a ball. After squeezing out a few remaining drops of whey, she plopped the soft yellow blob into her butter dish, which she claimed was as old as she was, though I didn't believe that for a second, for it looked brand new.

Grandma Rye's butter bell

Before that year ended, Mama got a refrigerator similar to Grandma's, and she and Daddy were even talking about buying a freezer.

28

How to Catch a Mess of Fish

Grandma Rye, as well as Granddaddy Tip, liked me best. I was sure of that, and I didn't feel a bit guilty about it. After all, other family members favored my sisters. Uncle Harold liked Patsy best, maybe because Patsy was his first niece, born to his only sister. True, he went off and joined the War Department soon after she was born, but Mama said he wrote letters asking about Patsy, and when he returned, he doted on her. Patsy's full name was Laura Patricia, so naturally her namesake, Daddy's baby sister, was also crazy about her niece.

Daddy's other sister, Aunt Clara Mae, thought the sun rose and set on Anetha. I never knew what the basis was for this adoration. Was it because they were both skinny as cane stalks? Anetha's greatest bond, though, was with Granddaddy Rye. Wherever Granddaddy Rye went, Anetha tagged along, even if he just went outside to milk the cow or shell corn for the chickens. I felt a tad jealous of their close relationship, since Granddaddy Rye never said much to me. Anetha claimed when the two of them got off to themselves, they carried on serious conversations. One had to do with his clothes.

"He told me one time," Anetha said, "that 'he was so *pore* he had no clothes to wear.' Then he says, 'Guess I'll just have to go off to the swamp and let the skeeters eat me.'"

Anetha said she felt sorry for Granddaddy Rye that day and offered him the nickel she had in her pocket, but he refused it.

He was pretty easygoing, though I did see him get mad one cold winter day when we sisters spent the day at his and Grandma's house. After playing in the yard, we ran inside to warm up by the oil heater, which stood in front of a now boarded-up fireplace. As we gathered around the heater, Hampton, the teenager Granddaddy had recently hired to help around the place, walked in. His father worked as a tenant farmer on Mr. Saunders's farm.

Hampton liked to play tricks on us girls, and that day was no exception. He walked over and picked up a big pair of scissors somebody had left lying on top of the heater. The heater stood so tall I couldn't see its top, so I didn't actually see him pick up the scissors—I think he used a folded handkerchief from his pocket to keep from burning his hand. Holding them by the pointed end, he offered them to Anetha. She took them by the handles.

"Owooowwch!" she screamed and dropped them. Their points jabbed the wood floor next to her feet. Granddaddy must have heard her scream. He came rushing inside, and when he saw Anetha's red hand and found out what happened, his face turned the same color. I thought I saw steam rise off the top of his balding head. He fired Hampton on the spot.

Whether Granddaddy would have fired Hampton if Patsy or I had the burned hand, I don't know, but no matter, I respected Granddaddy, and I liked what he'd done. I also liked the way he treated Grandma, his "Shug," and I admired his many skills.

For one thing, he could blow perfectly shaped smoke rings. From the O of his lips came the smoke shaped like a wedding band. It stretched wider and wider as it floated up and disappeared into the air. He made me want to smoke, so I could blow smoke rings like that.

At one time, he'd been a convict guard. He said he never had to shoot a prisoner, but he sure knew how to shoot a gun. He showed off his marksmanship every year at Christmastime when he used his rifle to shoot down mistletoe, and when he went hunting. He never returned empty-handed.

People in the community considered Granddaddy a top-notch dog trainer too. He trained his hunting dogs to sniff out quail and to point and retrieve the birds, squirrels, and rabbits he killed. At one time, to earn extra cash, Mama said he trained dogs for lots of people. One was Mr. Richard Sears, of Sears and Roebuck fame. According to local lore, Mr. Sears moved into the area in the early 1900s to make his fortune from lumber products. Legend has it that because Sears wanted the trains that hauled his lumber to arrive on time, he gave watches to every train engineer. At the time, he owned the Sears Watch Company.

I guess his dogs didn't have to be trained by a certain time, though, because he never gave Granddaddy a watch.

Granddaddy was also a good fisherman, and when he headed to the river, Anetha wasn't the only one who wanted to go with him.

"Shug, I'm going down to the Suwannee for a little while," we heard him say to Grandma late one afternoon. All three of us immediately ran to his side.

"If you girls want to go," he said, "go hop in the truck."

We were halfway to the river when Anetha threw up her hands and said, "Granddaddy! We forgot our fishing poles!" Normally, we fished with cane poles and worms—wigglers or grubs.

"We don't need poles today," he said.

If we weren't going fishing, I wished I'd stayed home with Grandma, but it was too late to change my mind.

At the river, Granddaddy took two buckets from the truck bed and headed down the river bank. Trim and agile, he quickly descended the steep bank ahead of us. His boat, floating near the river's edge, was tied to a cypress knee and buttressed by other knees of varying heights. Many stuck out of the water two feet or more, while others barely broke the surface. At the time, I thought all cypress trees grew knees like that. Later I learned that a cypress tree on dry ground won't grow knees. Nobody knows the reason. Some say the knees that grow in water help the roots take in oxygen, while others say they just keep the trees, which can grow to 150 feet, from toppling over in waterlogged soil.

Granddaddy pulled the boat over so it touched the riverbank and told us to hop in. With us seated, he untied the boat, set the buckets and one foot in, and shoved off. Once away from the bank, he sat on the other bench seat, picked up an oar, and began to row, guiding us upriver against the swift current.

"So, we're just going for a ride?" Anetha asked.

"Yeah, but we're apt to find some fish," Granddaddy said.

I was puzzled but sat still between my older sisters as Granddaddy paddled along the dark river. It was near dusk now, and no sound could be heard except the buzz of an occasional mosquito hawk and dripping water as Granddaddy lifted the oar from the river on one side and then the other. Slowly, we made our way upriver, staying fairly close to the bank. Near a giant rock on the Suwannee County side (Lafayette County was on the opposite bank), Granddaddy slowed the boat, grabbed a low, overhanging branch and swung the boat around so it clunked against a rock.

He tied up to the tree, slid one hand down one of its low branches, and found another rope. He tugged it, and up from the water came a chicken-wire contraption full of thrashing fish. Wow! A dozen or more perch, mullet, and catfish. Granddaddy unlatched a flap on one end of the barrel-shaped cage and poured the fish into one of the buckets. We had ourselves a mess of fish.

He reached into the other bucket and pulled something out.

"What's that?" Anetha asked as I wondered the same thing.

"Corn pones your Grandma baked last night. The fish love 'em."

After tossing a handful of corn pones into the open end of the wire contraption, he latched the flap. Meanwhile, I studied the other end of it and what was inside: two cone-shaped funnels each tapered to a hole about the size of a man's fist.

"The fish swim in through there," Granddaddy said, pointing to the first opening, "but once inside, they're too dumb to find their way back out."

"So, it's a trap!" Patsy said.

"Well, we don't call it a *trap*," Granddaddy whispered with a slight chuckle as he put the cage back in the water and let it sink out of sight. "We call it a *basket*."

With no more talk, Granddaddy guided the boat to another spot and repeated the process, filling the other bucket with live fish.

I didn't have a clue that Granddaddy's "baskets" were against the law. Neither did Anetha when she later bragged to her friend's father about her great fisherman grandfather, along with details of how he caught dozens of fish with nothing more than corn pones for bait.

29

Trapped

Our dog Tommy was asleep under the wooden steps of the front porch, his head resting on one paw, the one he lifted when we told him to shake hands. Spanish moss swayed in the breeze. Cows grazed in the pasture. Chickens waddled around the yard, scratching and pecking at the ground, searching for food. Our chickens were what people would later start calling "free-range" chickens.

There can be pluses and minuses to letting chickens roam free, though. On the minus side, we kids had to watch where we stepped with bare feet, or else we ended up with chicken poop caught between our toes. Cold poop stopped us in our tracks, made us shake that foot to get rid of it. That was bad enough, but a fresh, warm, and gooey glob made you search for some way to clean it off. Leaves, moss, anything.

On the plus side, our free-range chickens took care of roaches and scorpions that could have crawled into our house. Being very old, the house had holes and cracks that practically announced, "Enter here." Yet I never saw a roach or scorpion inside. And thanks to the chickens, my sisters and I didn't have to go far to find feathers, the paraphernalia needed when we went in search of doodlebugs.

Equipped with chicken feathers that lazy, breezy morning, we lay on our bellies and eased ourselves like inchworms into the crawl space under the porch. Tommy, still asleep under the steps, raised one eyelid and let his sleepy eye follow us. He inhaled and let out a big sigh as his eyelid closed.

Under the house, we could always find doodlebugs, which some people call ant lions, but finding them required effort. They lived in the soft sand below "holes" they formed themselves. The shape of the their holes reminded me of the cone-shaped paper cups stored in a canister next to a giant upside-down water bottle in Sharples, the department store in Live Oak.

If I hadn't seen it with my own eyes, I would never have believed that a tiny doodlebug, not as big as a pencil eraser, could form a perfectly shaped cone in the sand by turning 'round and 'round as it flipped its tiny forked tail.

Under the house, my sisters and I spread out to claim a spot. In position, our elbows on the ground, we each brushed the tip of a feather across the edge of a cone-shaped crater we'd chosen. I watched my hole intently as my feather nudged a few grains of sand down the steep slope. This would fool the doodlebug into thinking an ant had fallen into its trap and was trying to escape.

When our boy cousins visited, they caught ants and dropped them into the little craters and watched as the doodlebugs came to the surface and devoured the squirming ants. I thought that was mean, but I guess the ant lions thought it was great. Still, my sisters and I preferred to coax the doodlebugs to the surface so we could scoop them up and play with them.

I stared into my crater, waiting for signs of movement. Nothing.

Since I knew that the harder an ant tried to climb out of a doodlebug's trap, the more grains of sand would tumble down, I brushed the edge again, harder.

"I got one!" Patsy blurted.

"Me too." Anetha squealed.

I scooped up a handful of sand from my crater.

"Me too!"

But did I really have one? I separated my fingers slowly to let grains of sand trickle out between my fingers. And then I felt it.

"Oooo—it tickles—it tickles!" With most of the sand gone, the doodlebug, in an attempt to hide, was trying to burrow into the creases of my cupped palm.

We compared the ones we'd caught and traded them back and forth. Their shape reminded me of the horseshoe crabs I'd seen at Dekle Beach, over on the Gulf coast, but the horseshoe crabs were much larger, closer to the size of a gopher tortoise, and had just one spike instead of a forked tail like a doodlebug.

Eventually we released the doodlebugs and watched as they scurried about, making designs in the dry sand. After a while, they tunneled down and disappeared.

We never killed one if we could help it. That would have been like killing a toy.

The day still seemed ordinary when we crawled from under the house and went exploring in the edge of the woods. Some neighbors talked of seeing panthers and wildcats in those woods, but the worst we'd ever seen was a snake.

Patsy spotted a cicada—or its clear, amber-colored shell—clinging to a spindly trunk of an oak tree. She pulled it off the bark and stuck it on the front of her dress. As usual, the empty shell had a slit down its back. Mama had told us the insect escaped through that opening. The claws clung to Patsy's dress as we trounced on through the woods, but it fell off and got lost when we rolled a half-rotted log over to see what we might find underneath. Nothing but grubs, the ugly white worms that reminded me of maggots, but Granddaddy liked to fish with them, saying he caught more fish with them than with wigglers.

Anetha discovered a leaf with something strange attached to it—tan, about the size of a bird's egg. We ran to the house to show it to Mama. "It's a cocoon—spun with silk," she said, "the beginning of a moth." *Silk?* Then we should try to find more cocoons so Mama could use them to make silk to make us some britches. But Mama said she didn't know how to weave silk. Up until then, I thought Mama knew how to make everything.

Instead of going back to the woods, we ended up on our "playground." Daddy had given us an empty drum, a fifty-five gallon oil barrel.

Patsy hopped up onto the overturned barrel, spread her feet apart and her arms wide as she got her balance, and began rolling it across the yard. The idea was to see how far she could roll before falling off.

Daddy had also given us a wide board about ten feet long that we used to make two pieces of play equipment. If we set it across the barrel, we made a seesaw. To create a jumping board, we laid it across eight or ten stacked-up bricks.

Our jumping board was similar to a seesaw except you *stood* on the board. If one person was heavier, the heavier one took a step or two toward the center until the board balanced on the bricks. When one jumped up and landed, she sent the other flying. When that one landed—on the board, hopefully!—her weight sent the other one into the air. Sometimes, we missed the board completely. Other times we landed half on, half off, which caused the board to jackknife, the bricks to fall apart, and scraped knees. But none of us ever broke a bone.

In addition to our barrel, seesaw, and jump board, we had the best swing around. Some of our friends had rope swings with a tire or a stuffed croker sack attached. Too bad. When it rained, the tires held water and the croker sack got soaked. Our swing, which Daddy made for us, had a board seat. The swing was attached to a high limb of the oak tree by a heavy chain. How Daddy attached that chain to that limb, about twenty feet off the ground, I don't know. He didn't own a ladder that tall, and I never saw him climb the tree.

We usually took turns on the swing, pushing one another. But if two of us happened to be jumping board or seesawing, the one left out would stand on the swing's seat and pump to get it going. When possible, we asked a stronger person to push us, but Mama and Daddy usually stayed too busy. On tobacco-gathering day, I always asked Alfred Boatright. He was nearly grown, but we shared the same birthday, so we were buddies. He'd push me so hard the seat would almost slide out from under my bottom. And at the highest point of each lap, I could see the top of our house. I could have grabbed a handful of leaves from a high branch but I was afraid to let go of the chain.

Because of the board seat that dried quickly after a rain, plus the long chain, our swing was the envy of kids in our community. When Daddy built something like that swing or the outhouse, he did it right.

Speaking of the outhouse, when one of us needed to visit the outhouse, the others usually went along. That tradition probably got started when Uncle Itchy first built the outhouse and I was afraid to go in there by myself.

So that's where we were that day—inside the outhouse—when Mama started yelling at us and we got real scared.

Moments earlier, we had seen her at the sliding kitchen window, a new feature of the house that Daddy had recently installed. From the new window, Mama could see our swing and play area. And with the back kitchen window shutter open, she could see the backyard and the pasture beyond the fence.

She told Daddy that night that she'd seen us swinging and jumping board and thought we were still on the east side of the house when she heard a squeak that sounded like it came from the wire fence out back. She looked out the sliding window, saw we had disappeared, and figured we were climbing the sagging fence, something Daddy had forbidden us to do. She walked over to the back window, planning to yell at us, "Get off that fence before I get a switch." But instead of seeing us climbing the fence, she saw the big Brahma bull butting his head against it.

"I stood there watching that bull for a few seconds," Mama said to Daddy. "I watched as he backed away, but he was staring at that fence like he intended to come over it. That's when I ran out to find out where the girls were."

I knew what happened next. It was stamped in my memory.

"Girls! Girls!" Mama hollered to us, panic in her voice. "Where are you?"

"In the toilet," Patsy hollered back.

"Stay in there!" Mama said. "Don't come out!"

Why would Mama want us to stay in the toilet?

Sitting on the toilet seat, I no longer had to "go." I jumped off the bench seat and pulled up my scratchy muslin britches. I could hardly pull them up. With the hot sun beating down on the tin roof, I was all sweaty.

"Stay put! Stay put!" Mama screamed. "Don't open that door! The bull's in the yard!"

We didn't know exactly where Mama was, where the bull was, or what was happening, and we began bawling.

"After the bull jumped the fence and got closer to the toilet, he could hear the girls crying," Mama told Daddy. "Boy! He started pawing at the sand and it looked like he planned to ram that toilet. Oh! He looked mad. I held my breath, not knowing what to do. I was afraid he might turn the outhouse over with the girls in it."

With the door shut, the outhouse was very dark, and it was getting hotter by the minute.

Eventually, the bull saw some shucks on the ground, Mama said, where the girls had shelled corn for the chickens. He trotted over there and began to eat the shucks.

"With him distracted," Mama said to Daddy, "I grabbed a pitch-fork leaning against the house."

Why that pitchfork was there, I don't know. Daddy normally kept equipment like shovels, rakes, and the pitchfork stored under the packhouse shelter. We were just lucky, I guess.

"About the time I grabbed the pitchfork," Mama continued, "that bull turned and stared at me. I froze, but I had it ready if he charged. Thank goodness he soon spotted the heifers in the cow lot and headed toward them."

Soon spotted the heifers? It didn't seem *soon* to me. It seemed like forever that we stayed trapped in the outhouse. But finally, Mama threw the door open.

"Run! Run to the house!" she yelled as she stood guard, armed with the pitchfork.

Mama didn't have to tell us twice.

Nor did she have to tell Daddy twice to fix that sagging fence or get rid of that mean bull. Before Daddy went to bed that night, the bull was back in the pasture and the fence had been repaired.

30

Aunt Oleta and the Old Ward Place

Mama unlatched and pushed open the door-like shutter to the right of the fireplace to let in fresh air and light. Rusty hinges creaked as the heavy shutter swung out and slammed against the outside of the house. Rays of sunlight filtered through the oak tree that held our swing, casting a dappled pattern on the age-darkened, tongue-and-groove paneled walls. "Third-grade sealing material," Daddy called it. Or did he say "ceiling" material? (I much preferred Grandma's light-colored walls to our dark ones and would never have guessed that paneling like ours would one day be painted white and sold as something special called *beadboard*.)

"You girls set the table while I finish breakfast," Mama said as she walked into the kitchen. "We've got a lot to do today. Your Uncle Ira and Aunt Oleta will leave Miami with the boys early this morning, so your cousins will be here before dark."

Uncle Ira reminded me of Daddy. They both joked around a lot and favored one another, though unlike Daddy, Uncle Ira wore wire-rimmed glasses and plastered down his hair with Brylcreem. He had married one of Mama's best friends, Oleta Ward. In fact, Aunt Oleta grew up in the house we now called home, and many people still referred to our place as "The old Ward place."

Mama said she used to walk with Aunt Oleta to Ladyland School, and by the time they were teenagers, they were best friends. "We'd roll one another's hair, polish each other's fingernails, and pluck each other's eyebrows."

That made Aunt Oleta's teenage years sound rosy, but I also overheard conversations between adults about sadness and tragedy. For one thing, Aunt Oleta's father died of blood poisoning after a shaving cut became infected on hog-killing day. Soon after his death, Oleta's mother, who everybody called Daisy, married Ozie Hurst, a young man as close in age to her daughters as to Daisy. This caused gossip. And then, somebody up and murdered him.

It happened one night when Ozie took the family to see a free outdoor movie in Mayo. As they made their way home from Mayo, in the swamp near Luraville, a truck zoomed up from behind and forced Ozie's car off the road. Men in the truck fired shots. Several bullets found their target.

The killers testified at the trial that they just intended "to put a scare into Ozie, to teach him a lesson because they thought he'd been "up to no good." They "had to shoot him," they said, when he went for his gun.

In time, I learned that Great-Granddaddy Tip was called to testify at the trial against his neighbors, who were accused of the murder—people he had known for years. In court, Granddaddy swore on the Bible to tell the truth, the whole truth, and nothing but, after which the lawyers bombarded him with questions about what he knew.[3]

Q. You lived there during the month of October of this year and prior thereto?

A. Yes, sir.

Q. Just prior to the time that O. O. Hurst was shot and died,

---

[3] Transcript of trial: In Circuit Court, Third Judicial Circuit of the State of Florida, in and for Suwannee County. Regular fall term, 1937. November 16–18.

did [the defendant] come to your house?

A. He came there before that.

Q. About how long was it before that time that he came to your house?

A. I don't remember. I reckon two or three weeks.

Q. Was it the night they had the prize fight between Joe Lewis and another man?

A. That was the first time.

Q. Was anyone with him at that time?

Granddaddy Tip provided the names of the other men.

Q. Did they come up in the car together?

A. They had been to Warren's and they rode back by my house.

Q. They went from Marvin Warren's over to your home?

A. Yes, sir.

Q. When they got to your house, did they have a conversation with you about O. O. Hurst?

A. Yes, sir.

Q. In that conversation did they make a statement to you as to what they were going to do to Hurst or what they wanted to do to him?

A. Yes, sir.

Q. State to the court the entire conversation and the statements made there at your house.

A. He said that he was going to kill him, and that he had something to do it with, and he picked up the shotgun out of the back of the car.

Q. He made the statement that he was going to kill O. O. Hurst, and that he had the thing to do it with right there?

A. Yes, sir.

Q. What else was said?

A. I cannot recall all that was said, but I asked him to let that be the last thing that he ever did. I told him the condition his wife and children would be left in, if he did anything like that.

The accused men ended up in prison, but back in the Ladyland Community, Mama said life went on about the same. She said Daisy then tied the knot for a third time, but her luck didn't change. Her new husband cut all the hard timber on "the old Ward place" and took off with the money, leaving the family almost destitute. To make ends meet, Daisy sold her car and made arrangements with a sharecropper to farm the land. Plus, Aunt Oleta, still a teenager, took a job as a maid at a Branford hotel.

Mama loved telling about how Aunt Oleta and Uncle Ira met.

"My daddy took Oleta back and forth to her Branford job in his truck," she said. "One night, instead of taking Oleta straight home, they stopped off at our house. I told Oleta I had a date that night with C. G. Howell. She was still there when C.G. drove up, and he had his brother Ira with him. He'd planned to drop Ira off someplace when we got to Live Oak. But when Ira and Oleta saw each other, it was love at first sight. They went out with us that night and ended up beating your daddy and me to the altar."

From the kitchen, Mama called to my sisters and me with some aggravation in her voice, "Girls, I said to set the table. We've got lots to do today."

Patsy went to the kitchen and brought back five plates. Anetha thought our dishes were absolutely beautiful: cream-colored and silver-rimmed, with decals of pink and white roses (Homer Laughlin, Virginia Rose, Mama said). But I liked Grandma's blue willow pattern better.

Patsy laid the plates around the dining table and I added forks and spoons. Anetha went to the water shelf in the hallway to fill all the glasses. Mama had given up on making us drink milk.

In the kitchen a few minutes later, I watched as Mama flipped hot grease over eggs in an iron skillet. After the clear part of the eggs turned white and a thin layer of white covered the yellow, she transferred the sunny-side-up eggs to a platter that held fried ham. "Here, Susanette, you can set the biscuits on the table," Mama said, handing a platter to me. "But be careful," she said as I slowly made my way to the table.

Mama set a bowl of grits and the platter of ham and eggs on the table, and we took our usual seats. Mama always sat closest to the kitchen since, during the meal, she often had to fetch something she'd forgotten. She always had me sit on her right. Daddy took his seat on the other side of her, and Anetha and Patsy sat directly across from them. We bowed our heads and Daddy rushed through "Bless this food to the nourishment of our bodies for Christ's sake. Amen."

The serving dishes made their way around the table. I helped myself to a fried egg, smothered it with grits, and added a dollop of butter. I mashed and stirred everything together and spread the yellow-tinged grits and eggs across pink and white flowers and let the mixture congeal. For each bite, I ran my fork from one side of the plate to the other, making stripes until my plate resembled a pie.

"I forgot the jelly," Mama said, shoving her chair back to get up, but a leg of her chair dropped into a hole in the floor—a hole as big as my fist. "C.G.!" Mama yelled as she threw her hands out to catch her balance. Her chair had almost toppled over.

"C.G.," Mama said more calmly as she returned to the table with a Mason jar of blackberry jelly, "I wish you'd fix that blasted hole."

"Blasted hole" was right, considering how it got there. If you lay on the floor and put your nose to it, you could see through to the ground below.

According to what I'd heard, the hole was put there not long before Mama and Daddy bought the house. Over time, I'd picked up snippets of conversation about it. "A shooting . . . the Richardsons' little boy . . . blood, lots of it." In time, I learned more.

After Daisy's third husband had left her, she decided to move out of her house and let a sharecropper family, the Richardsons, move in. Mr. Richardson, with the help of his boys, would farm her 240 acres and share the profits with Daisy.

As it turned out, though, Mr. Richardson had a drinking problem, and a night of drinking in Live Oak turned ugly. How he got to town, nobody knew. He didn't own a vehicle. And where he got the liquor was a mystery since Suwannee County was a dry county. Supposedly, another man drove him home that night and went inside with him. There in the Ward house (now our house), the driver demanded money that Richardson supposedly owed him, and a fight broke out. One of them had a shotgun. It went off, not once, but twice. One shot blasted a hole in the floor. The other went through one of the Richardson boys. The driver escaped through an open window as the boy lay bleeding.

Another of the kids ran to get Granddaddy Rye, but by the time they got back with his truck to take the bleeding boy to the doctor, the boy had bled to death.

If there was a trial, I never heard it mentioned. Folks just said, "It was a tragic accident that would never have happened if the men had been sober."

I was glad Daddy didn't drink.

After that tragedy, Daddy said Daisy Ward was looking to make new arrangements, and it so happened that he, with plans to marry Mama, was looking for a place to rent where he could farm the land. Daisy agreed to rent her place to him beginning on January 1, 1941. But a few months after he and Mama married in August of 1940, he learned that the Richardsons did not intend to move.

Daddy received the surprising news from Granny, who heard it from the Richardson children. They often stopped in at Granny's house on their way to Ladyland when the weather was cold, and she talked with them as they warmed up by the fireplace. She knew about Daddy and Mama's plans to rent the old Ward place and said to the kids one morning, "Well, I guess y'all will be moving at the end of the year." One of the boys answered that they wouldn't be moving because his daddy (Mr. Richardson) was buying the place.

Daddy investigated and learned that Daisy, who was by then living down in Clearwater, had fallen behind on her property taxes. Mr. Richardson planned to pay the back taxes and claim the place for himself. Daddy contacted Daisy and told her what he'd heard. She said she didn't have the money to pay the taxes, but she told Daddy she'd rather he have the place than the Richardson fellow. She said if Daddy would pay the back taxes as well as pay for her to get a divorce from the man who'd run off with her timber money, she'd sign the place over to Daddy.

As Daddy and Mama began discussing the purchase of the Ward place, friends and neighbors tried to discourage them, telling them the place was haunted, that all kinds of bad things had happened there, and that bad things might happen to them. But Mama and Daddy bought "the old Ward place" anyway, all 240 acres.

31

Want to See a Lizard Nest?

When we expected company, Mama cleaned till the house sparkled. She also worked out the sleeping arrangements ahead of time and put clean linens on the beds, including starched-and-ironed embroidered pillowcases on all feather pillows. Preparations seemed especially important to Mama when Aunt Oleta visited, perhaps because Mama had heard comments made by South Florida relatives about how nice Aunt Oleta kept her Hialeah home: "Every time a wall gets a scuff mark, Oleta has Ira repaint. I'll bet the paint on every wall in that house is an inch thick". . . "You can eat off Oleta's floors." I'd heard the remarks myself, and those talking sounded jealous.

When I eventually got to see that Hialeah house, I fell in love with it, especially its pastel-painted walls and shiny tile floors that looked like a checkerboard. I vowed when I married and had my own house, mine would be as neat and clean as Aunt Oleta's. I planned to dress like her too.

She wasted no fabric when making herself an outfit. Her snug-fitting clothes showed off her curvy figure. As for her hairstyle, I wasn't sure about that. She wore straight bangs like my sisters, but the back of her head looked like she went to a barbershop instead of a beauty shop.

One thing I noticed about Aunt Oleta. When visiting, she didn't sit around expecting somebody to wait on her. She'd go to the kitchen and help cook meals as if she were home, and I guess she was since she grew up in our house, though Mama said the house wasn't quite the same as when Aunt Oleta was a kid named Oleta Ward and Mama lived down the road from her. "The Wards had a freestanding kitchen back then," Mama told me. "A boardwalk connected it to the back porch."

With company on the way now, even the outhouse was ready, equipped with store-bought toilet paper, a luxury when we had plenty of pages left in an old *Sears and Roebuck* catalog.

While Mama was inside, still preparing for company or the noon dinner, we sisters were outside, drawing a hopscotch design in the dirt when we heard a squeak and looked up. I expected to see Mama going into the outdoor toilet. But instead of Mama, a calf had poked its head into the outhouse.

For a few days, we had been feeding the calf extra milk from a bottle. I'm not sure exactly why.

"Look!" I said.

At the sound of my voice, the calf went "Baa-a-a—," jumped back, and took off running,

Mama snapped the picture as I killed a flea I found on the calf and Anetha holds the bottle.

toilet paper clinging to its tongue.

"Ee-ee-ee-ee—" went the spinning toilet paper dispenser as the calf ran in zigzags and circles, bucking like a horse—toilet paper streaming behind.

"Ma-ma-a-a!" we yelled at the top of our lungs.

Hearing the commotion, Mama ran from the house and took chase, finally getting close enough to yank the trailing toilet paper from the calf's tongue.

"I guess the calf mistook the toilet paper for a salt lick," Mama told Daddy at noon when he came in to eat dinner. Daddy kept a salt block in the cow lot for the animals. He said it "fulfilled some nutritional need."

By the time Daddy heard about the incident, of course, Mama had put the calf back into the pasture with its mother, and we'd collected all that precious toilet paper and re-rolled it as best we could on its cardboard tube for our company.

Uncle Ira's family arrived late that afternoon. *Yippee*, I thought as their wood-paneled station wagon made its way down the lane. But I soon thought *Yuck* when all the hugging and kissing got underway. Mama and Daddy never kissed us, even when they tucked us into bed at night, so all that affection made me antsy. With greetings finally over, they took suitcases and baby Eddie into the house, and my sisters and I took Jimmy with us to do our chores.

Every afternoon, we shucked and shelled corn for the chickens, letting the dry corn kernels fall to the ground. The chickens came running and pecked at the ground around our bare feet—Jimmy was now shoeless, like us.

Next, we all gathered eggs. "Why are some of the eggs brown? Jimmy asked.

We explained that White Leghorn chickens lay white eggs and Rhode Island Reds lay brown ones. It amazed me how much our city cousins still had to learn.

Jimmy didn't know about lizard nests either.

"Want to see a lizard nest?" Patsy asked him the next afternoon after a hard thunderstorm. Water had poured from the sky.

"Yeah," Jimmy said. "Where?"

"Over in that tree," Patsy said as she headed to an oak in the front yard with a low-hanging branch. "Up there," she said point-ing. "See it? Right up in there."

Jimmy craned his head this way and that, like a chicken looking for a bug in a bush.

"I can't see it. How big is it?"

"It ain't real big," Anetha chimed in, "but we can see it from way over here." I stood next to her.

When Jimmy stood directly under the branch, looking up where Patsy pointed, she jerked the tip of the low branch and ran. Rain-water pelted Jimmy's face. We doubled over in laughter as Jimmy spit and sputtered and mopped water off his face with the neck of his T-shirt.

We also taught our cousins about certain plants—told them to steer clear of sandspurs, prickly pears, and stinging nettle, though that was easier said than done. If you got a sandspur in the sole of your foot and pulled it out with your fingers, you then had a sand-spur stuck in your finger.

The prickly pear's yellow blossoms were pretty, but we knew not to pick one. Even if you avoided being stuck by the cactus's two-inch long thorns, you'd end up with hair-like thorns (glochids) in your fingers. Because they're nearly invisible, they're nearly impos-sible to remove.

Stinging nettles were the absolute worst. Their little white flow-ers gave them away if they were in bloom, but if not, they blended in with other weeds, and you'd brush against them before you knew what had happened. It didn't take long to know you'd made a mistake. Your skin started itching like you had poison ivy and welts formed.

Speaking of poison ivy, Mama had taught us to recognize it by its three leaves. Poison oak too. Both were prevalent in the nearby woods and along the banks of the Suwannee River. If a person is allergic to the oil in its leaves, stems, vines, and roots, they'll break out in blisters that will itch for weeks. Mama said she was allergic, so we probably would be too.

Patsy, however, decided one day that she was *not* allergic to poison ivy. To prove it to Anetha and me, she grabbed a handful of poison-ivy leaves and rubbed them up and down and all over her arms and legs. To further make her point, she even stuck out her tongue and rubbed the leaves on it. Later that day, she proudly showed us that she had no blisters or itchy rash whatsoever. We were impressed. But within three days, Patsy was scratching instead of bragging. The rash got so bad, especially in and around her mouth, that Mama considered taking her to the doctor.

Even some of the plants in our vegetable garden made me itch—things like cucumbers, squash, and okra. I hated picking them. Anetha, on the other hand, loved working in the garden because she liked eating raw vegetables as she picked—lettuce, tomatoes, cucumbers, peas—she even liked raw corn.

I didn't care much for vegetables period, much less raw ones, but I did like to chew on "sour weed," a spindly plant that shot up each spring and turned our cow pasture from green to coral.

We often ate blackberries on the spot, but we knew to stay away from nightshade's berries, which were also black. Anytime Mama or Daddy came across a nightshade plant, they pulled it up. According to them, it was one of the deadliest plants around. Some people called it belladonna; others called its berries *death cherries*.

I couldn't understand why God created such plants. Thankfully, he also created many that provided entertainment for us kids—the pokeberry bush, for example. Mama said that some people used its leaves in salad. We didn't, but when the berries ripened in late summer, my sisters and I picked and mashed them, then used their purple juice for finger paint.

Crotalaria plants also provided beauty and entertainment. In the early summer, we picked its leaves and pretended they were tobacco. We'd get a ball of twine and practice stringing the leaves onto a stick. All three of us aspired to, one day, move up from lowly "tobacco hander" to "stringer" and we knew we needed practice.

In late summer, the crotalaria plants put out yellow snapdragon-like blooms, and as the blooms drop off the stalks, pale green seed pods form. We'd press the pods to hear them pop. If left to dry, the seeds inside would rattle, sounding like a rattle-snake's rattle. Some people called the plant *Rattle Box.*

Crotalaria (Rattle Box)

The plant that provided the most enjoyment, though, was corn. Every spring Daddy planted a big patch of field corn, plus several long rows of Dixie Queen, a variety of sweet corn. By mid-May, the silks sprouting from the top of each ear glistened in the sun like Rapunzel's hair. When there weren't chores to do, Patsy, Anetha, and I headed for the corn rows. We'd go from plant to plant, plaiting the silks on each and every ear we could reach. On some, we plaited one large braid; on others, we made two or three pigtails.

As the ears matured, the silks changed from creamy white to golden to green and purple tinged. We continued to braid the silks until they dried out and turned brown. But Daddy caught us one day.

"Quit that," he said, "It's bad for the corn."

How could it be bad when the braids were so beautiful?

Only much later did I learn about the birds and bees as it applies to corn. The tassels on the top of

each stalk are the (male) flowers that produce pollen, which drifts down to fertilize the silks (female); and each silk corresponds to a single "potential" kernel that, without pollen, won't form.

There was a small window of time, Mama said when corn was at its peak for eating it on the cob or making creamed-style corn.

Our family worked together to break the corn (harvest it). At first, I found this task almost impossible. I'd twist and twist and twist, sometimes breaking the stalk instead of breaking off the ear. But I finally got the hang of it: yank and twist at the same time and the ear pops right off.

We'd fill a trailer and Daddy would haul it to the house and park the tractor and trailer under the oak tree that held our swing. That seemed to be the spot where many activities took place. We'd take chairs from the front porch and set them up in the shade near the trailer. Then, Daddy shucked the ears as Mama, Grandma Rye, and us girls sat in the chairs and silked. Silking corn was a long, tedious process. Each of us used a paring knife to dig the silks from between rows of kernels. Mama and Grandma didn't like to see even a single silk left, so they reinspected the ears we kids silked.

Sometimes green worms got into the ears while in the field and ate the kernels around the tip. When we went to silk it, often a worm was still there, eating away and leaving behind their yucky brown goo, so that part of the ear had to be cut off and discarded. Other times, we'd come to ears that were not filled in completely with kernels. *Hmm-m-m. Wonder why?*

At noon on silking day, we always ate corn-on-the-cob, usually with fried chicken and fresh vegetables such as sliced tomatoes and peas from the garden. That afternoon, we carried all the other ears of silked corn into the kitchen where Mama and Grandma cut off the tips of the kernels with a sharp knife and scraped the cobs clean with the dull, back edge of the knife, making cream-style corn. Mama cooked it with a little butter and salt before she ladled it into cartons and let it cool before placing it in the big deep-freezer we now had in the open hall of our house.

Harvesting all the ears of Dixie Queen sweet corn, around the first of June took several days. We also harvested a few ears from the field-corn patch, though most of the field-corn was left in the patch until the whole stalk dried out. In early fall, Daddy would break all the dried ears off and sell some of the corn. But he always stored a good bit of it in the packhouse so it could be used as feed for the chickens and pigs throughout the year.

Granddaddy stored his dry corn in a corn crib and occasionally he'd shell some and put it in the sugar kettle and boil it for his pigs. The pigs would squeal and fight over that soft-boiled corn when he poured it into their trough. Daddy never boiled corn for our pigs since he didn't own a sugar kettle. And even if he had owned a kettle, I don't think he would baby his pigs like Granddaddy did.

Eventually, I noticed, though, that Granddaddy only babied his pigs with boiled corn in the weeks leading up to hog-killing day.

32

My Miami Grandmother

Every summer, we looked forward to a visit from Grandmama Midgett, who lived in Miami.

"Is she a midget?" kids asked when I mentioned her name.

"No," I'd say emphatically. But then I had to explain that Daddy's father died about a month after Daddy turned eight, and my step granddaddy's last name was Midgett. The two of them lived in Miami with Grandmama Midgett's oldest daughter, Aunt Clara Mae, who was married to Uncle Bob, Granddaddy Midgett's son. So they were all doubly related.

Sometimes they all drove up to our farm together, along with Uncle Bob and Aunt Clara Mae's children. Other times, Grandmama Midgett caught a ride with a friend or relative who happened to be headed north. No matter how she got to our house, though, she arrived with a paper sack containing a surprise for us kids: socks, fabric for a new dress, or colorful barrettes for our hair. As for her own hair—short, wavy, fluffy, and silver white—she wore no clips of any kind. She just brushed it back from her Miami tanned face so that one wave dipped and cast a faint shadow on her forehead.

Although we saw her only once a year, we looked at pictures of her year 'round. I liked the one of her and Granddaddy Midgett in

which he sported an all-white
suit, and Grandmama standing
next to him, wore a dark fitted
suit that showed off her slen-
der figure. When she visited
us each summer, though, she
packed mostly dresses made of
soft-and-cool floral rayons with
skirts that swirled when she
walked. If she wore accessories,
she chose a strand of pearls,
a gold pin, or a white hanky
tucked into a breast pocket so
only its lace edges overflowed. I
adored the way she dressed, especially her high-heeled shoes,
with tiny toe cutouts, and her
pocketbook that matched her shoes.

Grandmama Midgett holds me during
my first family trip to Miami.

One day I peeked inside her black patent purse she'd left lying
on the bed. It opened with a tiny gold knob that required pulling back with both my thumbs. Inside, I found an assortment of
items, but I focused on a tortoiseshell-backed mirror. I took it out
and looked at my reflection from different angles before putting
it back. She'd never know, I thought. But as I closed the purse, it
made a loud click, so I jumped off the bed and ran from the room
as fast as I could. I did not want Grandmama Midgett to be mad
with me.

Because of her pretty clothes, the citrus fruit she shipped to us
every winter, and the gifts she brought each summer, I thought
she and Granddaddy Midgett were rich. At the time, I knew little
about the life she'd lived after Daddy's father died. I never pictured
her as a single woman with a seventh-grade education, trying to
raise five hungry children.

Daddy told me about it, years later.

"After my daddy died," he said, "my mama tried to farm other people's land—sharecropping—just as my daddy had done. I remember seeing her plant corn by hand, walking along the row, dropping the kernels, and covering them up, pushing the sand with her bare feet."

I could not imagine Grandmama Midgett with bare, dirty feet.

Daddy said he once saw his mother pen up somebody else's open-range cow and calf to get milk for her children. He also saw her second husband, a man named Pat Sullivan, walk out on her while she lay in bed too sick to get up. "The scoundrel!" Daddy said, "He never did come back, and Mama never heard from him again."

After that, Daddy said they moved from Suwannee County to Jacksonville where his mother went to work for an older man. She kept house and cooked for him.

"We all moved in with him," Daddy said, but that didn't last long. "The man came home drunk one night and expected more from her than housekeeping, so Mama threw the man out—out of his own house."

After that, though, Daddy said his mother got sick and needed surgery. That's when Daddy ended up in an orphanage in Jacksonville. But he eventually made it back to Suwannee County to live with an uncle and then his cousin, Joe. During that period of time, his mother, still in Jacksonville, met and married Charles Midgett, who had a good government job. That, Daddy said, made it possible for her to get her younger children out of the orphanage.

Though I saw Grandmama Midgett only once a year, I was crazy about her and felt honored the night she asked to sit next to me at the supper table.

Mama had cooked hoecakes—pancakes made with corn meal. Mama preferred making hoecakes during hot weather, rather than cornbread or biscuits, which required a hot oven. She always measured all the hoecake ingredients very, very precisely—a handful of freshly ground cornmeal, half a handful of flour, a clump of lard, an egg or two, a pinch of salt and baking powder, and just enough fresh cow milk to make the mixture into a batter.

She placed an iron skillet on the stove, turned on the flame, and added a dollop of lard to the skillet. The lard soon melted, covering the bottom of the skillet. A few seconds later, to check the temperature, Mama sprinkled in a few drops of water. If the water danced, she knew it was hot enough. She then poured the batter into five separate puddles, cutting off the stream when each puddle was about three-inches wide. In less than a minute, bubbles formed on the surface of each puddle and began to pop—time to flip them. Mama's hoecakes turned out brown and crispy on the outside but warm and tender inside.

My mouth watered as I sat down for supper at my designated spot. It was summer, so our dining table had been moved to the open hallway. Mama sat on one side of me—to make sure I took at least one bite of everything. I was thrilled to have Grandmama Midgett on the other side.

Anetha said the God-is-great-God-is-good blessing, and the bowls and platters of food made their way around the table.

"Here, honey," Mama said to me, "I'm giving you just a few bites of turnip greens."

I detested greens and almost gagged as Mama spooned the greens, roots and all, onto my plate. Thank goodness for hoecakes; they helped me get things like turnips and rutabagas down without throwing up. To keep from tasting the yucky vegetable, I'd wrap a piece of the hoecake around a bit of the yucky stuff and swallow it whole. I knew I had to clean my plate in order to get dessert. That night we had no prepared dessert, but for me, hoecakes slathered with cane syrup ranked up there with cake or pie.

After cleaning my place, I asked for more hoecakes and the syrup jar. Grandmama Midgett held the platter of hoecakes over my plate, and I dragged two onto my plate with my fork. After covering them with syrup, I rolled up a hoecake with my fingers and stuffed it into my mouth. *Yummy*, I thought as I chewed and licked my sticky fingers.

As I began rolling up the second hoecake, Grandmama Midgett cleared her throat and picked up my fork.

"Here, Susanette, let me show you," she said with her husky voice, which sounded as if she smoked, but she didn't.

With the fork, she cut my remaining hoecake into several small pieces and held the fork out for me to take. Recognizing that she wanted me to use the fork—and wanting to please her—I took it, stuck its tines into all the cut pieces on my plate—stab, stab, stab, stab—and put them into my mouth.

Laughter erupted around the table. I looked up to see what was funny. All eyes stared at me. *What? I'd used my fork like Grandma wanted!*

After I'd heard the Susanette-and-the-hoecake story about a dozen times, I finally got it.

In years to come, I would write letters to my Miami grandmother. Mama told me to ask her questions and she would answer me. Mama was right. She answered every letter I wrote.

Dear Grandmama Midgett,
How are you doing? I hope you are doing very good. We are all
doing very good.
    Love, Susanette

***

Dear Susanette,
Thank you for your sweet letter. We are all doing fine.
I just finished making a dress for Clara Mae.
Write again soon.
    Love,
    Grandmama Midgett

***

Dear Grandmama Midgett,
How are you doing now? I hope that you are doing very good.
Did Aunt Clara Mae like her new dress? What color was it?
    Love, Susanette

We had no telephone, so our letters kept us connected between summers, between the times she arrived carrying a paper sack filled with goodies for us kids. The rest of the family wrote her too, and sometimes a letter came that she'd addressed to our whole family. That was nice. But the letters that came with my name alone on the envelope put a big grin on my face.

33

Nothing Is Impossible

Mama made me mad as a wet cat one Sunday when she told my Sunday school teacher I slept with the chickens. Why would Mama say such a thing? I never slept with the chickens. I slept on the cot with my sisters. Always.

Well, except when I fell asleep on a church pew. That happened because we practically lived in church. Anytime the church doors opened, we showed up—for Sunday school and preaching service on Sunday morning, for training union every Sunday night, and for Wednesday night prayer meeting. We attended occasional all-day sings with dinner on the grounds, helped with the annual cemetery clean-up, and attended week-long revival services, spring and fall. My sisters and I also went to Vacation Bible School each summer—my favorite church activity—and our family seldom missed a wedding or funeral at Philadelphia Baptist.

According to Daddy, our church got its name not from that big city in Pennsylvania but from one of the seven churches mentioned in the book of Revelations. "Philadelphia means brotherly love," he said. Daddy knew all about our church's history, since his grandfather served as one of its first deacons. Seven local families organized the church in 1876, he said. One of them donated land,

and the men in the new congregation cut trees on the property to build a log church, which also served as a school.

In 1903, a white frame building replaced the old log church. Inside this new church—our church—three rows of hand-built pews could seat about 70 people. If more than that showed up, which often happened for a funeral, the men gave up their seats for women and children, and the men stood at the back of the church or outside, where they could smoke or spit.

The church had no steeple or fancy stained-glass windows. The pews had no padding either, and during a long preaching service, they began to feel more like stone than wood. Sometimes my dangling feet fell asleep. Other times, my whole body did.

Whenever Mama noticed me yawning or nodding off, she'd lean me over until my head rested in her lap. As I lay stretched out on the pew, Mama stroked my hair and tugged at my curls—perhaps absentmindedly—wrapping strands around her fingers or stretching each ringlet to its full length before letting it spring back. Mama's touch gave me a warm feeling all over and always put me right to sleep.

My getting mad with Mama for telling my Sunday school teacher I went to bed with the chickens happened during a nighttime revival service. When we arrived for the service, Daddy went in one direction, Patsy and Anetha went in another, and I followed Mama. She chose a pew behind my Sunday school teacher, who turned around to talk to us. Mrs. Ross was beautiful. Her eyes exactly matched her dark wavy hair. As she and Mama talked, she looked at me and said to Mama, "Susanette's already looking sleepy." She smiled at me, then pursed her crimson lips as she slowly brought them together over her white, white teeth.

"Yeah. Susanette goes to bed with the chickens," Mama said.

"Mama! I don't sleep with the chickens!" I protested, pulling on her arm. "Mama—"

"Sh-h-h," she said, patting my legs as our minister stood to introduce the visiting preacher and Mrs. Ross turned to face forward.

I was so mad with Mama right then that I didn't know what to do. What if Mrs. Ross told her son Al, who was in my training union class? Would he tell his older brothers? And who all would *they* tell? Mama knew perfectly well where I slept, and it was *not* with the chickens. I looked up at her staring straight ahead and said to myself, When I grow up, I won't wear that puny "natural" lipstick Mama wears—orangey-looking in the tube but pale pink on your lips. My lips will be bright red like Mrs. Ross's.

Despite being angry with Mama, I soon lay down with my head in her lap and she began tugging my curls. Although I still wanted straight hair that could be plaited, I recognized that curls did have benefits. I liked the feel of Mama's fingers twisting them. Plus, Daddy often said I reminded him of the little curly-headed girl on the Sunbeam bread wrapper.

I fell fast asleep on the church pew that night, but awoke with a start to the preacher's shouting, "Nothing is impossible if you be-lieeeve!" I sat up straight.

"It's God's Word!" the preacher bellowed, slamming his fist against the lectern. Did he think the congregation sat on Daddy's back forty? *Amens* bounced off the walls of the church. This re-vival preacher evidently thought our whole congregation had hearing problems like Granddaddy Tip—who wasn't even there. He attended Patmos Primitive Baptist Church, which met just once a month so the men could wash one another's feet. I'd visited once. Men brought in a bucket of water and washed each other's feet right there on the front pew in front of God and everybody. I thought that a strange custom. But I thought it even stranger that the church had no piano.

Philadelphia's revival preacher raised one arm toward Heaven and thrust the other toward the congregation, a splayed Bible hanging over his outstretched palm.

"Open your Holy Bibles to Matthew 17:20," he commanded. As people in the pews flipped through onionskin pages of their Good Books trying to find Matthew, the preacher yanked his Bible toward his barrel chest, pushed on the nosepiece of his black-frame glasses with one finger, and read, "Verily I say unto you, if ye have faith as a grain of mustard seed, ye shall say unto this mountain, Remove hence to yonder place; and it shall remove; and nothing shall be impossible unto you." He stopped then, as preachers tend to do after a Scripture reading, waiting for the words to sink in.

"Nothing is impossible," he repeated before lowering his voice to a whisper and breathed the words, "if you be-lieeeve." After a moment of silence, *Amens* from the congregation overlapped one another. "Amen!" . . . "men!" . . . "en!"

"Let us pray," the preacher said, as he closed his Bible and dropped to one knee beside the lectern. All men kneeled.

Daddy was on his knees across the aisle from Mama and me. I had heard him say once that he felt closer to God on his knees. That made no sense to me. On his knees, Daddy was closer to the ground, to Hell, which I knew was deep underground, the place where the Devil lived.

The women never knelt. They stayed put, keeping their heads nearer to God, their eyes closed. I did as the ladies did. Except, as the prayer went on and on, I opened my eyes enough to see my hands. I interlocked my fingers, made a double fist, and recited under my breath: "There's the church, there's the steeple, open the

door and there's the people."

I preferred Sunday school to a revival service like this with a shouting preacher and prayers that went on forever. I liked Mrs. Ross's calm, soft voice and the stories she told, like the one about Jesus turning water into wine—though that story did confuse me. Daddy said wine was "bad and nobody should drink it." So why did Jesus turn perfectly good water into something bad?

When the prayer ended, the preacher wiped his brow with a wrinkled white handkerchief, returned it to his back pocket, then turned the service over to Clarice Boatright, our choir director, for the invitational hymn. This was when we—all of us unsaved souls—were supposed to walk down the aisle to accept Jesus as our personal Savior, something I was much too afraid to do.

Clarice told us the hymn's page number and motioned for the choir and the congregation to stand. As piano music filled the air, she waved one arm in a graceful and continuous figure eight. Her hymnal lay cradled like a baby on her bad arm. According to family members, she'd had limited use of that arm since birth. She was now married to Daddy's first cousin, Doc Boatright, a farmer like Daddy. I thought Doc was very handsome. I liked the way he parted his hair near the middle and plastered it down with Brylcreem. He and Clarice made the perfect couple. Her porcelain-smooth skin showed off her sparkling blue eyes, like sunlight on freshwater springs. Their boys, Wendell, Donald Ray, and Marlyn—close in age to my sisters and me—had inherited their parents' good looks. I could imagine my sisters and me marrying the Boatright boys one day in a triple wedding.

As Clarice directed the invitational hymn, I whispered the words, "Just as I am without one plea." I didn't sing loud anymore, not since Patsy said what she did after the Christmas concert. Before the program, Clarice had told us preschoolers she wanted us to sing so loud that Jesus in Heaven could hear us. I followed directions but was sorry I did after Patsy said on the way home that I drowned out everybody else and embarrassed her.

As the invitational hymn dragged on, I thought of what Mrs. Ross told us in Sunday school, about Jesus walking on the Sea of Galilee, and then I thought of what the preacher said—if you had the faith of a mustard seed, you could move mountains. If a person had the faith of a mustard seed, could he also walk on water like Jesus did? If Granddaddy Rye had enough faith, could he step out of his boat onto the river? I didn't know whether he had that much, or any faith for that matter. He never went to church with us, though Grandma Rye did. She squeezed into Granddaddy's truck with us nearly every Sunday morning.

Looking across the church aisle, I noticed rotund Mr. Curtis Johnson sitting near Daddy. What if Mr. Johnson wanted to walk on water or move a mountain? Might he need the faith of a watermelon seed?

34

Walking on Water

Our family piled into Granddaddy's truck one Saturday morning, ready for a trip to town. We lived closer to Branford and Mayo,
but Daddy preferred Live Oak because it had everything—the
livestock market, tobacco warehouses, and the Commercial Bank
where he borrowed money to plant crops.

"I need to buy Susanette some shoes today," Mama said to Daddy
as we headed out. I couldn't believe my ears. I'd always worn my
sisters' hand-me-downs. But I'd been complaining that my shoes
were too tight and Anetha's and Patsy's shoes still fit them.

Upon learning I was getting new shoes, I could hardly sit still.
The trip to Live Oak seemed to take longer than usual. After passing our grandparents' house, we passed the farms and homes of
the Bennetts, Wards, Touchtons, Johnsons, Gambles, Knights,
Boatrights, Lands, and Allisons, all people we knew from church,
before turning onto the paved road.

Thank goodness Daddy drove a little faster on Highway 51. As we
approached other vehicles, he nodded and lifted an index finger
off the steering wheel. In town, he took the usual route, north on
Ohio Avenue (US129), which went by the courthouse, a stately yellow brick building with arched windows and a clock on its dome

that faced east, west, north, and south.

"It's four minutes after eleven o'clock," Patsy announced as soon as the clock came into view.

Daddy turned onto Warren Street, a block short of US90, and parked in an angled spot. The truck's tires bumped the curb of the sidewalk that provided access to the back entrances of several dry goods stores facing Howard Street (US90). On occasion, members of our family compared those stores—discussed which one carried the best merchandise. Granddaddy Rye said Sharples, hands down, reminding everybody, "You get what you pay for." He shopped Sharples for shoes, socks, hats, khaki shirts and trousers, and cotton handkerchiefs. Grandma went there for shoes, slips and bloomers (Mama made all Grandma's dresses). Mama and Daddy shopped Sharples only for shoes.

"Hold my hand," Mama said, as I jumped from the running board to the pavement. We entered the store through the convenient back door. Mr. Joe Sharples, dressed in a white shirt and bow tie, creased trousers, and highly shined shoes, greeted us. He wore his hair like Doc Boatright, parted in the middle and slicked down, not a single hair out of place.

"Mrs. Howell, what can I do for you all today?"

"Susanette needs shoes," Mama said as I hopped onto one of the upholstered chrome chairs in the shoe area.

"Let's take a look," he said, dragging a stool over so it sat in front of me. After removing my tight and scuffed hand-me-downs, he placed my socked feet, one by one, on a metal board and measured them with the board's sliding gauge.

"I'll be right back," he said, as he walked toward a fabric curtain that served as a door to a storage area. He returned with a shoebox, lifted its lid, rustled his hand in the tissue paper, and pulled out the prettiest shoe I'd ever seen—reddish leather, decorated with tiny cutouts and buckle straps.

I raised a foot to meet the shoe.

"Nope, give me your right foot."

Using a shoehorn, Mr. Sharples slipped my right foot into the shoe, buckled it tight, and pressed hard with his thumb to feel where my big toe ended.

"Plenty of growing room," he said to Mama as he pulled out the other shoe, slipped it on my other socked foot, and buckled it.

"There, now, young lady," he said, slapping my feet together and smiling. "Walk around and see how they feel."

I walked 'round and 'round, admiring the reflection of the shoes in the slanted mirror on his stool.

"Do they hurt anywh—"

"No, ma'am!" I said, cutting Mama off and shaking my head hard. "Can I keep 'em on, Mama? Can I wear 'em? Ple-e-e-ease."

"I guess so—if you're sure they don't hurt anywhere."

She then walked with Mr. Sharples to the checkout counter where she signed a credit slip. Mr. Sharples, like most town merchants, extended credit to farm families who paid their bills after they harvested and sold their crops. Now behind the counter, Mr. Sharples put my old shoes in the new shoe box, tied it with string and handed it to me.

"Okay, girls," Mama said, as she pushed against the heavy back door, "Let's go see if we can find your daddy."

"It's twenty-three minutes after eleven o'clock," Patsy informed us. Who cared. *I* had new red shoes.

In Live Oak, we often had to wait for Daddy to finish his business, so we'd wait in the public restroom on the courthouse square. The facility included several stalls, plus a separate rest area furnished with a dozen or more porch rockers. The woman who took care of the public restroom called herself a "Christian Scientist." She stacked pamphlets about her religion on tables and windowsills, hoping to convert others to what Daddy called "a heathern religion." Live Oak was made up mostly of Baptists like us, with a sprinkling of Methodists and Presbyterians, people who would not be caught dead reading such "scientific" literature. If anybody picked up a brochure, they used it to fan their sweaty faces.

Lucky for us, on that particular day, we didn't have to wait in the restroom. We saw Daddy talking with some men on the shady courthouse square, not far from the red brick jailhouse where men with sad faces clutched window bars and stared out at freedom.

All around the courthouse square, free people sat on park benches, and men leaned against live oaks and date palms as they jawed with fellow farmers about crops—corn, cotton, peanuts, watermelon, and tobacco. Most smoked or chewed. Pigeons waddled to and fro on the sidewalk, pecking at overripe dates. An occasional splatter of dark tobacco juice hit the sidewalk, causing the squatty birds to scatter.

The men who surrounded Daddy were laughing when we walked up. No doubt he had told one of his many jokes. We waited a while for Daddy to end his conversation. Then he walked with us across the street to Dr. Culpepper's air-conditioned drugstore. We sat together in a booth, and a woman from behind the soda fountain's marble counter came over to take our order. Everybody asked for a Co-Cola, except me. I ordered my drink of choice, ice water.

When we got to the bottom of our drinks and our straws made sucking sounds, Daddy said, "Okay, we'd better go get a few groceries and head home."

"It's ten minutes till twelve o'clock," Patsy said as we walked to the truck, "nearly time to eat."

In Webb's Grocery, owned and operated by Broward and Corrine Webb, Anetha and I helped Mama collect grocery items while Patsy followed Daddy to the meat counter.

It wasn't until after we got back into the truck to go home that I learned from Mama and Daddy's conversation what Patsy did while at the meat counter. She was in big trouble.

Daddy had stood at the meat counter, joking with Miss Corrine as she sliced meat for another customer. After finishing the slicing, she reached into the refrigerated case, broke herself off half a wiener to eat (this was before wieners came pre-packaged), and tossed the other half back into the cooler. Daddy—joking around—reached in and took the other half of her wiener and ate it, after which Patsy reached in and helped herself to a whole wiener.

"No, Patsy, don't do that," Daddy said to her, but it was too late. She'd already bitten off a chunk. So he told Miss Corrine to add Patsy's wiener to his credit slip.

In the car, Daddy began reprimanding Patsy.

"Patsy, taking something that's not yours is stealing. You can't just help yourself to anything you want in a sto—"

"Now wait a minute, C. G. Howell," Mama said, cutting Daddy off. "You're the one that started it. You're the one that was joking around and set a bad example for Patsy—so don't go jumping all over Patsy."

Daddy revved the engine and sped down the highway. Nobody said a word for several miles.

"Look a yonder, Ethel," Daddy said, breaking the silence as we turned ono the unpaved Philadelphia Church road. "Look at them rain clouds to the south. It's raining back at home."

"I sure hope so," Mama said, with more seriousness than excitement. "We sure need it."

I was too young to fully appreciate the need for rain, not recognizing that without rain the crops could fail and the bank could take the farm along with the house we lived in.

If Daddy said it was raining back home, then it was. He might be wrong about some things, such as taking bites of wieners in grocery stores, but he was seldom wrong about the weather.

By the time he drove the eighteen miles home, the rain clouds had moved to the west, but Daddy was on cloud nine when he saw puddles dotting our sandy yard.

"We really got a good soaking rain," he said.

Everybody jumped out of Granddaddy's borrowed truck and began hauling paper sacks of groceries into the house, except me. I bent over a puddle, looked at my reflection, and at the sand at the bottom of the puddle. The water was pretty clear and it didn't look very deep.

Nothing is impossible if you believe . . . if you have the faith of a mustard seed . . . Jesus walked on the Sea of Galilee . . . .

Standing on one leg, I extended the other over the water. I carefully lowered the sole of my new red shoe to the surface of the puddle and stepped—Splat! My foot plunged to the bottom.

My failed experiment in the power of faith might have ended there if it hadn't been such a hot day. The water felt so nice and cool. In went my other foot. Splash! Splash! Splash! Water flowed in and out the tiny cutwork in my shoes, wetting my socks. I jumped and splashed with both feet, enjoying the feel of splatters landing high on my legs. I ran to another puddle. Splash! Then, another. What funny squishy noises my socks made.

About that time, Patsy pranced down the front steps and waltzed over to me.

"Daddy said to tell you to go get his belt."

If Daddy had ever whipped me before that day, I don't remember it, yet I knew what "get his belt" meant.

Knowing I was in hot water, I stood frozen in the cool puddle, then began to cry. Slowly, I trudged into the house and into the bedroom. Through tears, I spied Daddy's black belt on the bed.

What followed is as vivid today as it was that new-red-shoe day. Daddy kept saying how I had ruined a perfectly good pair of shoes—not even paid for—as the lashes of his belt left welts on my bare legs. As he continued to swing the belt, I promised Daddy, God, and myself that I would never ever try to walk on water again.

35

Punishment and Wonderment

After what felt like forever, the lashes stopped. Daddy released his grip on me, and I flopped to the floor, bawling.

"O.K., dry it up," Daddy said after half a minute. My bottom and legs still throbbed, but I tried to muffle my sobs. "That hurt me more than it did you," he said, towering over me as he threaded his belt through his trousers' belt loops. "You know why I had to whip you, right?"

"Yes . . . (sniff) . . . sir."

"Why?"

"'Cause (sniff) . . . I ruined my new shoes?"

"And?"

"'Cause you love me?"

"Right," Daddy said.

In church, I'd often heard, "Spare the rod and spoil the child." The preacher said that parents who didn't punish their children didn't love them. So Daddy loved me.

When I learned that the Bible verse actually mentioned only *sons*, not

> He that spareth his rod hateth his son; but he that loveth him chasteneth him betimes.
>
> —Proverbs 13:24

daughters, I wondered why Daddy didn't know that. His Bible, with thumb tabs and a concordance, was tattered and finger-smudged from use.

I should have been thankful, I guess, that Daddy used a belt instead of a rod as mentioned in Proverbs. I knew some fathers who took up the equivalent of a rod. I once saw Daddy's uncle break a five-foot-long tobacco stick, about an inch thick, over the back of one of his boys for talking back. Yet I'd heard Daddy say that this uncle was his favorite, the one he most respected.

Just as Daddy respected that uncle, I looked up to Daddy. But my feelings were confusing: fear . . . love . . . respect . . . all mixed together—the same way I felt about God—the all-powerful One, the One who knew and saw everything. I knew in my heart that Daddy would give his life for me, just like the preacher said God the Father did for his only Son—even though I wasn't the son Daddy had wanted.

For some reason, I didn't fear Mama, even though she regularly punished my sisters and me for misbehaving. Maybe it was because her spankings didn't hurt like Daddy's whippings. Comparing the two was the equivalent of comparing a flea bite to stings from a swarm of bumblebees. Mama never made us bend over one of her knees either, as Daddy did, so he could clamp us in place with his other knee. Mama just grabbed an arm. That left us free to run around and around her, lessening the impact of her swats.

Occasionally, Mama made us find a switch and take it to her, though, just as Daddy made me get his belt. One day when she told Patsy, "Bring me a switch," Patsy took her a flimsy dog fennel, which broke on the first whack. I couldn't believe Mama didn't make Patsy get another. She didn't. But she also didn't forget Patsy's trick. Every time one of us got in trouble after that, Mama said, "Bring me a switch off the peach tree." That small tree in the backyard yielded unbreakable switches. A peach tree switch stung like the dickens when it hit bare legs.

Mama also had a few other methods of punishment.

"Come here, Anetha," she said one day when my sisters wouldn't stop arguing with one another. Using one of our crayons, Mama drew a circle on the inside of a low window pane in the front room and told Anetha to kneel there and put her nose in the circle.

"Patsy, go out on the porch and put your nose against the same circle," she ordered. "And y'all stay put until you can stop fussing."

Anytime Mama used that punishment, two of us had to sit nose to nose for as long as it took, with just the glass separating us. Soon, one stuck out her tongue. The other crossed her eyes. One made an ugly face. The other made a funny face. And before long, we were giggling.

"Okay," Mama would tell us then. "Now get up and hug one another."

Of course, the bed-wetting punishment, which applied only to me, also continued. When I woke up wet, I still rubbed my nose on the wet mattress. That beat Mama's standing over me, hand on my neck making me do it. Now, when we three sisters got up at the same time, I lagged behind and punished myself after they left. Some mornings, all alone in the room, I thought about skipping the ritual. Would Mama know? But the preacher said God knew and saw our every move.

I believed whatever the preacher said, since he quoted from the Bible, which he said was the Word of God. I didn't understand, though, what he said about God, Jesus, and the Holy Spirit being separate, but also One. How could that be?

No matter how much I tried to picture them as One, I pictured them separate. I thought God lived in the clouds and looked like Great-Granddaddy Tip, except God had long white hair and a beard that was even longer. I imagined the Holy Spirit as a ghost-like swirl of smoke because the preacher sometimes called Him the "Holy Ghost." And I pictured Jesus as a living man, like the drawings of Him in our Sunday school book. I thought He looked kind and gentle, like a man who would never whip one of the children who crowded around Him in the pictures. Then again, the preacher said Jesus once got so angry with people for selling stuff inside His temple that He turned over their money tables and threw them out on the street. I pictured them tumbling down the steps and landing on their heads.

That made me wonder what would happen if I accidentally peed on a church pew while asleep, my head resting in Mama's lap. Would peeing on a church pew anger Jesus? Would that be a bigger sin than wetting the cot at home? Surely, it would be. And what would be my punishment?

I also wondered why adults didn't get punished for things they did wrong or for arguing. Sometimes Mama and Daddy fussed, but nobody made them put their noses in a circle on the window.

The issue I heard them argue about the most was the rearrangement of furniture.

"Confound it, Ethel!" Daddy would say when he bumped into something Mama had recently moved. "Why can't you just leave the dad-blamed furniture in one place?"

"'Cause I like a change, C.G., and that change didn't cost a dime."

Only if Daddy helped was he okay with the new arrangement. That happened when we got a refrigerator that year, 1949. It wouldn't fit in the kitchen, so Daddy and Mama scooted her sewing machine closer to the buffet to create a spot for the refrigerator in the front room. Then when they got the freezer, it went in the hall where there was nothing to rearrange.

Later on, I learned that one of my parents' worst arguments took place when I was just three months old. Mama told me they'd gone to Miami around Christmastime to visit Daddy's relatives and show me off. Anetha was barely walking at the time, and Patsy was just two. We were on the way home, near Green Cove Springs, when Daddy decided his Model A needed an oil change. The car was one he'd practically built himself, using a rusty chassis

Granddaddy Rye gave him and the Model A body he got from somebody else. Mama thought the car's oil change could wait until we got back to Suwannee County, but Daddy insisted it couldn't because his car had reached the mileage point when a change was absolutely required.

"I was nursing you," Mama said, "so I had to go into the gas station's filthy bathroom to do that. Women didn't nurse in public back then. And I had a hard time keeping Anetha and Patsy—so tired from the long drive—from lying down on that grimy bathroom floor."

Mama shook her head as she added, "I got so mad with your daddy that day that I thought about leaving him!"

Mama looked as if she still held a grudge against Daddy about that long-ago experience.

One other time, Mama said she got so mad with Daddy that she "wanted to kill him." I knew, of course, that Mama didn't really mean that. Or if she did, she didn't go through with it. The disagreement she spoke of had to do with her milk cow. I didn't witness that "fight," but I knew Mama's milking routine and she added the details.

Daddy usually stayed busy doing other jobs at milking time, so the milking chore always fell to Mama. She said she actually enjoyed milking, although at times, the task presented problems, like when Anetha was a baby.

"Patsy was real jealous of Anetha," Mama said, "having been used to getting all the attention. She would bite her baby sister every chance she got. So before I went out to milk the cow, I had to tie Patsy to a bedpost." I smiled every time Mama told that story because I liked imagining Patsy tied up so she couldn't move.

After we were old enough to walk, Mama let us go with her when she milked the cow, unless the outside temperature dipped to freezing. On such days, she built a roaring fire in the fireplace, set three straight-back dining chairs a distance from the blaze, made each of us sit in one, and ordered us not to budge until she got back. If one of us got up from the chair, we knew another sister would tattle and we'd get punished. I don't know why we never made a pact to all stand at once so nobody could be the tattletale. Probably because none of us trusted the others to stick to the plan.

Because Mama milked a cow every day, she got attached to them—gave them names. Most of all, Mama favored Betty, a brown Jersey, with curved horns about a foot long.

When Mama went to milk Betty one morning—the day she ended up so mad with Daddy she wanted to kill him—Daddy was nearby, sharpening a plow. Mama did the usual preparations. On the ground, she set a galvanized bucket of feed that Daddy had made up. The feed contained hay, dry corn (ground-up corn—shucks, kernels, cobs and all) and some old cane syrup. The sweet mixture would keep the cow standing still while Mama milked. She squatted in front of Betty's hind legs, set her white enamel milk bucket under the cow's teats, and began pulling and squeezing with both hands.

"Before I took all of the cow's milk," Mama said, "I'd usually stop to let her calf suck a while. That's what I did that morning. Then I pulled Betty's calf off. As I hitched the calf to a post with a rope, so I could finish milking, another cow's calf ran over and tried to suck Betty. She never seemed to mind my taking her milk, but she evidently didn't like having another cow's calf take it. She whirled her head around, caught that strange calf with her horns, and gave it a flip. The calf did a somersault and hit the dirt. It was able to get up—wasn't really hurt. I was a little annoyed with Betty, but she didn't deserve what came next.

"C.G. evidently didn't see the calf trying to suck the wrong cow," Mama continued. "He just saw Betty horn and flip the calf, and that made him mad as fire. He picked up a broken fence rail and hauled off and hit Betty over the head with it. The blow knocked off one of her horns. Boy! Did I get mad with him! Betty would never have hurt one of us like he'd hurt her. I'd milked Betty when her bag was so sore she could hardly stand for me to touch it, yet she *never* tried to kick me."

Mama also got upset with Daddy when he said things that embarrassed her, like what he said to his old high school buddy, who was helping him with some farm work. His buddy ate the noon dinner with us, and hours later, when we were about to sit down for supper, Daddy said to him in front of all of us, "Now, George Frederick, I want you to help yourself tonight at supper, but I don't want you to eat like you did at noon today." Daddy's friend looked puzzled.

"Yeah," Daddy continued, "Ethel whispered to me after we finished dinner that she would hate to have to put in a sack and carry on her back what you put in your stomach today."

"I said no such thing!" Mama protested as Daddy chuckled.

In the future, Mama brought up that incident anytime we expected guests for a meal. She'd remind Daddy that he'd better not embarrass her again with such a comment as he'd made to George Frederick. But Daddy's antics continued. He would tell guests at the table to eat up but to please not put their feet on the table. That annoyed Mama too.

He joked around with people he hardly knew too—though I have to admit, most people acted as if they thought he was funny. Granted, his humor did land him a stand-up routine at the Suwannee River Jamboree. The outdoor show, held every Saturday night in Live Oak, featured musicians along with skits and jokes mocking all sorts of people.

Sometimes at home Daddy would mimic people he knew, like Mr. Goodley Hingson, who pronounced "just" as "thes." And he enjoyed quoting Aunt Daisy, the one he lived with as a teenager, the one who had a high-pitched voice and used words that stood for profanity. Daddy forbade us to use those words, even though he used one himself when he told Aunt Daisy's clabber story.

"Aunt Daisy hired a colored man named Robert to drive her over to her daughter's house one day," Daddy said. "Willie Mae was expecting a baby and she loved clabber, so Aunt Daisy decided to take her daughter a bowlful."

I hated milk, period, and couldn't understand how Willie Mae or anybody could eat stinky sour and clotted milk.

"Aunt Daisy got into the car," Daddy said, "and set the uncovered bowl in her lap. On

---

Suwannee River Jamboree
In the 1950s, this Saturday night show was turned into a weekly three-hour radio show on Live Oak's radio station, WNER, and was syndicated across the Southeast.

The Stanley Brothers (Carter and Ralph Stanley), known for their Bluegrass music, which included lots of banjo pickin', headlined the Jamboree from 1958-1962.

The popularity of Bluegrass began to steadily decline after that. But in the year 2000, the movie *Oh, Brother, Where Art Thou*, starring George Clooney, revived it.

---

the drive to Willie Mae's house, something ran out in front of the car, and the driver had to slam on the brakes. Clabber sloshed up and coated Aunt Daisy's face, hair, and dress. 'Robert! Why in tarnation did you do that?' she yelled at the driver. The colored man tried to explain, but Aunt Daisy, batting her clabber-coated eyelashes, flung her hands apart and spat, 'And thar's Willie Mae's *dern* clabber!'"

Daddy batted his eyes and flung his own hands out as if he were Aunt Daisy herself, exclaiming over spilt clabber. Listeners always laughed, and Daddy did too.

I liked when Daddy entertained and laughed. I wasn't afraid of him then, his belt snug around his waist.

36

Fire and a Burning Desire

My sisters and I were in the middle of a marbles game, and I was trying to get them to switch to a game of hopscotch the day Mama's oil stove caught fire.

Patsy had drawn a circle the size of a dinner plate in the sand. Into the circle, she dropped a handful of marbles. Squatting, she held the shooter marble in her curled pointer finger, her thumb behind it. Pressing her knuckles against the ground, she aimed at a marble near the farthest edge of the circle. Thump! Clack! The shooter knocked the marble from the circle. Thump! Clack! There went another. According to the rules, she kept going until she missed. The object of the game? To collect the most marbles. After Patsy collected four marbles, Anetha shot two out before missing.

"It's your turn, Sooz-net," Patsy said.

Too chubby to squat and shoot, I lay on my stomach on the sand, propped myself on my left elbow and got my right hand in position. Thump . . . the marble rolled only a few inches and died.

"This ain't no fun!" I said as I got up, brushing sand off. "It's a boy's game, anyway."

"Look!" Patsy said. "Watch me." She demonstrated, knocking another marble out.

"Let's play hopscotch," I said and picked up a stick to draw the diagram. Too bad the sand was dry and soft. I liked to draw on damp, smooth sand, so the lines looked sharp, as if carved in stone.

"No, we gotta finish this game first," Patsy said.

"Come on," I begged, "I'm drawing the—

"Girls!" Mama yelled from the porch. "Go get your granddaddy!"

"Ma'am?" We hollered back, thinking we'd misunderstood.

"Go get your granddaddy! Hurry! The stove's on fire!"

My sisters dropped their marbles, I dropped my stick, and off we ran. Patsy and Anetha soon got ahead of me. When I looked back, Mama had disappeared from the porch, and dark smoke billowed from the side kitchen window.

The soles of our feet hardly touched the ground as we ran. Even so, they were about blistered from the scorching sand by the time we reached the shaded road near our grandparents' house. While running, we hadn't taken the time to slide them under the hot layer of sand to reach cooler dirt or to step off to cool them in grass.

"Granddaddy!" Patsy and Anetha yelled. "Our stove's on fire!"

Granddaddy Rye hopped on his gray Ford (Ferguson) tractor, which had a trailer attached, and drove toward us. We hopped in, he put the tractor in high gear, and off we bounced toward home. I'd never seen Granddaddy drive his tractor that fast. As we rounded the last bend in the road, I saw our house—still standing—and no smoke at all.

Mama met us on the porch, saying, "I smothered the fire with a quilt." The singed and tattered patchwork quilt lay on the floor in the open hall.

When Daddy came home later that day from his job in town, he said, "Good thing the oil reservoir [attached to one side of the stove] was low on oil." He fixed the stove, and as I recall, we never even missed a meal.

"Whatcha gonna fix?" I asked Mama a day or two later when I saw her light the oven in the middle of the afternoon. If she planned to bake a cake, I wanted to stick around to lick the bowl. Turns out, it was pies.

She never made just one pie, saying it was just as easy to make two as one. Before mixing up the dough for crust, she prepared the spot where she rolled it out. She laid a clean dish towel on the cook table, which sat in the middle of the kitchen, directly under the light bulb that dangled from smoke-darkened overhead rafters. She dusted flour on the clean cloth and on her rolling pin. In a bowl, she mixed up flour, salt, baking powder, lard (always in a liquid state in warm weather), and a tiny bit of water with a fork until the mixture stuck together and formed a big ball. After dividing the stiff dough into two balls, she rolled one on the floured cloth until it grew to about a foot in diameter and was nearly as thin as the cover of our hardback storybook. She transferred it to a pie dish and cut off excess dough around the edges. She did the same with the other ball, after which she created a fancy fluted edge on each by pinching the dough between her fingers and giving it a slight twist.

When she made a pecan, sweet potato, egg custard, or fruit-filled pie, she added the filling before she baked the crust. But if she made cream-filled pies, she baked the pie crusts first, then filled them with lemon custard, or with coconut and chocolate filling (recipe p. 432), and topped them with meringue.

She was making cream-filled pies the day Patsy got her big surprise. Mama had already poured the cream fillings into the crusts when we joined her in the kitchen.

"Go back out and wash your hands," Mama said. "And use soap."

After washing our hands at the water shelf, Anetha and Patsy stood by the cook table while I dragged a straight-back chair from the dining table. I nudged it between them, climbed on its seat, and stood.

We licked the utensils and bowls that Mama had used to make the filling. Absorbed in that activity of scraping and licking, we didn't notice what ingredients Mama put in the green mixing bowl to make the meringue. But before long, as her manual eggbeater whirred, the stuff in the bowl began to look like whipped cream.

"Can I taste it?" Patsy asked, pointing her licked-clean finger at the white fluff.

"Me too," Anetha and I said in unison.

"Y'all need to wait a minute," Mama said, "it's not quite ready."

"Ple-e-e-ease," Patsy begged.

Mama did not like us to beg, so she surprised me when she stopped beating, leaned the eggbeater to one side, and let Patsy scoop up a dollop of fluff on her finger. Anetha and I were about to stick our fingers in too, when Patsy's "Mm-m-m" turned to "Agh-a-a-ack!"

"I told you to wait," Mama said as Patsy ran outside to spit. "I haven't yet added the sugar. Right now, it's just whipped egg whites."

Mama also loved baking cakes. Occasionally, she made a special kind—either sponge, angel-food, a jelly-roll, or fruitcake (at Christmas)—but mostly she stuck to making layer cakes. She'd bake the batter in three layers and let us eat one layer warm, fresh from the oven, without icing.

Daddy liked coconut cake—coconut sprinkled over seven-minute frosting (p. 437). My favorite was yellow cake with cream icing. Granny taught Mama how to make the cream icing (p. 431). Its main ingredients were fresh cow cream and granulated sugar. Mama cooked it until all the sugar crystals dissolved. After taking it off the heat, she added a teaspoon of vanilla and beat it vigorously by hand, the same way she whipped white divinity or chocolate fudge, until the creamy mixture began to lose its high gloss and look satiny as donut glaze. She poured and smeared that satiny warm icing between the cake layers, the sides, and the top. On every birthday, I asked for cream icing on my cake, and Mama usually obliged. After icing the cake, she decorated it with pink plastic birds that held the candles. Between birthdays, the pink birds slept in a covered tin on a kitchen shelf.

By midafternoon of my fifth birthday, my cake was ready. Mama had already let us lick the bowls and spoons. She'd also let us poke blue candles into the pink birds. I could hardly wait for Daddy to get home so we could eat supper. Then everybody could gather around and sing Happy Birthday to me, watch me blow out my candles, and help me eat cake.

That night, when the candles were finally lit, I closed my eyes tight and made my wish, the same one I made when I said my prayers at night and when I wished upon a star: If only I could stop having accidents in my sleep.

To feel better, I reminded myself that I wasn't the only person in the family with bad habits. Anetha sucked her thumb. Mama had been after her to stop it. Mama got her hopes up when Anetha's "sucking" thumb got smashed in Granddaddy's truck door. She bandaged Anetha's thumb with lots of gauze and rags and tape so it was too big to fit in Anetha's mouth. Mama assumed that would do the trick. But Anetha showed her adaptability by switching to her other thumb. Before that, Mama had tried dipping Anetha's thumbs in hot pepper sauce, thinking that would stop her. But that's when Anetha showed her toughness. She sucked a little at a time until she sucked the hot off.

As for Patsy's habit, she sleepwalked. I don't think Mama ever came up with a remedy for that. I don't know why she didn't tie her to the bed like she said she had to do back when Patsy bit Anetha due to jealousy. The sleepwalking seemed dangerous. Especially after Mama caught Patsy walking around in the middle of the night carrying sharp scissors. When Mama questioned her, she said she needed to cut chewing gum out of her hair, but Mama found no gum stuck in her hair. And the next morning, Patsy remembered nothing about walking in the night with scissors.

As for my nighttime accidents, I'd kept up my punishment in private. But that changed right after my fifth birthday. I was rubbing my nose lightly on the mattress and didn't hear Mama's steps in the hall. But I did hear the hinge of the door squeak. Fearing I'd been caught rubbing too lightly, I rubbed harder to make sure Mama saw I was doing it properly.

"Susanette," Mama said as she walked over to the bed and lifted my head. "Honey, you don't have to do that anymore."

"I don't?"

"You don't.

I felt as if half my birthday wish had come true. But the next time I had an accident and skipped the nose-rubbing ritual, I felt guiltier than ever.

37

Playing House on the Drew Estate
1950

My sisters and I padded around barefoot on the floor of our playhouse and giggled about the trick Patsy had played on Mama earlier that morning. She scared Mama with nothing more than a piece of jewelry. Granted, the brooch looked like a spider about three inches in diameter. The spider pin, with a purple stone for its belly, resembled a type of spider most people call a Granddaddy longlegs. Their spindly legs gave me the heebie-jeebies, but Patsy was never afraid of them. She would let a grandpa spider crawl up her arm, shoulder, neck, and into her hair.

Where Patsy got the spider pin, I don't know—probably from a friend at school or church. She left it on Mama and Daddy's unmade bed early that morning.

After we helped with the breakfast dishes, we followed Mama across the open hall to make beds and sweep up before going out to play. Mama, broom in hand, pushed the bedroom door open. Without the overhead light on, the room remained fairly dark, since the porch roof limited the amount of light coming through the front windows. But Mama's razor sharp eyes evidently spied the "spider" right away. She swept her hand across the rumpled sheet to knock the critter to the floor where she could step on it.

But when her hand hit the pin, which Patsy had left unclasped, Mama jerked back, raised the broom up high, then went Whop! Whop! Whop!

"Mama, it ain't real!" Patsy yelled as Mama beat the spider brooch with the broom.

"Honey, don't tell me it ain't real!" Mama shot back as she gave it another Whop. "It *stung* me!"

I think it was the legs that finally made Mama realize Patsy was right. They didn't curl up like the legs of a dead spider.

I half expected Mama to turn the broom on all three of her giggling daughters, but Mama laughed too as she shook her head.

"Y'all run on outdoors, now," Mama said after we finished making the bed. Outside, we headed for our playhouse, which sat in the edge of the woods—woods that still belonged to descendants of George Franklin Drew.

The Drew estate not only owned the land in front of our house that Daddy often burned off, but hundreds of acres along the banks of the Suwannee.

My sisters and I had no concern about land ownership, especially since Mama had helped us choose the site for our playhouse, under the shade of oaks, where the ground was soft from decayed leaves. Mama showed us how to pound stobs—broken tobacco sticks with sharp ends—into the soft ground with a brick until each stob stuck up about two feet. We spaced them about a yard apart. On the stobs, we laid narrow boards of various lengths that we found under Daddy's packhouse shelter. The boards, connecting one stob to another, served as boundaries, or walls, for the room.

Though Mama started us out, we soon got the hang of construction. Over time, we used more and more stobs and created additional rooms. To furnish our abode, we rolled in several small logs. And we made trip after trip to the family dump, scavenging for small rusty cans, brown vanilla flavoring bottles, and clear glass bottles to serve as vases. Then we'd go in search of flowers to put in our vases. Depending on the season, we might pick wood violets, black-eyed Susans, crotalaria blossoms or some other flower. The flower I thought most beautiful was the maypop. Mama said it was also called passion flower. She pointed out its "crown of thorns," saying it represented the Crucifixion of Christ.

If we found no flowers, we'd stuff wild fern fronds or other greenery into the vases.

Using the aluminum pots and pans brought to us by Santa, we also pretended to cook. For food, we picked whatever was in season: blackberries, grapes, persimmons. Sometimes we picked wild citron melons the size of grapefruits and pretended they were cannonball watermelons. They were always green inside, and we knew not to eat them. "Only pigs like the taste of citrons," Mama said. Daddy didn't even want the cows to eat citrons because he said the wild melons would make the cow's milk taste bitter.

Each time we exited our playhouse, we carefully moved a board aside and put it back to close "the door." Outside, we mounted our "horses"—small persimmon trees and oak saplings that bent and bounced under our weight.

When we saw Daddy coming in from the field at noon on his Farmall, a trail of dust following, we knew it was time to go to the house for dinner. Daddy didn't carry a timepiece, but he could tell time by the sun, almost to the minute. As we washed our hands in the pan of water on the shelf in the open hall, Mama called to us. "Don't forget to use soap—and then set the table."

Soon after all of us sat down to eat, Daddy said he was going to Luraville that afternoon to talk with Mr. Drew.

"What about?" Mama asked.

"About trading him our twenty acres near the river for his twenty out front."

"Good," Mama said as she dumped a spoonful of yucky squash on my plate.

I'd heard Mama say more than once that she wanted to own that land. "If somebody else was to buy that land out there," she said, "they might cut down all the trees and build another house under our noses—or even put in a smelly pigsty."

"Y'all want to ride with me to Luraville?" Daddy asked. I hoped Mama would say yes, and she did.

My sisters and I had been to Luraville, situated on Highway 51 between Live Oak and Mayo, with Granddaddy Rye a number of times. According to him, it was once a bustling town with several mercantile stores, lots of homes, a school, a post office, and several churches. But now, the town consisted of maybe a dozen homes, a church, a store that sold groceries, kerosene, and gasoline, and a gristmill. Granddaddy went to the mill regularly to have dry corn run though grinding wheels to produce coarse grits or fine corn meal. I don't remember so much the mechanics or size of the grinders as the white corn dust. It swirled in the air and the man working there was coated with it—his dark hair, eyebrows, eyelashes, and even the hairs on his arms were white with dust.

I could hardly wait to go to Luraville with Daddy that afternoon, but we still had hours to kill. So after helping Mama with the dishes, my sisters and I headed back outside and walked down the lane next to one of Daddy's fields, where he'd found an arrowhead the week before. All we found that afternoon, though, were rabbit and snake tracks and one shard of pottery we picked up, knowing it would make a good scoop for spooning up make-believe food in our playhouse.

Daddy borrowed Granddaddy Rye's truck for the trip to Luraville. We left home before sundown. I looked forward to seeing what the Drew home looked like. I anticipated a mansion, since Mr. Herbert Drew was a descendent of a governor. As it turned out, the Drew home, located a few blocks beyond the gristmill and general store, looked no fancier than my grandparents' white frame house.

Daddy parked the truck under a tree, a good distance from the house, and told us we could wait there, after which he got out and walked to the front door and knocked. The screen door opened, and Daddy went inside. Mama said the men would be talking business, and we didn't need to go with Daddy. But I kept thinking that surely Mrs. Drew would come out and invite us to go sit on the porch and offer us iced tea or something, since that's what Mama would have done if she had seen people sitting in a vehicle in front of our house.

Alas, nobody came out, and nobody invited us to go anywhere. So we sat and sat and waited and waited with nothing to do but squirm in the cab of that truck. Daddy could talk and talk and I hated sitting and waiting for him. I wished we had stayed home. No mansion. No tea. No nothing! I was wondering just how long it might take Daddy when Mama interrupted my thoughts.

"Look, girls, at the hummingbirds. The Drews have feeders for them." She pointed to several small contraptions hanging from low branches of the trees.

Hummingbirds? I'd never in my life seen one. They were greenish, but seemed to turn different colors as they flitted about, catching the last rays of light from the setting sun. They darted here and there and hovered near the feeders, their wings a blur.

"Can we get closer?" Anetha asked.

"No, we'd better watch from here," Mama said. "We might scare them away."

As we sat entranced, Daddy came out the door of the house with a man right behind him.

"Get out and come on over and take a look at our hummingbirds," the man yelled to us. "I didn't know that you ladies were out here in the truck."

It was Mr. Drew, a short man with graying hair, nothing like the fancy-dressed man I'd expected. He wore a white dress shirt, but its long sleeves had been rolled up to his elbows. He apologized that his wife wasn't there to greet us. "She's a schoolteacher in Live

Oak, and she often spends nights at our house in town."

Two homes. Yep. They're rich. Wonder what that town house looks like. But Mr. Drew acted like an ordinary person. He gave us a tour around the outside of the house, telling us how he mixed up sugar water for the hummingbird feeders, and which feeders and flowers the tiny birds liked best.

Now that we were out of the truck watching the hummingbirds, I was in no rush to go home—until I began to notice more mosquitoes than hummingbirds.

"What'd Drew say about swapping the two 20-acre plots?" Mama asked on the ride home.

"He'll think about it."

In the years to come, my sisters and I continued to play make believe in our house in the Drew woods, and Daddy kept pestering Mr. Drew about the trade. When we bumped into him on the sidewalk in Live Oak one day, Daddy asked, "Any decision yet on our trade?"

"Not yet," was Mr. Drew's reply.

But nobody ever built another house under our noses. No one ever erected a stinky pigsty. And best of all, nobody ever showed up at the front door of our playhouse to evict my sisters and me from the Drew estate, which, in my mind, was all that mattered.

38

Don't Go Plundering

"Don't go plundering," Mama said when my sisters and I headed out to Grandma's. She'd said that more times than I could count, but Grandma never told us we couldn't look around her house. So we often went room by room, amusing ourselves with discoveries or playing with something we'd already found. Window shades, for example. Grandma's living room had scalloped ones with fancy satin fringe. We'd pull them down, let them up, pull them down, let them up—until they accidentally zoomed to the top with a Blap! Blap! Blap! Unable to reach them, we moved on.

The dining room had no shades, but I adored the ruffled swag curtains trimmed with pea-green ball fringe, which perfectly matched the hand-painted cookie jar behind the glass door of the china cabinet, a cookie jar that held chewing gum.

That day, when we arrived, we headed straight to the dining room. "Grandma, can we have a stick of chewing gum?" Patsy asked.

"Sure," Grandma said from the kitchen. "Can you reach it? Get a half-stick for me too, and chew it for me." Grandma thought chewing gum, straight from the wrapper, tasted too sweet, so she let one of us chew it for a while to get the sweet out.

One day when I told a friend we chewed Grandma's gum, she said, "Eeewww, that's gross" and made an awful face. So I grossed her out even more by telling her what Mama had told us—that when we were babies with no teeth, she used to chew tough food— things like fried steak—before transferring it to our mouths.

Grandma's cookie jar usually held more than one flavor of gum, and we all wanted a different kind. Grandma liked Beechnut or Doublemint; Patsy liked Dentyne, but I didn't because it burned my mouth; and Anetha liked Juicy Fruit. I liked Juicy Fruit too, until I tasted Spearmint and that became my favorite. I also liked Chicklets, with the thin candy coating.

Gum in mouths, we asked to look through Grandma's collection of flour sacks stored behind a buffet door.

Grandma and Mama both bought flour by the ten-pound sack. At home, Mama emptied the flour into a large tin can, one with a tight-fitting lid to keep bugs out. Then she ripped out the sack's seam by pulling threads that unzipped it. (Every time I tried to do that, I caused the seam to pucker up instead of unzip.) After opening the sack, Mama soaked off the paper label and washed it. Then she had a half-yard of cloth to make herself an apron or to make us a sundress.

Grandma didn't do much sewing, so she saved her sacks for us. If we wanted a dress with a full skirt and puffy sleeves, we needed two sacks. So that day, we spread Grandma's sacks on the dining table and rummaged through them, looking for two alike. I passed over the dull browns and grayish greens, preferring pinks, pale blues, and bright yellows. Often, the colors

> **Sacks Used for Fabric**
> Women picked out flour, sugar, beans, rice, cornmeal and even the feed and fertilizer for the family farm based on which fabrics they desired. So there was heated competition among manufacturers of flour, sugar, feed, etc., to produce the most attractive and desirable prints. Artists were hired to design these prints.
> *http://www.buchanancountyhistory.com/feedsack.php.*

were nearly identical on two fabrics, but the prints would be different. Other times, it was just the opposite.

While Patsy and Anetha sorted and switched, tossed and traded, I unfolded the fabrics I liked best, put them up against my chest, and stared in the mirror above the buffet. The foot tall mirror, which stretched from one side of the buffet to another, hung by a cord so it tilted out at the top, giving me a good view of myself. I ended up with two pink-flowered sacks.

After making our selections, we crammed the leftovers back where we'd found them, and laid our choices on the buffet amongst the clutter. Grandma was a good housekeeper, but everybody who came by the buffet dropped something on it—mail, papers, tacks, so she kept the surface of the buffet covered with a linen scarf that had embroidered flowers on each end.

Grandma and Mama were always embroidering scarves or pillowcases, adding flowers, butterflies, birds—or words. Mama had recently embroidered *His* and *Hers* on a set of pillowcases, and Grandma had pillowcases with blue satin embroidery that said

Sweet Dreams.

"Will you teach us to crochet?" Patsy asked Grandma as she fingered a crocheted doily on the ornate table next to the buffet.

"We can try that later," Grandma said. "I need to cook dinner now."

Mama didn't crochet, so her favorite type of needlework besides embroidery was hemstitching. She'd pull out several threads from a piece of linen, about two inches from the edges, after which she used a needle and thread to tie up a few threads at a time, creating a pattern.

While Grandma cooked dinner, we continued looking around. We skipped over the top drawer of the buffet, though, because we already knew it contained Grandma's silverware. It was evidently very old for the silver on the tips of the forks and spoons had worn off. Grandma said it was silver plated. Mama disliked

One of Grandma's crocheted doilies. This one reminded me of dancing ladies wearing floor-length dresses, which Grandma said girls and ladies wore when she was growing up, even in the daytime.

silver-plate for that reason and the fact that it needed to be polished. At home, we ate with stainless steel.

Anetha whispered that she once saw a pistol in Grandma's silverware drawer. I didn't know whether to believe her or not. She said she asked Grandma about it, and Grandma fussed at Granddaddy—told him, "Find a better place to store that thing." Anetha said Granddaddy later told her it was a Luger, a pistol that Uncle Harold brought back from South America. But Anetha didn't have a clue where Granddaddy put the gun after it disappeared from the buffet drawer.

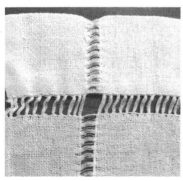

Mama's hemstitching on a dresser scarf

We opened the bottom drawer. Nothing there but yellowed papers and letters, stuff Mama would toss in the trash at home. Why was Grandma keeping all those old papers and letters? I didn't know, or care that one of the documents was a homestead deed, signed by President William McKinley in 1899, granting a hundred and sixty acres to Asbery Lanier (Granddaddy Tip). Nor did I know that the saved letters in the drawer were the ones Uncle Harold had sent home from faraway places—with money inside—for them to build the new house.

Our next stop was the front bedroom, but we stopped at a big picture on the living room wall, a picture of a setter dog and her puppies with floppy ears. Patsy put her finger on the glass, counting the puppies for the umpteenth time, as if we didn't already know the number.

"Fifteen!" she announced.

In the front bedroom, we lifted the lid off a box of Cody powder and smelled it, then opened the bureau's top drawer to find an assortment of jewelry. We opened Grandma's gold locket, which had a diamond chip in the center, and looked at the photos of her and Granddaddy, taken before they married. We tried on her shell necklace that had a tiny gold ball between each pink-tinged sea-shell. We fingered a delicate gold lavaliere that held a blue sap-phire, and I held up Grandma's rose gold, fleur-de-lis pin, that had a hook on the back for securing a lady's breast watch.

In the same drawer, we took out the teeny ivory-colored spyglass we'd looked through many times before. It was only as long as a paper match (from a match book), and not as big around as a pen-cil. Yet when held to the light, the entire Lord's Prayer could be read. Granddaddy Rye had told us the prayer was written on a grain of rice. Patsy read, "Our Father, who art in Heaven, hallowed be . . ." as Anetha and I picked up other objects in the drawer. One was a brooch with a woman's face carved in it. Grandma called it a cameo. She said her brother Alonzo gave it to his mother. But now that Granny was gone, Grandma Rye wore it.

Patsy found the item Granddaddy Rye called a "watch fob," an alligator carved into a slice of deer horn. "A convict carved that for me," Granddaddy had told us when he wore it, hanging from his pocket-watch chain.

The piece of Grandma's jewelry that I liked best was never in the bureau drawer. It was on her finger. "Your granddaddy gave this ring to me after we married," she said one day as I put my eyes close to the diamond in its six-prong setting and twisted the ring back and forth on her finger so I could see the colors of the rainbow. "Can I wear it?" I asked.

"I'm sorry, honey, I can't get it off my finger," Grandma said, pulling and twisting it, as if she were trying hard to take it off. That ring was as much a part of Grandma's hand as her fingernails, which she kept trimmed short.

As Patsy, Anetha, and I continued "looking around" our grandparents' bedroom, Anetha spotted Grandma's animal-hide purse on the shelf at the top of their wardrobe, a freestanding closet Granddaddy had built. Standing on Grandma's well-made bed that she kept covered with a pale green spread, we managed to pull the purse down off that high shelf—a shelf where we also spotted shotgun shells and a box of bullets, but no gun.

Anetha was the one who had her hands on the purse first and tried to open it. *Was it locked? What might be inside if it was locked? Lots of money? The Luger?* As Anetha kept trying to open it, Patsy kept trying to snatch it away from her, so she could try.

"Turn that thing thataway," Patsy said, pointing to a little dangly piece of metal.

Patsy was so smart. Anetha turned that thing and it opened right up. But to our disappointment, there wasn't a thing inside except a tiny rectangular tortoiseshell mirror.

"Gen-you-wine leather," Patsy said emphatically, pointing to writing on the pocket that held the mirror. But as far as I was concerned, my sisters could have that old empty purse. I wanted to locate Grandma's red silky robe. I felt around in the dark wardrobe and found it. I rubbed the soft fabric against my face. The robe—floor-length, berry-colored, and trimmed with white piping—was a Christmas gift from Uncle Harold and Aunt Louise. I thought it was the prettiest thing ever. But Grandma never wore it.

"It's too pretty to wear for every day," Grandma said when I'd asked her why. "I'm saving it in case I ever have to go to the hospital." I guess Grandma knew what she was doing, because, sometime later, Dr. Black, her doctor in Live Oak, sent her to a specialist in Jacksonville, who put her in the hospital. When we kids asked what was wrong, the adults said, "female trouble." I never got to see Grandma wear the robe since Jacksonville was too far away for us to go for a visit. Besides, if the Jacksonville Hospital was like the one in Live Oak, visitors under twelve years of age were not allowed past the waiting room doors. Anyway, Grandma was now back at home.

Our next stop: the bathroom. After closing the door, we slid open the drawer of the green cabinet, a cabinet that Mama said had been a "secretary," before she sawed off the top of it as a 4-H Club project when she was a teenager. Now it had just a cubbyhole and two drawers. Inside one drawer we investigated items that interested us. One was a small glass jar filled with clear liquid and something I thought was a tapeworm, but Patsy said it was pork rind that Granddaddy Rye planned to use for fish bait. We tried to open it, but the top was screwed on too tight. Why did adults do that? Anetha took a brown speckled sea shell (a cowry) from the drawer and put it to her ear, saying she could hear the sea, while I picked up the case that held the "shot needle," a glass hypodermic syringe that Grandma had probably used to give Granny shots. I pulled out the plunger, filled it with water, and we took turns squirting water into the bathtub, a bathtub that was now connected to the drain. For quite a while, Granddaddy didn't have the money to connect it, so the tub sat with labels still glued to it, serving as a dirty-clothes container. Granddaddy didn't borrow money if he could help it since he didn't like owing people.

In the other drawer of the green cabinet, we found a bulbous rubber object as big as a man's fist. One part, which stuck straight out, was the size of a cigar and had tiny holes in it. We had no clue what it was or what it was used for, but we filled it with water, and squeezed the bulb part with both hands. Water shot out in all directions from that cigar-like tube.

Somehow, our dresses got wet, so we headed to the front porch to dry off. As usual, Granddaddy Tip sat glued to his rocker. I knew I was still his favorite—could do no wrong in his eyes—but I was beginning to think I was too grown up to sit in his lap. So instead of climbing up on his knees, I followed my sisters' lead and each of us stepped up onto one of the ledges that supported the porch columns. To keep from falling off my narrow ledge, I held on to the column with both hands.

We began to march 'round and 'round.

"Girls, you better get down from there before you fall," Granddaddy Tip said as we made our way around one column and then another.

"Girls, I said get down before you get hurt—you're gonna break a leg!"

I don't know how many times he cautioned before he said under his breath, "Hard-headed young'uns. Cain't tell 'em a thing." With that, I almost fell from the ledge. My great-granddaddy—the one who loved me unconditionally, the one in whose eyes I could do no wrong, the one who called me his "prettiest little girl in the county o" had just called me a "hard-headed young'un!" Though I didn't fall from the ledge, I knew I'd fallen from his grace.

Part IV
Special Days

39

My First Day at Ladyland

If Mama made me a new dress before I started school, I don't re-member it. What I remember is her spending half a day giving my sisters Toni permanents.

"This will make your hair pretty and curly like Susanette's," Mama said as she took supplies out of a small box. Mama's compli-ment made me stand tall, but I soon slumped when all her atten-tion turned to my sisters and all I could do was sit and watch.

After cutting their hair—long, straight hair I'd always envied—and having them shampoo it, she started the process. She parted their wet hair into square sections and clamped each section in place with a wide aluminum clip—the same kind of clip she used in her own hair after a shampoo, to make a crisp wave that would last a day or two. As Mama worked her way across and around Pat-sy's head, and then Anetha's, she divided the sections into rows. With a comb, she would pull a strip of hair straight out, wrap it with a small square of tissue paper—similar to the papers Grand-daddy used to roll cigarettes—and roll the hair up onto a tiny plas-tic rod and lower a clamp that fastened it into place, tight against the scalp.

"Ouch! That pulls," Patsy and Anetha kept saying when Mama

twisted the rollers too tight. Yet, I still felt envious that they were getting attention I was not.

When their heads were covered with rollers, Mama tucked cotton batting around their faces. She then placed a towel around each of their necks, unscrewed the cap from a bottle of permanent-wave solution, and began dripping the white liquid over the rollers. The solution stunk to high heaven, and they complained, saying it was stinging their noses and eyes, even though their eyes were shut tight. Only after I saw how long they had to sit with that stinking stuff on their heads did I let go of my envy. Finally, Mama had them bend their heads over the kitchen sink Daddy had recently installed, and she poured pitchers full of water over their heads to wash the permanent-wave solution out. (The sink had no faucets, but it had a drain hole to let the water drain out under the house.)

After their permanents, my sisters ended up with frizzy mops of hair that stuck straight out. Mama said she must have left the solution on too long. (See Anetha's hair in our class photo, p. 290).

On the first day of school, the three of us set out swinging our lunch boxes, with our dog Tommy following. We stopped at our grandparents' house to say hello and continued to school, walking the road alongside Granddaddy's fence. Once we got to school, Tommy turned and headed back home.

Having been inside the school for Halloween parties, Patsy's school play, and many potluck suppers sponsored by Mama's Home Demonstration Club, I knew the layout of the building. Third, fourth and fifth grades met in the first classroom on the left. Patsy went in that door where her teacher, Mrs. Hunter, Mama's close friend, greeted her. (They had been friends since the two of them entered first grade at Ladyland.)

Anetha and I walked on down the hall, past the classroom for sixth, seventh, and eighth graders, and at the last door on the right,

Mrs. Johnson said, "Good morning, girls. Come on in and find a seat." The doors and windows in all the rooms stood wide open. The dog days of summer were past, but cool weather wouldn't arrive for another two months.

Patsy and Anetha really liked Mrs. Johnson, so I knew I would too. She reminded me of Mama, except she wore bright red lipstick and heels higher than Mama wore.

"First graders sit here," Anetha told me, pointing to the side of the room next to the hall and blackboard. "You can pick a seat, but if you talk too much, Mrs. Johnson will move you." After we stowed our lunch boxes in the cloakroom, I sat in the first seat I came to, at the back of the room, and Anetha took a seat near the open windows.

After the school bus arrived, the room filled up. As it turned out, I already knew all of the kids in my class: Billy George, Drew Allen, Jean Evans, Jerry O'Neal, Lynn Herring, Annie Lou Hingson, and my cousin, Myra Boatright. After everyone took seats, Mrs. Johnson told us the rules: no gum chewing in class and no talking unless you raised your hand first.

Mama had also laid down a rule.

"I don't ever want to hear about y'all getting into a fight at school," she'd said, and then added, "unless somebody spits on you. That's grounds for a fight. In fact, I'd *expect* you to hit anybody who spit on you."

I didn't know why Mama thought somebody might spit on us. Nobody had ever spit on me before, but I would definitely hit them if they did.

Mrs. Johnson also told us we should follow the golden rule: "Do unto others as you would have them do unto you." She held up a twelve-inch ruler and showed us that those words were printed across the ruler. As she talked on, my mind wandered. I rubbed my palms over the flat writing surface of my desk—my very own desk. Other than a few initials carved into its surface, the varnished desktop felt smooth as glass. That wasn't the case, though, for its underside. *What is that?* I wondered as I fingered stuff underneath. When Mrs. Johnson looked out the window, I bent over and looked under the desk. *Yuck! Someone had stuck wads of spitty chewing gum under my desk.*

I thought of what Mama had said about somebody spitting on us and I felt as if my fingers had been spit upon, but who should I hit? I rubbed my hands on the skirt of my dress and twisted the fabric around each of my fingers to wipe away nasty germs. At home, we knew better than to stick gum under a tabletop. But Mama let us lay the gum on the sides of our plates to save it for later. After all, a five-stick pack of gum cost a nickel.

I continued wiping my fingers on my skirt while Mrs. Johnson passed out sheets of ruled paper on which she had printed our names. *Susanette* extended all the way across the top of mine. "Copy your name on each of the solid lines below," she said. Meanwhile, she had the second graders write their names in beautiful script. I loved the look of the *S* on the alphabet border over the blackboard. I could hardly wait to learn script.

But in order to be promoted to second grade, I knew I must learn how to print all my ABCs and learn the numbers to a hundred. With chalk, Mrs. Johnson had written a chart on the blackboard:

1	2	3	4	5	6	7	8	9	10
11	12	13	14	15	16	17	18	19	20
21	22	23	24	25	26	27	28	29	30
31	32	33	34	35	36	37	38	39	40
41	42	43	44	45	46	47	48	49	50
51	52	53	54	55	56	57	58	59	60
61	62	63	64	65	66	67	68	69	70
71	72	73	74	75	76	77	78	79	80
81	82	83	84	85	86	87	88	89	90
91	92	93	94	95	96	97	98	99	100

I'd never seen anything as scary as this chart. How in the world would I ever learn all that?

Around midmorning, the school bell pierced the silence with a "B-r-r-i-n-g" and the second graders jumped up from their desks.

"Wait a minute," Mrs. Johnson said. "I need to tell the first graders about the bell. One long ring is for dismissal for morning and afternoon recess, for the lunch break, and for dismissal at 3:15. But if you hear three short rings, it's a fire drill. You are to rise from your seat, leave all belongings behind, and march single file in an orderly fashion out of the room, down the hall and through the back door. Okay, now it's recess. You can go outside."

Mrs. Johnson didn't say how many rings we'd hear if the school actually caught on fire, and I never did find out in all my years at Ladyland School.

Under the shade of big oaks in the front schoolyard, we girls joined hands to form a circle and danced 'round and 'round, over and over, singing, "Ring around the rosy, pocket full of posy. Up the ladder! Down the ladder! Ginny-Ginny-squat!" The last girl to squat was out.

We also played "London Bridge," making the motions as we sang:

London Bridge is falling down, falling down, falling down,
London Bridge is falling down, my fair lady.
Take a key and lock her up, lock her up, lock her up.
Take a key and lock her up, my fair lady.
How'll we build it up, build it up, build it up?
How'll we build it up, my fair lady?
Build it up with silver and gold, silver and gold, silver and gold.
Build it up with silver and gold, my fair lady.

After several rounds of "London Bridge," we were hot and sweaty, so we climbed up on the shaded stile to cool off. Made of granite, the stile was sturdy enough to support a dozen or more kids, and it had been there forever, so Grandma and Mama said. "Back when your grandma and I went to Ladyland," Mama said, "the stile served as steps over the schoolyard's rail fence. The fence kept the hogs out. The stile took the place of a gate."

By the time my sisters and I went to Ladyland, no fence surrounded the school, thanks to a law requiring farmers to keep their animals corralled, but the stile remained. Now, instead of a walkway to cross the fence, the stile served as our resting area. The stone steps, about five inches thick, two feet wide and about five feet long, quickly cooled sweaty skin.

"Let's play drop the handkerchief," Ceil Carver said after a few minutes of stile sitting. She and Anetha were best friends. The school year before, Anetha had spent a night at Ceil's house and told me that Ceil slept on a feather mattress. *A feather mattress?* I now looked upon Ceil as a princess. Her real name was Celia, and I thought everybody should call her that because it sounded more princess-like.

To play drop the handkerchief, we formed a circle and joined hands, everybody except Ceil who held the hankie. Walking and skipping around the circle, she dropped it behind me. I whirled around and picked it up and ran after her. If I could tag her before she got back to my spot, she'd have to go stand inside the circle—in jail. But before I could tag her, she jumped into my vacant spot. Now it was my turn to skip around the circle. I dropped the handkerchief behind Nettie Crews. Big mistake. She was quick and caught me before I got halfway around. I ended up in jail. The game continued as others joined me in jail and the circle got smaller and smaller. By the time the bell rang, to end recess, those of us in jail were packed together like pickled pigs' feet in a jar.

We ran to the pump and drank handfuls of water before going inside. While one person worked the handle of the iron pump, others could cup their hands under the cool water and drink from their hands.

That afternoon, I learned another unwritten rule: if a fellow classmate misbehaves while the teacher is out of the room, all pupils (that's what the teacher called us kids) must join together in a hum, "U-m-m-m-m," and point fingers at the culprit.

That's exactly what we did when Mrs. Johnson stepped out of the room and we spotted Drew Allen chewing gum.

"U-m-m-m-m," we repeated over and over. Drew stuck his gum under his desk before Mrs. Johnson returned, but we continued with "U-m-m-m-m."

"What's going on," she asked Drew since all fingers pointed straight at him.

"I was chewing gum."

"Go stand in the corner."

The unwritten rules were sometimes confusing, though. You pointed fingers and made the accusatory *U-m-m-m-m* sound with the rest of the class, but if you quietly and discreetly went to the teacher on your own to report someone's misbehavior, you were called a *tattletale*. Sometimes I didn't learn an unwritten rule like that until I'd already broken it.

On occasion, when kids did something worse than talk out of turn or chew gum, the teacher punished them by striking their palms with the flat side of her ruler, the ruler that said, "Do unto others as you would have them do unto you."

40

The Suwannee County Fair

Yippee! One Tuesday in late October, we got out of school to go to the Suwannee County Fair, where there were carnival rides. We could have ridden the school bus, but Mama and Daddy wanted to go too, so Daddy drove us in Granddaddy's truck. As soon as he parked and we got inside the gate, Daddy went one way and Mama went another. We followed her.

Big mistake. Mama gawked at canned goods in booth after booth as we meandered through the exhibition area. While Mama lollygagged, looking at boring exhibits, I was busting to get to the carnival rides. To the merry-go-round, to be exact.

Mama looked at Mason jars filled with blackberry, grape, and mayhaw jelly . . . at fig and watermelon preserves . . . at quart after quart of white pears, yellow peaches, green beans, red tomatoes, and purple beets . . . and at pickled cucumbers and pickled pigs' feet. She also had to stop and look at the handmade items—crocheted doilies, embroidered scarves and pillowcases, ruffled aprons, and patchwork quilts.

I tugged on her arm each time she stopped dead still, but it did little good.

When we got to the booth marked LADYLAND, a blue ribbon

was attached to a jar of sweet pickles—hers. This was not really all that surprising to me. Mama was known for her fourteen-day pickles (recipe p. 435). She didn't consider her table set properly without them. But I wasn't interested in pickles or ribbons. I wanted to ride the merry-go-round. I kicked at the floor with my Mary Janes while Mama kept looking. I think she read every single label on every item in that Ladyland exhibit.

After what seemed like forever and a day, Mama finally said, "Okay, we can go look for your daddy now. He's got the money for the rides."

We found him checking out the fattened-up livestock in hay-strewn pens. Together, all five of us walked past cages of chickens and rabbits as we made our way to the carnival grounds, abuzz with throngs of people, scurrying this way and that, the smell of roasted peanuts and cotton candy in the air. Kids nibbled at their pink cotton candy and sucked straws sticking out of grape and cherry snow cones. Here and there, people munched on roasted peanuts, tossing the hulls on the ground. Others lined up at booths that served mustardy hot dogs and oniony hamburgers.

At a ticket booth, Daddy handed over a dollar bill for three strips of tickets. I think he got twelve for a dollar. Entry to the fair was waived on Tuesday for us school kids, but you had to pay for tickets if you wanted to ride or eat.

"Can we ride the merry-go-round first?" I asked.

"We'll see," Mama said, "Hold my hand."

"*Mama*, I'm in *first* grade!"

"Okay, then. But stay right beside me," she said.

Where is the merry-go-round? I asked a few seconds later.

Mama didn't answer. I looked up, but it wasn't Mama's face I saw. Where was Mama? A lady with the strange face hurried past me. I looked up again. It wasn't Mama. Everybody was taller than I was. Where'd Mama go? Where was Daddy? Patsy? Anetha? I stopped and turned all the way around looking for any face I would recognize, but I couldn't see through all the people. I jumped up high to see over some kids but got bumped to the ground. I tried to get up, but more and more people kept bumping into me. I finally got to my feet and turned around and around searching for familiar faces, for anybody I recognized. Nobody.

"Ma-m-a-a!" I cried out, but I could hardly hear myself above the din of voices and whirring motors. "Ma-m-a-a!" I screamed again. Scared, I began to cry.

"Honey, are you lost?" a lady said as she put her hand on my shoulder and then under my chin.

"I, I, I can't, can't find my maaa-ma!"

"Come with me," she said. "We'll find her." Taking my hand, she led me to the edge of the crowd and said we should look from there. Through tears, I searched faces but no Mama, no Daddy, no Patsy, no Anetha.

"What's your favorite ride at the fair," she asked.

"The, the, the merry-go-round," I said, still sobbing. "We, we wuz gonna . . . "

"You were about to ride the merry-go-round?" she asked.

"Yes, yes, ma'am."

"It's this way," she said, pointing. She took my hand and began leading me through throngs of people. We came to an opening and I saw the merry-go-round. Then I spotted Mama. She saw me at the same time. I ran toward her open arms, even though I knew she would scold me for not holding her hand. She bent over and hugged me like she never had before, then stood and, over and over, thanked the lady who'd led me there. Daddy joined the conversation and they talked on and on.

Meanwhile, the calliope music was blasting, so I tugged Mama's hand. Finally, she and Daddy said a final "thank you" to the lady, whose kind face I would never forget, but whose name I never learned. The carousel came to a stop as we stood in line. Kids got off the ride and ran through the exit gate, and a man motioned us forward. Mama handed our tickets to him, and I scrambled onto the round platform. Mama stepped on too, helped me climb onto a frosty gray horse, and stood next to me as the music started. I clutched the brass pole as my horse moved up and down and seemed to gallop faster and faster. Patsy and Anetha, in front of me, turned and waved, as the breeze dried the tears on my cheeks.

Next, we rode the boats, and then a choo-choo train. I thought both were fun, but Patsy complained, saying she was tired of "baby rides" and wanted to ride the Ferris wheel.

Mama said she had ridden it once and didn't like the queasy feeling it gave her, but persistent Patsy persuaded Anetha to ride it too. Mama didn't want them to go on the ride by themselves, so she said she'd get on with them and I could stay with Daddy.

The operator grabbed hold of a bench-like chair as it came down, swung a bar back to let three people off, then motioned for Mama and my sisters to take the empty seat. He locked them in, and off they went, waving as they moved backwards. I waved back as they went up, up, up into the blue sky. When they got to the top, I could see only the bottom of their seat, but I recognized Anetha's scream as they came down. Her face looked white as a sheet as their seat whirred past the operator, Mama called to him to please, please stop the ride, that her daughter was getting sick, but he didn't seem to hear. Each time they swooped passed, Mama pleaded, but the Ferris wheel kept going 'round and 'round.

"Anetha was sucking air going up and screaming bloody murder coming down," Patsy said after they got off, a grin on her face.

"I think that operator gave us a longer ride than usual," Mama said to Daddy.

Anetha staggered around but recovered quickly, and we headed off to check out the arcade. At one booth, teenagers threw darts at balloons. Mama said the darts were too dangerous for us, so we moved on. At another, teens tossed balls at holes in a fence. Patsy tried but missed one hole, so she won nothing.

The high shelves above the games held glitzy prizes and rows of giant Teddy bears. We asked Daddy if he would try to win a Teddy bear for us. He said the games were "rigged" and were a waste of hard-earned money. Yet I kept seeing kids walking around carrying Teddy bears bigger than life.

We came to a booth where children were picking up yellow plastic ducks, about the size of my fist, that floated along a water-filled trough. I wanted to pick up a duck, for it looked as if every kid was winning a prize, but Patsy said, "I ain't gone pick up no baby duck."

When I handed my duck to the man behind the water trough, like other kids were doing, he looked at its bottom and said, "Six."

"Mama, the duck is six like me," I said, for I had just celebrated my sixth birthday.

"That ain't the duck's age." Patsy said, like I was stupid. "That's the number for your prize."

I was sure Patsy was wrong until the man pulled my prize from a can labeled "6" and handed me a plastic whistle. It hurt my ears when I blew it.

"I wish I'd had this whistle when *you* got lost," I told Mama.

When we came to the House of Mirrors, our whole family went inside. Some mirrors made us appear fat and squatty, some skinny as toothpicks, and in others, we looked crooked as snakes.

A sign along the last part of the arcade advertised a "half-man/half-animal." Patsy wanted to see the creature, but Daddy mumbled something about it being a "hoax"—whatever that meant, and that it was time to go home anyway.

It was getting dark as we headed toward the exit. We passed a tent where a barker was yelling out, "Come one! Come all! See the fattest lady in the world!" A drawing on the sign above the entrance showed a fat lady with short blond curls and rosy cheeks, dressed in a short, ruffled, pink polka-dot dress. She was half lying, half sitting, propped on a big fluffy pillow, with one leg kicked over her head. Even her panties were ruffled, and her bosom looked as big as two cannonball watermelons.

"Can we go see the fat lady?" I asked.

"Whatcha think, Ethel?" Daddy said as he looked at Mama, lifting his eyebrows.

"We need to go home," Mama reminded him. "The girls have school tomorrow."

Daddy looked more disappointed than I felt as we left the Suwannee County Fair.

41

Not What It Seems

If I had to choose my least favorite holiday, I'd pick Halloween. There wasn't much to like about it. We didn't go trick-or-treating; I'd never even heard of such a thing. And if I had, who in their right mind would want to go trick-or-treating in our neck of the woods, where panthers and wildcats were said to roam at night. I certainly didn't. I had always been afraid of the dark. On nights when Mama handed me the bowl of leftover grits from supper and told me to "go feed the grits to the chickens," I'd go out but stand right behind the house near the steps, eat the grits myself, and run back up the steps to safety. Of course to be honest, I loved grits, hot or cold.

We celebrated Halloween, but we never decorated our house or carved a pumpkin into a jack-o'-lantern. Who would destroy a perfectly good pumpkin that could be used for making two pumpkin pies? All the jack-o'-lanterns I knew were made of orange construction paper. At school, Mrs. Johnson let us decorate our classroom with them, along with black cats and bats, in preparation for the school's Halloween party. It took place on Halloween night and included a bonfire and weenie roast, among other things.

For roasting the weenies, our family provided the skewers:

palmetto stalks we gathered in the woods. A few days before Halloween, Daddy drove his tractor to the swamp near the river, pulling the trailer with all of us in it. There, with a sharp knife, he cut stalks off palmetto bushes and handed them to Mama. With an equally sharp knife, she cut off each frond, leaving a strong, sharp-pointed stick about three feet long. My sisters and I made a pile of skewers in the trailer.

Around the bonfire on Halloween night, everyone picked up a palmetto stick and skewered a weenie. You were supposed to stick the point into the end of the weenie until about half the meat was secured on the saw-tooth stalk. But at least one kid would always stick the point through the middle of his weenie, leaving its ends flopping. About the time the weenie reached the fire, it broke in half and fell into the coals, which wasted a perfectly good weenie and stunk up the night air as it sizzled and burned to a crisp in the coals.

When the red skin on my weenie started to blister, I took it out of the fire and put it on a hot-dog bun with catsup. Others, like Daddy, would leave the weenie in the fire until it turned black as smut and put it on a bun with coleslaw.

After everybody ate their hot dogs, the party moved inside where some of us kids tried to win prizes by picking up ducks—kind of like I'd done at the carnival booth, but from a washtub of water. We also fished from a make-believe stream, casting the line over a barrier, and when we pulled the line back, we'd caught a small prize on the hook. Meanwhile, the brave kids like Patsy bobbed for apples. I didn't because I didn't like putting my head underwater any better than I liked going outside by myself after dark.

The last activity of the night was the spook house, set up in a cloakroom. I didn't want to go in there, but everybody kept insisting. All the kids crowded around the entrance and an older girl grabbed my hand. "Come on. It'll be fun." She practically dragged me into the spook house.

Once inside, there was pushing, shoving, hollering, and screaming, and I couldn't see my own hand in front of my face. My heart raced as I tried to turn around and feel my way back, but I was pushed forward by the mob of kids in there. Something wet brushed my face as a strange "ooooOOOAAaa!" grew louder and louder—I was being pulled and pushed where I didn't want to go. Kids were bumping into me. I stumbled over something and my feet began to rock. I lost my balance and fell—on what, I didn't know. I crawled across a wobbly wire surface and finally found something solid to stand on. "OooOOOoooooo, feel the brains." My hand was shoved into a slimy mess. "Now—feeeeel the E-Y-E-b-a-l-l-s! Ha! Ha! Ha! Ha-a-a-a." I was on the verge of tears by the time I escaped from the spook house to the bright lights of the classroom, where kids giggled and yelled, "That was fun! Let's go in again!"

They're crazy. There was no way they'd get me back in there.

On the way home, I still felt scared. Anetha said she didn't like the spook house either. She said she had started to eat a piece of candy she'd caught fishing when she went into the spook house; and after she came out, she threw the candy in the schoolyard because her hands had touched brains and eyeballs. Mama, Daddy, and Patsy tried to explain that it was all fake, that it was just wet Spanish moss that had brushed our faces, that ordinary bed springs had made it hard to walk, that cooked spaghetti felt like brains, that peeled grapes stood in for human eyeballs. *Why didn't they tell us that BEFORE we went into the spook house?*

As if that experience wasn't bad enough, a boy came to school the next day saying he had a finger to show us. He took a small matchbox from his pocket. A bloody finger lay on cotton in the matchbox, as if it had been cut off a live person. We crowded around to get a better look, but just then, the bell rang for us to take our seats.

Whose finger could that be? Who chopped it off? Him? I could not concentrate on what Mrs. Johnson was saying for thinking about that bloody finger, who might be missing one, and who had chopped it off. At recess, all the boys gathered around the boy with the bloody finger, clamoring to see it again. I didn't want to look again, but couldn't help myself. Argghh.

Finally, at lunchtime, I learned the truth. The matchbox had been stuffed with cotton and stained with ketchup. The boy's own finger was sticking up through a hole in the bottom of the box. Like the scary spook house, it was all fake.

Another Halloween, we went to a costume Halloween party at the Curls's home. Mama had let my sisters and me each pick out a false face (rubber mask) at McCrory's dime store. Mine was the face of a grungy old man clenching a glowing, red-tipped cigar stub between stained teeth. I went to the party wearing that mask, along with some of Daddy's old clothes, with sleeves and legs rolled up. I also carried a knapsack on a stick, like a hobo. At the party, I became the center of attention as everybody kept trying to guess who the old hobo was. Behind my mask, I felt very smug, and I ended up winning the contest. But on the way home, Patsy said I'd won only for being ugly.

Like I said, Halloween was my least favorite holiday.

42

Waiting for Polecat

As warm days gave way to cool, stalks of purple-tinged sugar cane announced autumn and the biggest social event of the year: my grandparents' annual cane grinding.

On our walk home from school one early November day, my sisters and I were happy to see a half-dozen cane stalks leaning against an oak tree in our grandparents' side yard. Granddaddy Rye stood nearby, shelling corn for the chickens.

We ran through the swinging gate, up the front steps, and greeted Granddaddy Tip, rocking on the porch. Inside, we dropped our lunch boxes on the dining table, said *hey* to Grandma Rye, and flew out the back door. As we ran up to Granddaddy Rye, he stopped turning the handle of his corn sheller, a cast iron contraption mounted to the tobacco rack. (The wooden rack held sticks of tobacco on tobacco gathering day before they were transported into the barn for curing.)

"Can I finish shelling the corn so you can cut us some cane?" Anetha asked.

Granddaddy stepped aside to let her operate his sheller. Anetha stuck a shucked ear into the sheller's mouth and turned the handle. Yellow kernels zinged and pinged, hitting the metal bucket below. Teeth inside the sheller stripped the cob *nekkid*, shooting kernels out on all sides. How I wished Daddy had a sheller like that. At home, we had to rub ears of dry corn with our fingers to pry the kernels loose, which sometimes caused scratches and blisters on my fingers.

After Granddaddy tossed kernels from the bucket into the chicken yard, he opened up his bone-handled pocketknife and began to strip a cane stalk so he could cut the cane into chunks we could chew. *Mm-m-m.* After chewing and sucking the juice from each chunk, we spit the leftover pulp on the ground and held out our hands for more. We could finish off a six-foot stalk in no time.

"Will you do another one?" I asked. But Granddaddy wiped the blade of his knife on his khaki trousers, flipped it shut, and put it back in his pocket, saying, "That's enough for today." Later I learned that Granddaddy knew something I didn't: too much cane juice can affect you like eating too many prunes.

Every year, Granddaddy raised enough sugarcane for both our families—enough for chewing, enough to produce a year's supply of syrup for all of us, and enough, even, to give a bottle of syrup to every family who came to the cane grinding, a tradition Great-Granddaddy Tip started long ago.

"Granddaddy Tip had always held his cane grinding just *before* the first frost," Mama said. Now of course, Granddaddy Rye did all the farming and took care of the place—and he had his own ideas about the best time to harvest cane. He checked the *Farmer's Almanac* to see when the first frost was predicted and planned to harvest right *after* that. "A *little* frost is good," he said. "It makes the cane juice sweeter." A really hard freeze, though, could cause the stalks to burst open in the field. As it so happened, cane grinding usually took place the Saturday before Thanksgiving.

As the day approached, Daddy and Granddaddy Rye, wielding machetes, chopped off the cane stalks close to the ground. They left just enough stubble that the cane would sprout again the next year. They harvested trailer-loads and hauled it to the yard where they stacked it near the cane mill, a double-barreled cast iron grinder that sat atop a sturdy railroad-tie scaffold.

Each barrel of the grinder was as big around as two of me, and each had big teeth on the outside—Daddy called them gears—that locked together in such a way that when one barrel of the mill turned, the other turned too.

For the cane grinding, Daddy and Granddaddy hoisted a beam nearly as big as an electric light pole above the mill and let it rest on a T-bar. They positioned it slightly off-center so the shorter end of the beam stuck up high, and the longer, heavier end nearly touched the ground. Atop the mill, Granddaddy bolted the beam in place, while Daddy used a heavy chain to connect the long end of the beam to the drawbar of the tractor.

Perhaps they also wire-brushed and greased the rusty mill, I don't remember. Sitting idle except for one day of the year and exposed to the weather, it was covered with rust.

Every year, when Great-Granddaddy Tip saw the tractor being hooked up to power the mill, he grumbled. He'd done that every year, Mama said, since her daddy switched to using a tractor to power the mill instead of a mule.

"When I was growing up," Mama said, "we kids would walk with the feed bucket in front of Roadie, Granddaddy Tip's mule, to get Roadie going around. Later on, we'd reward Roadie with cane juice. Boy, did he love that stuff."

Mama said Granddaddy Tip thought her daddy was out of his mind when he bought a tractor for plowing. "Aye, God, Buddy, that piece of equipment won't never take the place of a good mule. You won't put no corn in ya crib with that thing."

But Granddaddy Rye had proven him wrong where corn and all other crops were concerned.

In further preparation for grinding cane, the men rolled a metal drum over to the mill and stood it up to hold the juice. They also

Granddaddy poses, as if feeding cane stalks into the mill. Daddy sits on Granddaddy's Ford-Ferguson tractor with Patsy on his lap. (They must have posed for this picture because the barrel is missing its burlap strainer, and I can't imagine Daddy maneuvering the tractor in a perfect circle around the mill with nine-month-old Patsy on his lap.

placed a croker sack over the top of the drum and wired it in place to create a strainer that would keep out small pieces of cane stalks, leaves from overhanging oaks, and insects. Finally, Granddaddy set a metal trough in place to carry juice from the grinder to the drum.

Daddy hopped up onto the seat of the tractor, put it in low gear and eased his foot off the clutch. The tractor inched forward and the mill let out a high-pitched screech as it began to turn. As Granddaddy Rye fed cane stalks through the mill's grinders, juice trickled down the trough into the barrel. It took about ten stalks to produce a gallon of juice. Stalks came out the other side of the grinder as flat and dry as cardboard.

Friends and neighbors began arriving right away, making me wonder if they heard the screech of the mill. Visitors knew they could drink all the cane juice they wanted, get a taste of polecat— the candy that formed on the rim of the sugar kettle as the cane juice turned to syrup—and go home at the end of the day with a complimentary bottle of syrup.

Unfortunately, the event drew unwanted guests too: honey bees and yellow jackets. "They won't sting if you pay them no mind and let them have the sweet they came for," Mama said. I was never too sure about that. I don't recall that anybody ever got stung at my grandparents' cane grinding, but Anetha once came home from the Carver's cane grinding with a welt from a hornet.

Visitors pitched in, occasionally relieving Granddaddy from his bending over to pick up stalks to feed the mill. Visitors also helped themselves to cane juice as it ran down the trough, catching it in a cup or dipper before it went into the drum. We kids could do the same if we wanted to, but I preferred to chew the cane to get the juice out. One of the men standing around was always happy to take out his pocketknife, peel the cane, and cut off chunks for us kids.

After the drum filled about halfway, several men took it over to the sugar kettle and dumped it into the shallow, bowl-shaped vat. Five feet or so across, the vat held about 60 gallons. (The same vat was used to boil corn for the pigs and to scald dead hogs on hog-killing day, but on cane-grinding day, it had been washed clean.)

The flange of the vat rested on the edge of the brick furnace, which had a door-like opening near the ground where we tossed in wood. As soon as the kettle was full of juice, Granddaddy started a fire in the furnace. Smoke billowed from the chimney like a train engine stack. Once the fire glowed red, Granddaddy also tossed in spent cane stalks, a few at a time, getting rid of the "pummy" pile, the flattened stalks—which were too tough for any of the farm animals to eat.

As the juice came to a rolling boil, Granddaddy Rye stood next to the kettle, stirring it constantly with a wooden boat paddle. Daddy and other men took turns with a long-handled dipper with holes in it, skimming off scummy foam that rose to the top. These skimmings were dumped into an empty drum so the gunk could be fed to the hogs. Mama said that was one of the biggest changes from earlier cane grinding days; Granddaddy Tip used to turn the cane skimmings into white lightning.

Almost as intoxicating as Granddaddy Tip's white lightning was the aroma coming from the steam off the sugar kettle. As the steam evaporated, it flavored the cool air. People drew closer and closer to the kettle as they waited for polecat.

The cooking time varied, depending on the amount of juice in the kettle. It could take three or four hours. Even one hour felt too long when you were waiting for polecat. The sun had already slid behind the trees by the time the juice began to thicken. Though Granddaddy stirred it constantly, now, the cauldron of foamy golden bubbles gradually rose higher and higher. It was time.

Some of the menfolk quickly fashioned sticks from unspent cane stalks, similar to Popsicle sticks, and handed them out. When Granddaddy gave the word, people took turns going up to the hot foamy kettle to help themselves to a scoop of polecat. When I started up to get mine, Granddaddy took the stick from my hand—not trusting me near that bubbling vat. He ran my stick around the rim, just above the foam. As he pulled it away, a thread of candy trailed like a spider web.

"Blow on it now," Granddaddy said as he handed the stick to me. "You don't want to burn your tongue."

I blew on the clear amber glob, thick and gooey. If not eaten while still warm, it would harden. But that was okay because then, it was like licking a Sugar Daddy. Warm and chewy or hard like a sucker, polecat was mouthwatering.

Everybody I knew loved it—maybe because we got a taste of it only once a year. Mama told us how much everybody clamored for it when she was a little girl. She also told me a story about how somebody once tricked Granddaddy Tip at a cane grinding:

"It was late in the day and getting real cool outside, so the women and kids had gone in the house. That day, Uncle Lee (Granddaddy Tip's brother who lived nearby) was the one doing the stirring and skimming as the other men looked on and milled about. As the polecat was beginning to form, Dave Tomlinson, a neighbor, walked up. He and Granddaddy Tip were about the same size, and Granddaddy looked him up and down, admiring what he was wearing. 'Aye, God, Buddy,' Granddaddy Tip said, 'I shore do like them britches you got on!' 'Shore 'nough, Uncle Tip? Want to swap?' Granddaddy Tip agreed that he did, so the two men proceeded to take off their britches—right there in the middle of the yard! That's when Uncle Lee—knowing the men had their britches off—hollered toward the house, 'Polecat, girls! Come get the polecat!' The women started pouring out of the doors and kids jumped out of open windows, anxious to get to the sweet candy. Mr. Tomlinson and Granddaddy Tip had to run for cover."[4]

I couldn't imagine my great-granddaddy taking off his britches out there in the yard, but Mama said it was the truth.

Granddaddy Rye continued to stir the syrup as it thickened and turned darker. Now and then, he lifted the paddle and watched drops of amber drizzle back into the bubbling cauldron. This was the critical time, he said. Overcooking could cause sugar crystals to form, and a good syrup maker didn't want that. He kept a close watch, and when the drops were reluctant to fall from the paddle, he knew he could douse the fire.

The syrup had to be bottled up quickly and done with care since the liquid was so hot it could scald a person. The adults used a pot

---

[4] From C.G. and Ethel: A Family History, 2008

with a long handle to scoop it up. They filtered it through a clean piece of linen or a square from an old bed sheet into containers of all kinds—jars, jugs, bottles, and cans. For every ten gallons of juice, we ended up with about a gallon of syrup.

By the end of cane-grinding day, it was night. As everybody departed, Granddaddy Rye gave each family a bottle of hot syrup to take home. The rest of the filled containers would be stored in a dark place, except for one that would sit next to the salt and pepper shakers and sugar dish in the middle of our dining table, handy for pouring over pancakes, hoecakes, and biscuits.

43

Thanksgiving Day Scene

Our family's Thanksgiving Day scene looked nothing like Norman Rockwell's "Freedom from Want," painted in 1942. Instead of sitting around a dining table to feast on turkey, we sat around a campfire in the piney woods of Taylor County and ate fried fish, hush puppies, grits, and swamp cabbage. That is, *some* people ate swamp cabbage.

> **Norman Rockwell**
> During World War II, Rockwell painted the Four Freedoms series, inspired by a speech by Franklin D. Roosevelt, in which he described four principles for universal rights: Freedom from Want, Freedom of Speech, Freedom to Worship, and Freedom from Fear. The paintings were published in 1943 by *The Saturday Evening Post*. The United States Department of the Treasury later promoted war bonds by exhibiting the originals in sixteen cities.

On most Thanksgiving mornings our family, along with our grandparents, headed toward the Gulf, but we always stopped short of the salt water. We set up camp in a clearing dotted with palmetto bushes, surrounded by cabbage palms and stunted pines. The adults said it was "too windy to cook on the beach."

The year I turned six, the Hunters (Patsy's teacher and her family), joined us on Thanksgiving Day, and they brought along their

Swamp Cabbage

The cabbage palm will grow to 80-90 ft., but the heart is taken from trees 8-10 ft. high, including fronds.

To remove the central core (heart), the outer leaf stems are cut away and the trunk is severed about 3 ft. below the bud. The untrimmed swamp cabbage weighs 10-15 lbs.

At preparation time, boots (frond remnants) are stripped from the 3-ft. long section until the tender, closely wrapped central core (swamp cabbage) is reached. This cylindrical core is

Swamp cabbage heart, fanned out
http://manuredepot.com/

creamy white in color, and composed of layers of undeveloped fronds with the consistency, tenderness, and texture of regular cabbage.

Swamp cabbage may be prepared in various ways. The most popular is to cut it into thin slices like cole slaw and cook with meat seasoning until done. Cooking causes it to turn a brownish gray.

The cabbage or sabal palmetto palm became Florida's state tree in 1953. Cutting the bud of the palm kills the tree. Harvesting swamp cabbage without authorization is now prohibited. *http://edis.ifas.ufl.edu/*

rich relatives, the Summeralls. I knew the Summeralls had money because of their house—brand new and very modern. Every time we went to Live Oak, we passed it, an *L*-shaped ranch home that looked like two houses pushed together, one built with red brick, the other painted white. The home sat off Highway 51 in the dappled shade of longleaf pines, beside a pond surrounded by cattails. Next to the pond stood a shiny, purple gazing ball that sparkled in the sunlight and reflected on the pond's glass-like surface. That sparkling ball—bigger than my head—was about the prettiest thing I'd ever laid eyes on. How I wished we had one in our yard. But Mama would never hear of owning something that cost money and occupied space if it served no purpose but pretty.

Another feature of the Summeralls' house set it apart from other homes in the area. Instead of a peaked roof, its roof slanted in only one direction. Because the outside looked so different, I was really curious about the inside, and my curiosity got satisfied one day when Daddy stopped there. Mrs. Summerall invited us in while Daddy stayed outside and talked with her husband.

I'd never seen anything like it. To step into the living room, you had to step down, and then the floor felt as if you were walking on a cloud. I loved the soft feel. I wanted this soft stuff in my house when I grew up. But Mama said later, as Daddy drove us home, "That wall-to-wall carpet is totally impractical. It'll just trap dust and dirt. I wouldn't want that in my house." Mama's remark made me question what I wanted when I grew up. I didn't want dirt in my house, but I sure liked the softness of that carpet.

I was happy the Hunters and Summeralls would join us on Thanksgiving since that would give us playmates. I liked the Hunters two boys and figured I'd like the Summeralls's son. The first thing the three boys wanted to do, though, was climb a palm tree. For once, I was glad Daddy put all of us kids to work. He told us to start gathering up wood for a campfire while the adults unloaded vehicles.

The women had taken along everything needed to prepare a meal over a campfire: big cook pots, long-handled utensils, and several spiders (three-legged iron skillets under which a fire could be built). They'd also packed grits and corn meal, but that was about all the food they took. The rest of our Thanksgiving Day feast would depend on what the men caught in the Gulf or brought back from in the woods.

The men consolidated their guns, axes, and fishing gear, which included Mr. Summerall's net for seining fish. They placed everything in one truck, while the women used the bed of another truck to get pots and pans organized and prepare to cook. After we kids gathered the wood, the women started the campfires.

An hour or two later, the men returned with buckets of fish and a croker sack of swamp cabbage. I didn't know at the time that harvesting swamp cabbage—cutting the bud out of a sabal palmetto palm to get to the palm heart—killed the tree. I wonder if the grown-ups did.

As a few of the men scaled and gutted the fish, others worked on the cabbage, hacking off the outer boots (husks). When they got down to the creamy-white cabbage, they gave it to the women to chop up. That's when we kids ran over to get big chunks to play with. Each of us carefully unfolded a palm heart, the way we'd seen ladies open up old-fashioned silk or paper fans, and pretended to play our accordions. Open . . . close . . . open . . . close. For a moment, I thought I heard music, but the sound came from the wind whistling through palmetto fronds.

When the swamp cabbage began to bubble in a big pot over the fire, it gave off an awful stench. Thank goodness, the aroma of frying fish and hush puppies soon overpowered the cabbage.

Around high noon, the women called everybody to the "table." Pots and platters of food covered Mama's red-and-white-checked tablecloth that dressed up the tailgate of Granddaddy's pickup. With mouths watering, one of the men gave thanks, and we lined up to help ourselves. When my turn came, I helped myself to grits, a big piece of fish with the tail fin intact—I loved its crunch—and reached for a handful of hush puppies. *Ouch!* They had just come from hot grease.

Mama thought it best to cook hush puppies last, saying the dough would absorb the fish flavor, making the hush puppies taste better. Plus, she said cooking them last removed the fishy taste from the grease, so it could be reused for frying chicken or something else.

With my fingers burning from the hot hush puppies, I hurried to pick up a waxed paper cup of iced tea.

After the big dinner, the adults relaxed around the campfire as we kids played games like hide-and-seek and follow-the-leader. Around midafternoon, the adults broke camp and packed up the vehicles so we could ride on over to the coast. Sometimes we went to Jug Island, other times we went to Dekle or Keaton Beach. That day, we ended up at Dekle Beach.

Like every Thanksgiving, it was too cold to swim. So, while the men searched for oysters, we kids hopped, skipped, and jumped to the end of the rickety dock. If you leaned over and looked underneath, you could see oysters attached to pilings that supported the dock, which stretched out for what seemed like a mile across marsh and into the Gulf. The women followed, reminding us a time or two to be careful skipping along the dock or we might pick up a splinter. Later, back on shore, the women settled down on patchwork quilts they'd spread on the dry sand, while we chased scurrying fiddler crabs that ran sideways into their hiding holes in the water-packed sand. When we tired of that, we searched for washed-up horseshoe crabs and seashells.

The sun was beginning to set over the Gulf by the time we loaded up to go home. Everybody said their goodbyes and we headed out just as the sun slipped into the water.

I wonder, if Norman Rockwell had seen our Thanksgiving Day scene, would he have thought it worthy of his brush?

44

Christmas

Preparations for Christmas got underway right after Thanksgiving. First came the baking of fruitcakes: one for our family, one for my grandparents, and a third for Grandma to ship to Uncle Harold and his family in Indiana.

The baking took place at Grandma's. We spent most of the morning chopping nuts and candied fruit. Over the years, Grandma and Mama tried several recipes. Some called for citron and orange peel and strange spices I didn't care for. They eventually settled on a light fruitcake recipe that included lots of pecans, golden raisins, candied cherries and pineapple, with just enough batter to hold everything together. But, at the time, the fruitcakes were very dark.

Next, the arrival of Christmas seals from Father Flanagan's Boys Town reminded Mama that it was time to send Christmas cards. After she wrote notes in the cards and addressed envelopes, she let my sisters and me stick postage stamps on the front of each envelope, tuck in its flap, and add a Christmas seal to the back. We didn't seal the envelopes. Mama said that would cause the post office to classify the cards as first class instead of third. First class was too expensive.

With all the Christmas cards in the mail and on their way to faraway relatives, Mama turned her attention to decorating the house for Christmas. First came the holly wreath.

A holly tree stood at the edge of the sinkhole in the middle of Granddaddy's field, so we always went there for holly. As Mama cut off branches, she handed a few to each of us girls to carry home. Unfortunately, the points on the scalloped leaves stuck like thorns, and sometimes I wished Mama would forget about making a wreath. But back at home, after she bent a wire coat hanger into a circle, added the green holly with its bright red berries, and hung it on the door, I felt proud.

Next came mistletoe, something I could have done without. Mama always got Granddaddy Rye to shoot down a clump of mistletoe from an oak tree near their washhouse. He was glad to do it since he said the mistletoe was a parasite that would eventually suck the life right out of the tree. Mama hung sprigs of the mistletoe over doorways. From then until she took it down after Christmas, I'd run through doorways to avoid kisses—especially if we had company. Despite my speed, Cousin Alfred Boatright once caught me and gave me a peck on the cheek. Yuck! I wiped the kiss off on the hem of my dress. Alfred was one of my favorite people, but I did not like being kissed by anybody. I didn't care much for hugs either. I wished Mama wouldn't put up mistletoe.

About a week before Christmas, we always went in search of a tree on Mr. B. B. Saunders's property. Daddy laid his ax in the trailer attached to his Farmall and climbed up to the seat. After the rest of us piled into the trailer, he steered the tractor down the lane toward the river. About three-quarters of a mile from our house, Daddy veered off the dirt road into the woods, put his foot on the clutch, and let the tractor roll to a stop. We sprang from the confines of the trailer and headed out. Finding a perfectly shaped tree the right size was a challenge. Daddy usually grew impatient before we identified it.

"How about a short-leaf pine?" he said to Mama, brushing his hand over a scrawny tree.

"I'd rather a cedar," Mama said.

When we found what we thought might be the right one, Daddy wasted no time. With three heavy strokes of the ax, the tree lay sideways on the ground. Squatting in the trailer on the way home, I inhaled the cedar scent and wondered why such a pleasant smell was said to repel moths.

Back at home, Daddy set the tree in a white enamel bucket in the backyard, filled it with dry sand, and wet it, so it would hold the tree upright. "Where do you want it?" he asked Mama as he toted the bucketed tree into the front room.

"In that corner," Mama said, pointing to the spot where our Christmas tree always sat. "Turn it a little this way," Mama said as Daddy set it down. "Just a bit more. No, back a little. That's good." The tree's sparse side now faced the corner like a child who'd mis-behaved in school.

As soon as Mama dragged out the box of decorations, Patsy, Anetha, and I began grabbing ornaments. "Wait, girls," Mama said and picked up the string of lights. "Let's put these on first." Mak-ing that string of lights—heavy cone-shaped bulbs along red and green twisted wires—stay on the weak cedar branches required attaching a few wooden clothespins. Next we helped Mama add a rope made of tightly twisted foil. She tied one end near the top and we draped the rope back and forth, back and forth until it ran out. Below that, we added a colorful construction paper chain we'd made ourselves. Reaching to the tip top, Mama attached a tinfoil-covered cardboard star, then backed off to let us finish.

The ornaments—made of *unbreakable* plastic—included four white snowmen (two with red top hats, two with black); two white reindeer with multi-point antlers; two red Santa Clauses, including one with Scotch tape around his busted belly; and one Rudolph with just three legs. So much for *unbreakable*.

One year, we sprinkled artificial snow on our tree's branches,

but the slippery flakes filtered right
through the cedar branches and
landed on the linoleum floor. When
Christmas was over that year, I half
expected Mama to sweep the stuff
up and save it for the next Christmas, just as she saved the icicles
from year to year, but she threw out
the snow and never bought it again.

I thought each icicle should be
hung so it draped limp and straight.
But Anetha soon grew impatient

Unbreakable Rudolph

and began tossing them to the top of the tree where they landed
in a wad. Before long the two of us were fussing about the hanging
of icicles, which drew Mama's attention. "Don't make me sit y'all
down by the window and make you put your nose in a circle and
stare at one another," Mama called from the kitchen. She had never done that when it was freezing cold outside—and it was pretty
cold at that moment. *Who would she make go outside?*

The scent of cedar and the glow of our Christmas tree's red, green,
blue, and yellow lights reflected in our water glasses that night at
supper, making the room feel magical. I could hardly wait for Santa Claus to come down our chimney, for I knew he'd bring gifts,
just as he always had.

The year before, he had brought a doll for each of us! Each doll
had a hard head with eyes that opened and closed, and hard arms
and legs that attached to a soft, cotton-stuffed body. When you
laid them down on their backs, they cried *waa-waaaaa*. That was
the best present ever. Patsy was curious about what made the dolls
cry, though, and one day she decided to operate on her doll. She
cut the doll open with Mama's big scissors and found, among lots
of stuffing, an object the size of a snuff can. She removed it like a

doctor might remove an appendix. She then discovered that, by cupping her hands around the can as she turned it over, it made a *maa-maaaaaa* sound instead of *waa-waaaaa*. Anetha loved playing with Patsy's "cryer," so Patsy cut Anetha's doll open and took the cryer out of it too.

In years to come, the two of them would disagree over whether Anetha gave Patsy permission to do this. Patsy would say *absolutely*. Anetha would say *absolutely not*.

One year, Santa brought each of us a gold locket and matching ring with our initials engraved within two hearts. Unfortunately, Anetha and Patsy lost their rings while still in grade school. Anetha took hers off in church during prayer meeting one night and it fell through the grate of the furnace. Patsy lost hers in our yard but didn't know where. Anetha had the idea that a hen pecked it up and thought we should look in chicken poop for it. I don't remember whether or not we actually did that. Anetha later said, "We did." Patsy said, "We didn't."

On Christmas Eve night, Mama helped us hang our red stockings on three nails stuck in the mantel, and come morning, our stockings overflowed. Each of us dumped the contents onto the floor: an orange, a tangerine, a pair of socks, a box of Cracker Jacks, and a handful of nuts. Under the tree, Santa had left us a toy box and a set of Chinese checkers to share. But best of all, I got a navy and red plaid dress and a doll wearing a matching dress. The doll had human-looking hair, though Mama said it looked to her like it was made of lamb's wool.

Anetha got the same with a different color plaid. She loved combing her doll's hair, and before long, her baby looked as if it had stuck its fingers into an electrical outlet; the doll's hair struck straight out in every direction. I don't remember what Pasty got that year. Santa, having seen her cut open her doll and Anetha's doll, perhaps thought she was too old for dolls.

Our grandparents always came to eat the noontime Christmas dinner with us. Typically, it consisted of turkey, cornbread dressing, giblet gravy, cranberry sauce, butter beans, candied yams, ambrosia salad (chopped oranges, pineapple, cherries, coconut, and pecans), homemade yeast rolls, and sweet iced tea. And for dessert, we could choose between fruitcake or pie (pecan, pumpkin, or sweet potato).

I would have enjoyed our Christmas meal more if Mama had let me leave off the cornbread dressing and gravy. She thought dressing wasn't dressing without onion and celery, two vegetables that I detested. I cringed when she made me eat either. And she thought giblet gravy wasn't giblet gravy without bits of turkey gizzard and liver. The gizzard giblets, I liked, but I gagged when she made me eat liver, even a tiny bit.

Christmas was just one of the big events that took place in late December. The other was hog-killing day. Typically, Daddy and Granddaddy Rye scheduled this on a cool day between Christmas and New Year's, and I always looked forward to it. Not only did I enjoy the hustle and bustle of the day, I thought the hog-killing-day meal tasted better than the one we had on Christmas Day.

45

Cutting the Fat

On our wall calendar, Daddy had written across the date of Friday, December 28: *Hog Killing Day*. The adults probably prayed for perfect weather. If too cold, our fingers would feel like they were freezing when we worked with the bloody meat in open air. If too warm, flies and gnats would land on the pork and spread germs.

Where, I wondered, *do flies and gnats go during cold weather?*

Hog-killing day, like cane-grinding, took place at our grandparents' place since they owned all the necessary equipment: sturdy racks for bleeding and gutting the hogs, a sugar kettle that served as a vat for scalding the dead hogs, and several outdoor tables.

This annual event never drew a crowd the way cane-grindings did, but I always got excited about it. On this day, I felt grown up, for I was allowed to work right alongside those who were older. Everybody in the family had important jobs to do on hog-killing day, all except Great-Granddaddy Tip, who seldom left his porch rocker anymore.

We arrived at Grandma and Granddaddy's place well before daylight, and as always, the men immediately headed outside to fill the sugar kettle with water and build a fire under it. About a half-hour later, they returned, rubbing their hands together to warm them up, before heading out again with weapons. As they went through the back doorway, orange rays from the rising sun lit up their silhouettes: Granddaddy with his .22 rifle pointed upward; Daddy with a butcher knife pointed downward.

Within minutes, shots rang out.

Pow!... Pow!... Pow!... Pow!... Pow!... Pow!

I knew the procedure. I'd seen it once—didn't care to witness it again. But I saw it in my head anyway: Granddaddy put a bullet in the head of six fattened hogs. Each fell to the dirt. Daddy stuck each hog's neck with a butcher knife. Blood spurted from the puncture and soaked the dirt.

Daddy and Granddaddy worked fast to scald, scrape and string the hogs up by their hind legs, to bleed them. Supposedly, bleeding the hog made the butchering process less gruesome and produced whiter pork. An animal would bleed even better, Daddy said, if its throat was cut first, without a bullet to the head. But Daddy and Granddaddy couldn't bring themselves to do it that way.

"I hear a car," Patsy said.

My sisters and I ran outside. It was Kent and Allie Thomas in a truck. They always helped us on hog-killing day. When they lived in the house down the road from us, and she used to babysit us, they would walk to my grandparents' house on hog-killing day. But they'd recently moved. They now lived five or more miles up the road, not far from Philadelphia Baptist.

You couldn't ask for a nicer family than the Thomases. They didn't expect to be paid. But they knew from past experience that they wouldn't go home empty-handed.

As soon as they got out of the truck, my sisters and I followed Mama and Grandma out of the house to greet them. Mr. Thomas hurried out to help Daddy and Granddaddy. He'd arrived just in time to help them load the deadweight of the hogs onto a trailer to haul them over to the steaming sugar kettle.

There, working with one hog at a time, the men lowered each

into the vat of scalding water. They knew just how long to leave each beast in the water so the hair would come off easily when scraped with a dull knife or hog scraper. Daddy said if left too long in the hot water, the hairs would "set" and make them nearly impossible to remove.

After rolling a hog around in the near-boiling water for a short time, they manhandled it onto a large table next to the sugar kettle and worked fast to scrape off its bristly hair. Scraped clean, the animal's skin was whiter than my tummy. The hogs were now ready for hanging on racks.

Each of the two racks consisted of a six-foot-long, thick horizontal beam about six feet off the ground, supported by strong posts at each end. In preparation for hanging the limp, heavy hogs, the men cut slits in the hind legs of each hog, between the bone and Achilles tendon. This created an opening to slide in the *gambrel*, a foot-long, two-inch diameter piece of wood, whittled to rounded points at each end.

Standing under one of the sturdy racks, Daddy and Mr. Thomas lifted and stretched the hind legs of the first hog up on either side of the beam. As they held it in place, Granddaddy placed a gambrel on top of the beam, and threaded the hog's hind legs onto it, one on each side of the beam. To keep the legs from slipping off when the men let go of the hog's weight, Granddaddy tied its feet in place with *istle*, blades of *bear grass*, a strong-leafed plant, tough like yucca, which grew wild in the nearby woods. My sisters and I had helped Granddaddy gather the istle a few days before.

Once the first hog was secure, Daddy and Mr. Thomas let go and lifted the next hog, stretching its hind legs high so Granddaddy could thread the gambrel through the slits in its legs. Lifting and hanging those slippery hairless hogs—each weighing more than any man present—didn't look easy. But in just a few minutes, they had all six hogs hanging upside down, like shirts on clotheslines.

With a long butcher knife, they cut off each hog's head and set it aside. Blood drained from each neck and bloodied the Bahia grass.

Meanwhile, Mama, Allie, and Grandma scrubbed down the table where the men had scraped the hogs, so the table could be used for cutting up the carcasses. They also rearranged the other tables, which would be used for stripping the small intestines, cutting up fat, and packaging the meat.

Granddaddy set a washtub on the ground under one of the headless hogs, and as Daddy and Mr. Thomas held the body steady, Granddaddy slit its underbelly from its throat near the ground up to a point between its hind legs. Before the knife reached its highest point, guts tumbled into the tub—*ka-bloosh*!

After disemboweling each hog, they sawed the carcasses down the backs and transferred the sides of pork to the clean table where they would saw, chop, and carve the meat into hams, shoulders, loins, pork chops, ribs, and slabs of bacon.

As they cut, they left the outer skin on the hams. They also left it on the bacon so it would have a chewy rind when fried. But they cut off the skin and fat from most other cuts and tossed the chunks into white enamel dishpans.

When a pan was about half full of fat, they set it on the fat-cutting table. Now it was time for us kids to get to work.

"Be careful and don't cut yourself," Grandma said, "the knives are sharp"—like we didn't know that.

We all got started. With my paring knife, I stood on the side of the table next to Grandma and began to cut the chunks of fat into inch-size cubes, just as Grandma did. We tossed the chunks into another dishpan. Each time it filled up, Grandma dumped the pan of chunks into one of two iron washpots under which fires would be built that afternoon. (One year, we butchered twelve hogs instead of six and the fat wouldn't fit in two washpots. The men had to scrub out the sugar kettle, after scalding the hogs, and cook the fat in that.)

As Grandma and we kids continued to cut the fat and the men

kept carving the meat, Mama and Allie got busy with the guts. The small intestines had to be cleaned so they could be used for sausage casings or cooked into chitlins. Our family didn't care for chitlins at all. Mama cooked some for us once, and once was enough. I thought they tasted like our outhouse smelled. But lots of people liked them. Allie said they did—boiled for several hours with a little salt, pepper, and onion, and served up with vinegar.

Before Mama and Allie could clean the guts, of course, they had to snip here and there to untangle and separate the small intestines from one another and from all the other organs and fat. After they untangled a long strip, they would cut it off, stretch it out on the nearby table, and run the back edge of a case knife along its length to strip out the crap. The stinky mess fell into a hole in the ground, dug for that purpose. This hole would later be covered with dirt. Meanwhile, it was a nasty mess. I always kept my distance from it. I can only imagine how Cousin Bernice Lanier felt when she was a little girl and fell into such a hole.

After stripping the intestines, Mama and Allie rinsed them over and over in tubs of cool water, turning them inside out several times, scraping them again and again in fresh water, to make sure no smidgen of grit or slime remained. Finally, they put them in a pan, salted them down, and covered them with water. At the end of the day, Allie would take some home to cook as chitlins, but most would be kept for stuffing the next day with ground pork mixed with pepper and other spices.

Around eleven o'clock, Grandma went inside to fix dinner for everybody. Before long, the scent of frying meat made my mouth water. After Grandma called us for dinner, the Thomases followed us inside and sat at the little kitchen table where Grandma always rolled out biscuit dough and pie crust. The rest of us went into the dining room.

I asked Grandma once why colored folks always sat in the kitchen or on the back steps to eat. She said they didn't feel comfortable dining with us, though I never actually heard her ask them.

What a dinner Grandma cooked every hog-killing day! The side dishes might vary from one year to the next, but the meal always included hot biscuits and fried butterfly steaks—the freshly cut pork tenderloin that formerly rested next to the porkchop bone. The meat was nearly as tender as the buttered biscuits, which literally melted in your mouth.

After dinner, my sisters and I headed back to the fat-cutting table. Grandma stayed behind to wash the dishes, and Mama and Allie bolted a meat grinder to another table so they could grind up meat for sausage. Even the tongues would go into the grinder. I once heard someone say, "We eat every part of the pig except the oink." The feet, of course, were set aside so Mama could later make pickled pigs' feet for Great-Granddaddy Tip (recipe p. 435). He was the only one in the family who cared for them.

Around midafternoon, Granddaddy Rye started a fire under the two washpots, and about the time we finished our job of cutting all the fat, the bits of fat already in the washpots began to sizzle. It smelled like bacon frying and made me hungry all over again.

As the grease cooked out, crispy pieces floated to the top. Using a long-handled strainer, Grandma scooped out the cracklins after they browned sufficiently and tossed them into a clean dishpan lined with paper sacks for absorbing the excess grease. I reached to get a hot cracklin, but Mama stopped me.

"You girls go inside and wash your hands," she reminded, "before you start eatin' cracklins."

The first one I picked up with clean hands was so crispy it was gone in a flash, but the next one had a strip of rind that caused me to chew and chew.

After all the cracklins had been scooped out of the hot grease, Granddaddy doused the coals with sand, but left the grease in the pots to cool. Later, the women ladled it into lard cans for storage. Each lard can, with handles on each side, would hold five or six gallons. As the grease cooled, it would turn white and become semi-solid.

Mama and Grandma used lard throughout the year in breads, cakes, and piecrusts, and for frying anything and everything, from meat, fish, and chicken, to hush puppies, donuts, and pear and peach fritters.

In earlier times, Mama said they also used the cans of lard for storing meat they cured at home. She said the lard helped preserve the meat until eaten by keeping air and bugs off it and by providing insulation from hot summer temperatures.

Back then, she said, fresh cuts were packed in tubs of coarse salt for about six weeks (the salt drew most of the water out). The salted meat then hung in the smokehouse, a tightly constructed wooden shed without windows, in which a fire smoldered for one to two weeks.

They no longer cured their own meat or stored the cured meat in lard though. The flood had damaged the old smokehouse, which Great-Granddaddy Tip had built in the late 1800s. After the flood, Granddaddy Rye tried smoking meat in his tobacco barn, but the barn was much bigger than the 12'-square smokehouse, so smoking the meat in the barn didn't work as well.

Now, they took the meat to a place in Live Oak that would sugar cure the hams for them and they rented cold storage lockers for the fresh meat.

By the end of hog-killing day, all cuts of meat had been wrapped in white freezer paper, secured with masking tape, and labeled. Grandma and Mama always kept a few packages for our home freezers, but the bulk of the meat would be hauled to town.

Mama and Grandma helped the Thomases pack up, paying them with a fresh ham, a tin of lard, chitlins, and all of the hogs' heads. At one time, Mama said, she and Grandma kept one hog's head so they could put hog jowl in our black-eyed peas on New Year's Day, for good luck. But they now gambled with luck and just used any old piece of pork to season the peas.

They also gave Allie about half the cracklins since none of us cared much for cold cracklins. To me, it was like eating stale popcorn. And Mama and Grandma never bothered to add cracklins to cornbread batter, the way Allie said she did. Mama kept just enough for making a batch of lye soap that would do her the year.

That night when Daddy returned from hauling the meat to town, he said our hog-killing day had been a success: we and our grandparents had enough pork and lard to last another year, and everybody still had all their fingers.

46

Frozen Stiff

Soon after New Year's Day, Daddy and Granddaddy got together to butcher cows. They set aside two cold winter days: one to butcher Granddaddy's animal and another to butcher ours. Processing a single cow took the good part of a day.

One year Daddy would choose a female; another year, a steer, an "it." Turning the male into a steer made the meat tender, Daddy said. But the process, which Daddy called "castration" seemed awfully cruel to me. True, Daddy had quit using a knife for the procedure, but the clamp he'd switched to, which resembled giant pliers, couldn't have been any less painful for the calves. *What hurts more? Cutting your finger on a sharp knife or slamming it in a car door? Not that they were working with a finger.*

Animals chosen for slaughter were fattened up, fed ground-up corn in addition to grass. The cow slaughter took place when the morning air felt like the inside of a refrigerator. They butchered Granddaddy's animal at his place, and ours a week or two later in our cow lot since they needed no sugar kettle for scalding, as they did for a hog. "Hair on a cow," Daddy said, "is almost impossible to scrape off." So he and Granddaddy skinned the cow to get the hide off. To make that job easier, they hung the cow by its hind legs, like they did a hog. But cows were too heavy for two men to lift, so they used a tractor and pulley system.

The men never wanted the help of women or kids when butchering a cow. They didn't need the cow intestines cleaned since beef was never stuffed into sausage casings. And they didn't need us kids to chop fat since beef contains much less fat than pork. Whatever fat they found was ground up with the toughest cuts to make the hamburger meat juicier, or tossed out, buried with the guts.

But just because they didn't need or want our help didn't mean we kids weren't curious. During the day, we made frequent trips to the fence that separated our yard from the cow lot.

They used Daddy's Farmall, a pulley, and chains to hoist the cow up so they could attach its hind legs to the lowest branch of a shade tree. The tedious skinning process took a long time, after which they gutted the animal and sawed and cut up the carcass. After they finished the job around midafternoon, they loaded the beef into Granddaddy's truck to haul it to the cold storage locker in town.

I was glad I didn't have to go into that walk-in freezer on a cold January day. I'd been inside it the summer before when my sisters and I went to town with our grandparents. A trip to Live Oak with them always meant a visit with the North family—Aunt Ernestine, Uncle Jimmy, and Betty Jo, who lived right near the city limits of Live Oak. Aunt Ernestine was actually Grandma's first cousin, and Uncle Jimmy had become Granddaddy's fishing buddy.

"I see that Jimmy's home from his paper route," Granddaddy said to Grandma that summer day as we neared the city-limit sign. "Want to stop and say hello to Ernestine?"

Uncle Jimmy, who delivered *The Florida Times Union* all over town, sat on the porch smoking a cigarette.

"My goodness, you girls are growing like weeds," he said as we three bounded up the porch steps.

Aunt Ernestine pushed open the screen door and invited us in. Granddaddy parked himself next to Uncle Jimmy, straddling a straight-backed chair in his usual habit, and the rest of us went inside. Aunt Ernestine didn't seem like the kind of woman Grandma would take to. Her hair, cropped short, showed off big earbobs, and she took long strides like a man. But Grandma said they'd been friends since childhood.

Betty Jo, a teenager, stuck her head out of her bedroom door and invited Patsy, Anetha, and me in. The room was nice but felt hot and stuffy, so I didn't stay long before I went in search of Grandma. She sat at Aunt Ernestine's ultramodern chrome-and-Formica table. Aunt Ernestine stood in front of her refrigerator, the door open. Cool air spilled out as she pulled ice trays from the refrigerator's tiny freezer. Unlike Grandma's refrigerator, this freezer had no door of its own—just the refrigerator door closed it off.

After we all finished a glass of iced tea, we said our goodbyes and went on to Knight's grocery for Grandma to buy a sack of flour and sugar. From there, we went to the cold storage locker. "You girls want to go in and help me?" Granddaddy asked as he parked the truck. *Really? Daddy never lets us go inside with him.*

We entered through a door about five times thicker than a normal door. It slammed behind us. Our breath fogged the air in front of our faces. Granddaddy unlocked a numbered drawer and rummaged through it to find meat to take home for Grandma to cook. He handed packages to each of us. As I clasped the frozen food to my chest, I started to shiver. *How much longer?* I looked around the icy room. I began to feel scared. I had the urge to get out fast, but I knew that the ice-covered door was too heavy for me to open, especially with my arms full. My teeth started to chatter as Granddaddy unlocked and pulled open another drawer. He filled his own arms with packages.

"Okay, that should do us a couple of weeks," he finally said as he slammed the drawer shut, then fumbled in his pocket to find the key. Not finding it, he laid his packages on the floor and searched his pockets again. I was freezing. He finally found it, locked the drawers, picked up his packages, and headed toward the door. He pulled on the handle. The door didn't open. My heart skipped a beat. *How long before somebody will find us, our bodies frozen stiff?* Cold and scared, my body was shaking so hard I could hardly stand up. Granddaddy yanked the door again, harder this time. It sprang open. The outside air was like a warm blanket.

I hated feeling so cold I shivered. Winter was never my favorite season of the year. But I did enjoy a few cool-weather activities—such as quail hunting with Granddaddy and Joe, his bird dog.

Nose to the ground one chilly morning, Joe ran ahead of us in the hammock. Before long, he picked up the scent of a covey and stopped dead in his tracks, his nose pointed in the direction of the birds. Granddaddy whipped his shotgun into position, squinted one eye, sighted through the other, and gave Joe the nod. Joe took off running and scared the birds into the air. The barrel of Granddaddy's shotgun followed the birds as they flew up—Pow! Pow! Pow! One by one, the birds fell from the cloudless winter sky. Joe ran toward the birds and brought them back in his mouth, one at a time, and dropped them at Granddaddy's feet.

"Good boy, Joe," Granddaddy said as he rubbed Joe's neck hard and slid the birds into the big pocket of his khaki hunting jacket.

Joe was the only one of Granddaddy's dogs I ever knew, though we had photos of others. One picture showed Patsy, age two, riding Granddaddy's black dog, Bozo, like a horse; another showed Lady, rearing up on Granddaddy.

"That Lady was Daddy's all-time favorite dog," Mama said one day as she looked at the photo. "A man offered him a hundred dollars for her."

"But Granddaddy didn't take it, did he?" I said—more of a statement than a question, for I knew we wouldn't sell our dog Tommy for a million dollars.

"Daddy didn't want to," Mama said, looking sad, "but that was when times were really hard. Daddy couldn't find a job, and a hundred dollars was a lot of money. Yep. He took the money."

I was glad times weren't hard anymore because I wanted Granddaddy to keep Joe.

In addition to hunting with Joe and Granddaddy during cool weather, I liked to hang around when Daddy set fire to the cow pasture. He said the heat killed off the insect population so we'd have fewer bugs to damage the crops.

To burn a field, two adults worked as a team. One person set fire to one edge of the field while another set the opposite edge on fire, so the blazes could meet in the middle. After it burned and cooled, my sisters and I would enjoy stomping the charred grass to hear its crunch and feel it on the soles of our feet.

In addition to cool-weather *fun*, of course, we also had work to do. The tobacco crop, for example, got underway during the winter. The tiny seeds—even smaller than a poppy seed—were sown in large beds. My sisters and I helped keep the beds watered and weeds pulled for the next few weeks. By late February or early March, the seedlings would reach five to seven inches, at which time we'd help transplant them to the field. By then, my favorite season of the year was upon us. Spring.

47

Dogwood Blossoms and Easter Eggs

In early March, flowering trees in the hammock between our home and the Suwannee River announced the arrival of spring. Along the dark, leafless branches of wild Chickasaw plum trees, pindots of white blossoms opened up in clusters. A few days later, redbud trees showed off their pink blooms. Then came the Granddaddy Graybeard—that's what Mama called the tree—though its inch-long fringy white flowers looked nothing like Granddaddy Tip's stubby beard.

Mama pointed out a Granddaddy Graybeard (also called a fringe tree) one day at Running Springs, the same place she showed us a dogwood flower and explained its meaning. "Look here, girls," she said as she pulled a branch low enough that we could get a close-up look at its blossoms. She went on to explain that the dogwood flower symbolized Christ's Crucifixion.

We'd gone to the river that afternoon, the Sunday before Easter, for Daddy to check its level. After the flood of 1948, it was hard for him to rest easy when he started planting the crops.

"The four dogwood petals stand for the cross," Mama said, "and the holes here"—she pointed to the tip of each petal—"represent the nail holes in Christ's hands and feet when He was nailed to the cross."

I felt sick to my stomach every time I heard that gory story of Jesus's feet and hands being pierced with nails. Mama continued, "The center of the flower represents the crown of thorns they placed on His head, and these little red flecks on the petals represent His blood."

"When can we dye Easter eggs?" I asked.

"In a few days," Mama said, letting go of the branch.

Daddy climbed up the riverbank and announced what the river was doing—though I don't remember if he said it was rising or falling.

A few days later, Mama boiled two-dozen eggs, and set out the egg-dyeing equipment. In past years, we'd used food coloring, but this year, Mama seemed to have more money to spend. She bought a special Easter-egg dye kit. Inside the box, we found colored tablets, a clear wax crayon for drawing on the eggs, a wire ladle, and egg-sized pictures of bunnies, baby chicks, and flowers printed on tissue paper.

We put the colored tablets in teacups, and Mama added hot water and a little vinegar like the instructions said. We tried drawing on the eggs with the wax crayon but you couldn't see your picture until you took it out of the dye. My eggs surprised me when I ladled them onto the white muslin towel Mama had laid out. We tried transferring the pictures to the eggs by placing the tissue against the egg and wrapping it with a wet rag, but they came out blurry, so I left the rest of my eggs alone, thinking they were prettier plain. After the eggs cooled, Mama moved them to a big bowl on the table and hung up her pretty, new multicolored polka-dotted dish towel.

The next day, each of us took several eggs to school for our annual Easter egg hunt. All the kids brought eggs, and the older kids hid them along the edge of the woods behind the school. No windows overlooked that area, so nobody could peek.

When the bell rang at noon, we rushed out to hunt eggs. I was picking one up when a boy yelled, "I found the surprise egg!" Mrs. Johnson had decorated it to look like a baby chick.

Then, on Easter Sunday, we had an egg hunt at home. Elaine Boatright, who had no brothers or sisters, joined us. I was happy to see her but envious of her fancy Easter basket filled with chocolate bunnies and yellow marshmallow chicks. She said, "The Easter Bunny brought it." I'd never heard of an Easter Bunny and felt even more jealous. But when she shared her chocolate, my jealously melted with the chocolate in my mouth.

48

Easter Dresses

One of the highlights of Easter Sunday was having a new dress to wear. A few weeks before Easter, Mama and we sisters spent the better part of a Saturday at McCrory's in Live Oak searching through Simplicity pattern books and stacks of fabric that reached as high as Mama's shoulders. When all of us agreed on a dress we liked best, Mama bought the pattern in the size that would fit Anetha and me. At home, when she cut the fabric, she'd add a half inch at the side seams for Patsy.

Always, we chose a summer-weight fabric. Never mind that the weather would turn cold the day before Easter, forcing each of us to choose between wearing a sweater that would half cover our new dress, or go without and shiver through Sunday school and church.

Left to right: Anetha, Patsy, and me

One year, I shivered all the way to church because I wanted to show off my pretty Easter dress. I just knew my new dress would be the most admired in my Sunday school class. But as it turned out, another girl walked in wearing a dress even prettier than mine. In fact, she wore the prettiest dress I'd ever laid eyes on: sheer pink nylon, white lace, ruffles, ruffles, ruffles, and a big sash at the back.

I was flabbergasted since, until then, all of this girl's clothes were always dingy and dirty. She didn't seem to know what I'd been taught—that cleanliness was next to Godliness. But there she was, looking like Cinderella in that sheer pink dress.

During the church service, I pointed to her and told Mama I wanted a dress just like that next Easter. Then I felt bad, wondering if I'd hurt Mama's feelings.

"Turn your hymnals to page 292," the choir director said. "and let's stand and sing 'He Arose.'" That was my favorite Easter song.

He arose.

the grave. . .

Up from. . .

I liked the way it picked up speed and pitch.

The Sunday after Easter, the girl I was now calling "Cinderella" wore that beautiful pink dress again. And the next Sunday, she wore it again. And again. And again.

The more she wore that dress, though, the dirtier it looked, and by summer, it was filthy.

Now I was no longer jealous. I felt sorry for her, not having a Mama who recognized that cleanliness was next to Godliness. *Does her mother never wash clothes?* I wondered. *And does she never tell her children to wash their necks?* Mama washed clothes weekly and was forever checking our necks and ears to make sure we had scrubbed them good. After checking Patsy's neck one day, Mama decided Patsy hadn't done a good job.

"It's just a tan," Patsy said, but Mama was already soaping up a wet washrag.

Come here," Mama commanded.

"It ain't dirt," Patsy protested again, but obeyed Mama, who proceeded to scrub Patsy's neck until it was nearly raw. Finally, Mama admitted that it was a tan.

Another time, Mama accused Anetha of not brushing her teeth, saying her teeth looked brown! At the time, we used salt and soda to brush our teeth (toothpaste in a tube was too expensive). Mama proceeded to polish Anetha's teeth with Bab-O, not recognizing until later why Anetha's teeth were discolored; Mama had been giving her Geritol to build up her blood because she'd been looking puny.

One day I decided that if Cinderella's mother wouldn't teach her about washing, that I had to do it, and I came up with a plan.

When she showed up at church the next Sunday (with her grandmother, who was the one who always took her to church), I invited her to go home with me. Mama had said it was okay for me to invite her, and when Cinderella asked her grandmother's permission, it was granted.

At home after we'd finished eating the noon dinner, I asked Mama if I could take my friend to Grandma's house. Mama said okay, and off we went. My plan would work better at Grandma's house since she had a bathroom and we didn't.

Granddaddy Tip was on the porch when we arrived, Granddaddy Rye was outside somewhere, and Grandma was busy in the kitchen. None of them ever hovered over my sisters and me or any visitors that accompanied us; they just let us find our own entertainment, which was fine with me, especially now that I had a plan for the afternoon.

"Let's play house," I said to my friend. "I'll be the mother, and you pretend you're my little girl."

She agreed.

"Okay, sweetie," I said. "Come with me. It's time for your bath." I took her hand like I was her mommy and led her to the bathroom where I plugged the tub and filled it with water.

"Okay, sweetie, it's ready for you." Of course, I had to help her unbutton the back of her dirty pink dress.

Once she was in the tub, I began giving instructions.

"Okay, take this washrag and use that bar of soap while I start my chores."

I kept telling her exactly where to wash as I filled the sink, which Grandma called a lavatory, with water. "Wash your face . . . now your neck . . . ."

"Whatcha doin' with my dress?" she asked after I picked it and her panties up off the floor and wadded them so they would fit in the lavatory.

"Whatcha think I'm doing? It's *Monday*. Wash day," I said and pushed them down in the water. She didn't correct my saying it was Monday.

"Now you need to soap up your rag again and wash your arms and under them—and don't forget your ears."

On and on I instructed as I scrubbed her dirty clothes with a bar of soap. Finally, I rinsed them and pulled the plug for the last time, put the clothes in a towel, squeezed them, and ran outside where I hung the clothes and towel on Grandma's clothesline. The sun was out and the wind was blowing, so I thought the nylon clothes would be dry in no time—at least I hoped that.

"Now, let's play beauty shop," I said when I got back from outside.

Before she could protest, I put a dollop of Grandma's Lustre-Crème shampoo on her mousy hair and lathered it up.

"This is fun," she said as she leaned back and let me help her rinse out the shampoo.

"Okay, now you can get out of the tub, and you can be the mama and I'll be your little girl."

While she dried off, I drained and scrubbed the dark ring off the tub with a little Bab-O before adding more water and hopping in.

Surprisingly, as my "mama," she didn't pick up my clothes to wash them, and that was fine with me. She sat, wrapped in a towel, on the commode with the lid down as I bathed. I took my sweet time, hoping she would notice how careful I was to wash every spot. I went over each area more than once, shampooed my hair twice, and stayed in the tub until my fingers and toes were wrinkled—giving her clothes time to dry.

After what might have been a full hour, I got out, dried off, dressed, and ran out to see if her clothes were dry. They were, except a bit of dampness in the seams. She didn't seem to notice when she put them back on.

Once she was dressed, I neatly parted and combed her naturally curly hair. I could hardly believe how nice she looked. Her dress was clean. Her skin was clean. And when her previously limp and stringy hair dried, she had fluffy blond curls.

Back at home, I'm sure my family noticed but they said not a word. At church that night, I beamed with pride when somebody said how nice she looked.

On the way home, though, Patsy and Anetha started quizzing me, and when I told them what I had done, their mouths dropped open. "You gave her a bath?" . . . "Yuck!" . . . "You washed her clothes?" . . . "That's crazy!" . . . "You had to scrub the *tub*?"

They teased me about it for weeks. And to make matters worse, Cinderella went back to her old ways. All my effort was wasted.

Part V
Schooldays

49

First-Grade Goof-Ups

Anetha handed Mama a brown envelope addressed to Mrs. C. G. Howell. My sisters and I had picked up the mail on our way from school as we did every weekday. Mama, standing in the doorway of the kitchen, looked at the return address and said, "Probably y'all's new birth certificates."

Back when Patsy enrolled in first grade at age six and a half, nobody questioned her age. The same went for Anetha when she started the next year. But when Mama took me to register a year later, in 1950, the school wanted proof that I was old enough. Although I would turn six within two months of starting school, I had no proof because I'd been born at home. None of us had birth certificates. The teachers let me go ahead and register, but after the questioning, Mama applied for birth certificates for all of us.

When we received them, Mama opened the envelope and frowned, "Susanette's name is wrong." She pulled out a straight-backed chair at the dining table and sat. "They typed *Louise* Jeannette instead of *Susie* Jeannette."

"I can be *Louise* Jeannette!" I said, excited that I could then claim to be named after Aunt Louise. Everybody else in the family was named after somebody: Daddy after his father, Mama after her aunt, Patsy after Daddy's sister, Anetha after one of Daddy's high school classmates, and me—after nobody.

Aunt Louise, my namesake!

I'd seen her only once in my life, when she and Uncle Harold drove down with our young cousins from Gary, Indiana. But she wrote lots of letters to Grandma, often enclosing black-and-white snapshots. In one photo, she wore a fur coat as white as the snow in the background. The snow and fur contrasted starkly with her smooth dark complexion and dark silky hair. She was foreign born, beautiful, and the idea of having Aunt Louise's name made me giddy.

"I can be Louise Jeannette," I said again, but Mama ignored me, saying, "I'll have to write back to the State Board of Health and get this mess straightened out."

When Daddy came in, she told him about the mistake, saying, "I'll have to tell 'em to fix my name too. They typed Ethel *Mary* for the mother—on all *three* birth certificates."

Mama's middle name was Macie, but I'd heard her say she hated Macie. So why not leave it Ethel Mary? And why not leave my name Louise Jeannette? But nobody paid me any mind.

Now, just before Christmas, our corrected birth certificates had arrived in the mail. As Mama ripped into the second brown envelope she'd received this year, my sisters and I helped ourselves to still-warm oatmeal cookies (recipe p. 434) that lay on a muslin cloth on the kitchen table. This time, the certificates had no mistakes. And I, Susanette, was officially Susie Jeannette.

My sisters and I stopped at our grandparents' house on our way to Ladyland each morning and warmed up by their heater as the weather turned colder. Tommy waited patiently outside, wagging his tail. If frost blanketed the ground, Granddaddy would drive us the rest of the way in his pickup. As we climbed into its cab, Tommy turned and headed home.

On the coldest days, a wood-burning heater in the center of each classroom roared. Periodically, Mrs. Johnson sent a few boys out to tote in firewood. But our cold weather seldom lasted long, and I don't recall that the weather ever turned so cold we didn't go outside at recess and lunchtime to play games. Some games I enjoyed. Others I could have done without.

I liked "Mother, May I?" where one person played mother, and everybody else lined up and faced her as she gave instructions. The very first time I played the game, Anetha acted as the mother.

"Ceil," she called to her best friend. "Take four baby steps."

"May I?" Ceil asked.

"Yes, you may."

Ceil took four teeny-tiny steps toward Anetha.

"Nettie, take three little steps," Anetha told another classmate.

"May I?"

"Yes, you may."

First and second grade classes. Anetha (with permed hair) top left. Me, top right.

Nettie moved up.

"Susanette, take two giant steps."

Wow! That's way better than four baby steps or three little steps! Anetha's being nice to me since I'm her sister. Naturally, I took the longest steps possible.

"You forgot to ask 'May I?'" Anetha said. "Go back to the starting line."

Even though I often goofed when playing this game, I preferred it to Pop the Whip, where everybody joined hands and the leader pulled the rest along, running this way and that. The leader ran faster and faster, zigzagging, so it became impossible for the ones at the very end to hold on. I got flung off time and time again, sometimes landing with the skirt of my dress hiked up or ending up with a skinned knee.

I didn't care much for Red Rover either. We divided up into two groups and each team faced the other, standing about thirty feet apart. The goal? To steal members of the opposing team until only one team remained.

One team joined hands and formed a human barricade as they yelled at the other team to send somebody over. We might say, "Red Rover, Red Rover, send Billy right over." If we could prevent Billy's breaking through our chain of arms, we captured him for our team. If he broke through, Billy got to steal a member of our team for his. The boys would crash through so hard that I'd often let go rather than risk a broken arm.

Occasionally, we jumped rope, which was fun, though we younger kids usually got stuck turning the rope for the older ones. They'd pair up, or want to do *hot peas*, which meant we "turners" had to move our arms faster and faster, the way Mama moved her arms when she beat cake batter or when she made chocolate fudge or divinity candy.

We played dodgeball too, until I put a stop to that in late spring. A few of us girls, playing the game at lunchtime, took a break to go to the girls' outhouse. Naturally, we carried the ball with us to keep the boys from taking it. Inside, awaiting our turn to sit on one of the four holes on the bench seat, Myra and I bounced the ball back and forth on the floor. Just as one of the girls stood up, the ball bounced toward the vacant hole. I tried to grab it, but my grab shoved it through the hole. The ball was now in deep doo-doo, and I feared I was too.

Back in the classroom after lunch, everyone settled into their seats. I didn't tell the teacher what had happened, and I didn't see anybody tattle on me. But later in the afternoon as Mrs. Johnson stood in front of the classroom giving instructions, she stopped talking and stared at the hallway door behind me. I hadn't heard anybody walk up, but without even looking, I knew the principal stood in the doorway. Not the grandfatherly Mr. Rumbly, though. He had been the principal up until a few weeks before. Everybody loved him and was shocked and saddened when he died unexpectedly. The new principal (who also taught sixth, seventh and eighth grade) was Mr. Patterson, a stiff-standing man with jet black hair, Brylcreemed flat against his head. So far, I'd never seen him smile.

"What's this I hear about a lost ball?" he asked in a deep and gruff voice.

The room grew eerily quiet. Then, every classmate turned in their desks and looked back in my direction. *Are they looking at me or Mr. Patterson?*

"Well, speak up! Who's responsible?"

The room stayed quiet.

The inch-thick paddle the principal kept in his classroom was no secret. I dropped my head and slowly raised my hand. The pounding of my heart shut out everything else. *Will the principal's paddle be worse than Daddy's belt?*

"I'm sorry, sir," I said as I turned and looked up at him. He towered over me. "We—I mean—the ball—it bounced—I tried—"

"You know that was the only dodgeball this school had," he said, wagging his finger near my face. "Balls don't come cheap. That ball belonged to every student at this school . . . . And now it's gone. Down the toilet!" Disgust dripped from his words.

"Yes, sir," I said, looking down at his spit-shined shoes that matched his hair.

"You deserve a good paddling, young lady."

"Yes, sir," I said, wondering what the difference was between a good paddling and a bad paddling. None, I suspected.

He kept standing there, glaring at me, saying stuff I wasn't hearing because my mind was on his paddle. I wished he'd hush and get the punishment over with.

Finally, he addressed the class. "Well, students, you won't have a ball to play with now. The girls should have known better than to take that ball into the toilet."

To my surprise, Mr. Patterson then spun on the heels of his shiny shoes, disappeared into the hallway, and rang the dismissal bell.

No paddling? I'm not getting a whipping! I felt like giggling and crying at the same time.

On the walk home from school, I worried that Anetha would tell Patsy what had happened. Surprisingly, she didn't. She didn't tell Mama either when we got home. But a few days later, I got into trouble with Mama anyway when she heard me singing a song I'd heard the boys at school sing:

"In 1944,
my papa went to war.
He pulled the trigger,
and shot a n—"

"Come here!" Mama interrupted. "Where did you learn that?"

"Some boys at school were singing it."

Mama told me that the *N*-word I'd almost said offended colored people. I didn't quite understand why it was bad. Even Daddy said it. And everybody I knew used it when they talked about the nuts we got in our Christmas stockings.

"Can I say, '*Eenie, meenie, miney, Moe, Catch a—*"

"Catch a *fellow* by his toe," Mama said, cutting me off.

As for my misinformation about the people our soldiers were fighting against in 1944, Mama didn't bother to clear that up. And Daddy continued to use the word we kids were not supposed to say, though he would make a point of saying, "but they should have the same rights we have."

Mama explained to me at a later date that it was important to respect all races, but then she added, "of course whites and coloreds shouldn't marry." When I asked why, she said, "Red birds and blue birds don't mate, and that's the way it should be with people."

For a long, long time I thought I mostly agreed with Mama. It would be even longer before *integration* and *civil rights* would be talked about and acted upon.

But in time I would come to think that the human race would be better off if everybody in the whole world were the same caramel color of my favorite childhood candy.

50
Our Substitute Teacher
1951

When Anetha and I walked into our classroom one morning, Mrs. Johnson was nowhere in sight. Instead, Jeannette Land sat at our teacher's large wooden desk. *Huh? What's going on?*

Jeannette Land and her family attended our church, and I'd always felt a kinship to her since my middle name was Jeannette and we both had dark eyes and dark curly hair. In fact, I thought the two of us looked more alike than my sisters and I did.

"I'm Miss Land," Jeannette announced to the class. "I'm substituting for Mrs. Johnson because she's ill."

Calling Jeannette "Miss Land" would have been like calling Anetha "Miss Howell." So I avoided calling her anything.

At first, Jeannette took up where Mrs. Johnson left off, teaching us in much the same way. There were, of course, a few things we had to teach Jeannette, like who took the erasers out to dust them and who watered the spindly plants on the windowsill.

One morning while raising a window, Jeannette accidentally knocked over one of those plants. As the tin can toppled, she grabbed at it and ended up batting the thing to the floor, like I'd accidentally batted the dodgeball into the toilet. The tin can landed upside down next to Anetha's left foot and dirt spread across her shoe. Jeannette's mouth dropped open like a church choir member singing the *Doxology*. Everybody in the class let out a giggle. Or stifled one as I did.

"I'll get the broom?" Anetha said, shaking dirt off her foot.

"That would be nice," Jeannette said, her face turning red.

Anetha knew Mrs. Johnson stored the broom in the cloakroom; she and I had helped sweep up after school. Before sweeping, Mrs. Johnson always had us scatter red stuff across the floor, though. The red stuff looked like ground up pencil erasers; Mrs. Johnson said it contained oil to help control dust.

I thought the plant Jeannette had knocked to the floor should be tossed into the trash, but Anetha stuffed it back into its rusty tin, and Jeannette set it back on the windowsill.

For the rest of that school year, we spent less and less time on reading, spelling, and numbers, and more time with crayons, construction paper, scissors, and glue. One day, Jeannette announced that we were going to make three-dimensional houses. She demonstrated, cutting construction paper into different shapes—squares, rectangles, and triangles—folding, gluing, and taping pieces together in such a way that she created a boxy house with a peaked roof. She then turned us loose to make our own. First and second graders worked together, and before the day ended, we'd built ourselves a colorful village that covered the entire worktable.

I thought the project done, but the next day Jeannette brought in a box of Cut-Rite waxed paper. We measured the open windows of our houses with a ruler and cut squares and rectangles to fit the openings. We soon found that the glue we squeezed through the slit of the red rubber bottle cap didn't work, though. It rolled right off the waxed paper. So we switched to white paste, smearing it on with our fingers.

Another day, we made pinwheels from a sheet of construction paper, a pin, and a pencil, something Mama had already taught us to make. At recess, we took our pinwheels outside and ran around, letting them twirl like windmills.

I liked having Jeannette for a teacher and loved all the crafts, but I also missed Mrs. Johnson. I kept thinking she'd return after she recovered from whatever she had. But she didn't come back and didn't come back. Mama heard that nobody knew what was wrong with her, not even her doctors. She nearly died before they figured out she had lead poisoning.

By the time school started the next year, Mrs. Johnson had recovered enough to teach, and Jeannette went on with her education. She studied first at Stetson College in DeLand before transferring to the Ringling School of Art in Sarasota with plans to become an artist. At the time, we had no clue that she would soon be stricken with a disease that was becoming an epidemic. Polio.

51

How Daddy Got His Purple Jeep

Daddy still borrowed Granddaddy's old truck when we needed to go anywhere. But that changed near the end of my first school year, thanks to Daddy's cousin, Thomas Boatright, the one who fought overseas in the Big War. I'd heard bits and pieces about what happened during that war—about how the Nazis hated the Jews, how Japan hated us—but mostly I heard about Daddy's cousin Thomas and what happened to him during the war. It took place around the time I was born, but everybody still talked about it. Daddy said he remembered the day he heard that Thomas was missing like it was yesterday.

"I was at home working on my old Model A—the one I sold later to buy a tractor," Daddy said, "when one of the Boatright boys came down to our house and told me Thomas was missing."

Thomas's oldest sister, Winifred, later wrote down the details:[5]

"Thomas joined the Florida National Guard in October, 1940. World War II broke out and he found himself in the U.S. Army, headed for Europe. [Thomas's] first action was

---

[5] *Past Memories with the Joe A. Boatright Family,* by Winifred B. Padgett. Used with permission.

the invasion of the Anzio Beachhead in Italy on January 22, 1944. [The Allies] were under heavy fire. Thirty-seven men in his company hit the beach and helped establish a front line. Within about three weeks, 34 of those men were either dead or had been carried from the front line, wounded.

"On March 1, a German Patrol captured his buddies, and then they found him. He stated, 'There was nowhere to go.' He told us about a soldier being in the foxhole with him. The soldier had been shot 7 times from the waist up.

"We received a telegram April 13, 1944, that Thomas was missing in action.

"He was taken to a P.O.W. camp in Florence, Italy. He received a cup of water and one potato or a slice of bread per day. They put him in jail because he wouldn't give them any information and wouldn't salute a German officer. He was forced to stand for 13 days and nights in a cell that was too small to sit or lie down in."

"The Red Cross team visited the jail there and persuaded the Germans to release him from the cell. When he was captured, he weighed 128 pounds, and when he left the cell he weighed just 70 pounds. He was given two American food parcels, but he was so weak that he couldn't pick them up.

"Thomas related that he was eaten up with body lice while in the cell . . . .

"After a couple of weeks as a regular POW, he received a lucky break. He and some other men were assigned to work on farms [in Germany] . . . .

"After 14 months and three days, Thomas was released on May 3, 1945."

I wasn't yet a year old when Thomas returned from the war, so I don't know if he arrived to a parade or fanfare. But in the eyes of those I knew, he was a war hero.

Daddy and Thomas had always been close, and Mama liked his wife, Marie, so we often got together with them for a meal and for us kids to play with their daughter, Elaine, who was about my age.

Mama loved to tell a story about a visit with the Boatrights in which she had to insult Marie in order to get Patsy to eat what was on her plate. I think it happened before Elaine and I were born and when Anetha was just a baby.

As the platter of fried chicken and bowls of food were passed around the table that day, Mama said she added food to Patsy's plate—a drumstick, acre peas, and a dollop of mashed potatoes to which Marie had added a generous amount of black pepper. Patsy stared at the peppered potatoes, nudged Mama with her elbow, and pointed at the mashed potatoes. "Oh, Honey, don't worry," Mama said. "That's just some specks of trash that fell in the pot while Marie was boiling the potatoes."

Mama said Marie gave her a strange look before realizing Mama knew Patsy would not eat black pepper, but she *would* eat "specks of trash."

We saw the Boatrights often during tobacco gathering time when we traded work (they helped us, we helped them), and I enjoyed being around them—except I didn't like that Thomas was always tickling me. I'd beg him to stop but I'd be giggling as I begged, and he'd keep tickling until I was nearly out of breath. I don't think he ever did it when Mama was in the room. She would have had a fit. She couldn't stand to be tickled herself.

Every fall, the Boatrights invited us to pick up pecans from their orchard. Mama was always eager to do that since she needed lots of pecans for oatmeal cookies, brownies, fudge, divinity, and fruitcake. So, our family would spend half a day crawling around on the ground of the Boatrights's pecan orchard, picking up the nuts until we had several buckets filled. Then we'd wash up and spend the rest of the day inside, visiting with the Boatrights.

One day Daddy and Thomas wandered off to the porch, Marie

and Mama went to the kitchen, and we kids played with Elaine in the two rooms on the front of the house. In one room, she had everything imaginable—even a play kitchen, complete with a sink, stove, iron, and ironing board.

And in the other room, Elaine's mother had a mirrored vanity with a stool where we sat to comb one another's hair. Elaine's long hair had never been cut, yet it was curly. Clearly, what Mama said, "length pulls the curl out," wasn't true.

While combing Elaine's hair one day at her mother's vanity, I noticed a small velvet-covered box sitting on the vanity and asked her what was in it. She opened the box for me. Inside was a brooch—swirled gold wire with sparkling purple stones, as if sprinkled there. I thought it was the most beautiful pin I'd ever seen and decided then and there to look in McCrory's and Priest's dime store when we went to town to see if I could find one for Mama—or at least see how much it cost so I could get Patsy or Anetha to help me figure up how many dimes we'd need to save up to buy it.

I didn't know at the time that while I was drooling over that pretty purple-stoned brooch, Daddy and Thomas were talking about vehicles. Daddy was hoping to buy a car soon, and Thomas had been driving a purple Jeep for a couple of years. Well, he called it "maroon," but it was purple to me.

Daddy told Mama later about the offer Thomas had made him. "C.G.," Thomas said to Daddy, "I'm tired of making payments on that thing. You can have it if you'll just take over the payments."

So before my first school year ended, Daddy was making payments on and driving a 1947 purple Jeep.

52

Chicken Chores and More

Every day after school, my sisters and I had chores to do, but first, we headed to the kitchen for a snack. I always hoped for oatmeal cookies or bread pudding, my favorites. Whatever we found, we usually took it outside to eat it—even the bread pudding, since it required no plate or fork. Mama's bread pudding was never soft and gooey. Made from biscuits, it baked up so firm she could cut it into squares like brownies.

Sometimes we got so busy playing we forgot our chores. But Mama had a good memory.

"Okay, girls," she'd remind us, "Time to go feed the chickens and gather the eggs."

Feeding the chickens meant shelling corn, a job I hated. The job had to be done, no matter the weather. When it was hot, I especially hated shucking the dusty, weevil-eaten corn. The dust stuck to my sweaty skin and made me itch like crazy.

To pry the dry kernels off the cob, we had to rub the kernels hard with our thumbs. The kernels had tiny spurs on them that scratched my thumbs raw. How I wished we had a corn sheller like Granddaddy Rye, where you just slid the shucked ear into a chute and turned the handle.

As the kernels fell at our feet, the chickens came running. But our chickens must have been half blind. They were as apt to peck a toe as a corn kernel. I suppose we could have worn shoes, but who wears shoes when they can go barefoot?

We tossed the spent corncobs into a bucket to save for Daddy to grind up and add to the animal feed, though occasionally we kept a few that we took to the house.

"Can we make some corncob flowers for our playhouse?" Patsy asked Mama one afternoon as we dumped the corncobs on the kitchen table.

"Where are the eggs?" Mama asked.

"We'll gather 'em later."

"No, you'll do it now. Go find 'em while I finish ironing. I'm on the last of your daddy's shorts and handkerchiefs now. Then we'll make flowers."

I didn't like gathering eggs any more than I liked shelling corn—at least, not at home. Our chickens didn't have a special place to lay eggs as Grandma's chickens did—in cubbyholes Granddaddy had built up high around the henhouse. Our chickens laid theirs in the packhouse, which had just a front and back door on the bottom level and no windows. To find the eggs, we had to search dark corners and behind bags of feed, fertilizer, and bales of hay. As I searched, I kept expecting, any second, to walk my face into a spider web or trip over a scurrying mouse.

As soon as I found an egg, I made a cradle to hold it by gathering up the hem of my dress. Patsy and Anetha did the same, the way we'd seen Mama gather up her apron. She used to go with us to search for eggs, and she'd taught us not to mess with a hen settin' on a nest. To demonstrate what would happen, she reached toward the hen as if she planned to take the eggs from the nest. That hen started ruffling her feathers and making all kinds of racket like she was ready to fight Mama. Whoever came up with the saying "mad as a *wet* hen" got it wrong. "Mad as a *settin'* hen" is more like it.

Occasionally, after the hens had kept their eggs warm for a long time, we watched as the eggs began to crack and the little biddies struggled to get out and break free from their shells. The baby chicks were wet and ugly at first, but after their downy feathers dried, they became fluffy and yellow. Eventually, of course, they lost their yellow down and turned the color of their mothers.

Mama said White Leghorns were the best layers, but we also had Rhode Island Reds. When Mama used the eggs in cooking, she always checked as she cracked them to make sure they didn't have any red spots. If she saw a spot, she threw the egg out, for she said that indicated the egg had been fertilized. I thought that meant the hen had laid it too close to a bag of fertilizer in the barn, causing it to spoil.

"Can we make flowers now?" Anetha asked when we returned to the house with the eggs—a dozen or so in total, cradled in our gathered skirts.

"Yep. We can," Mama said, as she collapsed her padded wooden ironing board.

We put the eggs in a bowl, which Mama set inside the pie safe. They'd keep there until she fried them for breakfast, put them in a cake or pie, or traded them to Mr. O. C. Jones for something off his rolling store.

Mama sliced the corncobs the way you might a banana to put on cereal. Cutting a dry cob required a razor-sharp knife, but that wasn't a problem since Mama kept all her kitchen knives sharp. "You're more apt to cut yourself with a dull knife than a sharp one," she said more than once. That didn't make exact sense to me, but she was always sharpening her knives on a whetstone or having Daddy do it.

Speaking of Daddy, the wire he used for baling hay made perfect stems for our corncob flowers. Using wire cutters, Mama snipped it into pieces about seven inches long that we stuck into the soft center of each corncob slice. Next came the fun part—dyeing the cob flowers like Easter eggs.

Mama set several teacups on the cook table, filled them with water, and added red, yellow, and blue food coloring. Then, we got busy dipping.

"Look at my red one," Anetha said. "Ain't it purty?"

"I'm coloring mine yellow," I said, "like a buttercup."

Patsy had her flower in the blue dye but took it out and nudged my buttercup flower over with her blue one so she could put hers in yellow too.

"You messed mine up!" I said.

"Did not."

"Did too."

"Mama, Patsy messed up mine! It's turning green!" I didn't want a green flower. Whoever heard of a green flower?

"Well, you can dye another one yellow," Mama said. "Here, I'll give you some more cups so you can make orange and purple too."

Corncob flowers made with wooden skewers instead of wire.

As we dyed the corncob flowers, we put them into a Mason jar, and in spite of our bickering, we ended up with a bouquet as colorful as a rainbow.

"Beautiful!" Mama said, and I agreed completely.

Daddy noticed one day that our chickens were disappearing. "I think a fox is catching them," he said to Mama one morning. "We're gonna have to build a chicken yard with a high fence around it, like your daddy has."

Before long, one section of our yard had been cordoned off for the chickens. A tall fence surrounded it. Next, inside the fence, Daddy built a chicken coop. He called it a "brooder house."

Windows made of isinglass (mica sheets reinforced with wire) let in light during the day, and at night, the chickens could roost on the horizontal poles Daddy installed for them. He also equipped the space with electric lights, to keep baby chicks warm, even when the temperature dropped below freezing.

Mama and Daddy still ordered chicks a hundred at a time, and my sisters and I helped feed and water them daily. They drank from upside-down quart jars equipped with a special lid that served as a water trough. They'd lean their heads down to scoop water into their beaks and then lift their beaks toward the sky to let the water run down their throats.

As the chickens grew older, they were allowed out of the brooder house during the day where they could eat bugs and worms they found in the chicken yard, but we supplemented their bug-and-worm diet with chicken mash. And as they got older still, we, of course, shelled corn for them. Occasionally, we spread chopped-up oyster shells on the ground for them to eat so their eggshells would thicken.

The pullets seemed content to roam around in the chicken yard, but the roosters were always trying to fly over the tall fence, even though there was nothing on the other side of the fence to attract them. Mama said they were just showing off for the females. The roosters might think they were tough old birds, but Mama would wring their cocky little necks first—before she started with the pullets. She said the rooster meat got tough if she waited too long to butcher them. And they didn't fatten up like hens did. The hens made the best chicken pirleau (*puhr-low*), a chicken-and-rice dish as common to us as spaghetti is to Italians (recipe p. 429).

With the chickens confined to their own space now, we could walk barefoot in the yard close to the house, where we played, without stepping in poop. Another advantage to having a special place for the chickens was that gathering eggs was easier. For the most part, the hens laid their eggs around the chicken coop.

Though occasionally, one would lay an egg in a clump of weeds near the fence. Or one would make it over the high fence and lay it in the packhouse before Mama put her back in the chicken yard.

In earlier times, Mama might have just wrung that escaped chicken's neck and served it up for dinner. Back then, she'd surprise one, grabbing it by the neck as it scratched the ground looking for food. She'd swing it round and round until she heard the snap of its neck, then toss it to the ground. It always flopped around, its wings outstretched as if trying to fly. I didn't like to witness that. The sight of a struggling chicken always made my chest ache. Thank goodness Mama never made us kill a chicken. She did that job all by herself. Then, back in the kitchen, she'd bring a big pot of water to a boil, dip the chicken in that, and pull its feathers out. Sometimes she singed off the finest feather near the chicken's feet with a flame. Then, she might ask one of us to carefully go over the bird's skin and pull any pinfeathers out.

But now that we had a freezer, she sometimes butchered several chickens at once and put them in the deep freeze. On those days, she'd get Grandma to help her.

Over the years, Daddy and Mama ordered different breeds of chickens. While some might be better layers, Mama said she thought "white winedots" were the best tasting chicken, especially fried. (Later, I learned it was spelled Wyandotte, named after the Wyandot American Indians.)

As for myself, I could never tell any difference in the taste from one breed to another. But I did have a favorite piece—and believe me, I'd tried them all—wing, breast, pulley bone, short thigh, drumstick, back, neck, gizzard, liver, heart, and feet.

Mama never cooked chicken feet herself—said they were "too much trouble to clean for what little meat you got off them." But I tried a fried chicken foot at the Knights' house one Sunday and what meat was on the bony part reminded me of the gristly part of the gizzard, one of my favorite pieces. The crispy fried flour bits coating the foot made the thing pretty tasty. Still, Mama refused to fry chicken feet at home, and that was okay, since I liked the gizzard and loved the drumstick. Occasionally, I'd eat a pulley bone, too, just so I could use it to make a wish. Always the same wish. Oh, to sleep the night through and to wake up dry. *Would my wish ever come true?*

53

The Right One?

After my sisters and I helped Mama wash, dry, and put away the dishes one night after supper, our whole family moved out to the open hall in search of a cool breeze. School was out for the summer. I'd finished my first year with mostly Os.

As dusk gave way to darkness, the woods came alive with the soprano sounds of crickets and cicadas, punctuated by the occasional croak of a bullfrog. Daddy mocked the frogs, "Kneedeep. Kneedeep!"

From the edge of the porch, he pointed to the night sky, saying, "Look yonder at the Big Dipper." Or did he say "Little Dipper?" I could never identify either. Besides, I was more fascinated by the glow of lightning bugs as they floated from the woods into our yard.

Daddy walked over and pulled the string that turned on the naked light bulb in the open hall that shot through the center of our house. Tiny insects and fluttering moths flew to the bright light, making ping . . . ping . . . ping sounds as they hit the hot glass bulb.

Mama and Daddy each dragged a straight-backed chair under the light. She sat down to embroider a stamped scarf, and Daddy sat with his open Bible and Sunday school lesson book.

Meanwhile, my sisters and I jumped across wide boards that made up the porch floor to see who could jump the farthest.

There is a gap in my memory as to what happened next. I remember only that Anetha and I began to argue about something, and it escalated until we were yelling at one another. Daddy put down his Bible and started asking questions to get to the bottom of our argument. Anetha blamed me. I blamed her. And we kept arguing with one another.

"That's enough!" Daddy said suddenly and jumped to his feet, unbuckling his belt. "Y'all are both gonna get it. Then I'll know I got the right one."

My mouth dropped open and Anetha's eyes got as big as the tin saucers of our tea set.

One jerk and Daddy's belt snapped free from its loops. He doubled it over, clutching its buckle and tip in one hand. The sight, sound, and feel of what came next plays now in slow motion but high definition in my head: *Daddy plants himself on the edge of his chair, sits upright, spreads his knees wide, grabs me by one arm, flings me over one knee. The leather strap stings as it strikes my bottom and bare legs. After what seems like forever, he lets go and I sit on the floor bawling as Anetha gets the same treatment. I hear the leather strap hit her again and again. When Daddy finally releases her, she crawls across the floor and sits next to me.*

"Quit the squalling now," Daddy commanded, "or I'll give y'all something to cry about!"

Huddled together, backs to the hall wall, Anetha and I covered our faces and suffocated sobs. My chest felt as if it might burst as I held in the hurt.

Daddy sat back in his chair and picked up his Bible.

For a moment I heard no sound. Not even the crickets and cicadas in the woods.

54

Watermelon Teeth

One afternoon when my sisters and I stopped by our grand parents' house on the way home from school, Grandma seemed happier than I'd ever seen her.

"I got a letter from your Uncle Harold and Aunt Louise today," she said. "They're comin' to visit this summer! So you'll get to see your cousins Sheilah and Junior."

I'd seen these Indiana cousins only once in my life, but I remembered that Sheilah was close to my age and had curly hair like me. All I remembered about Junior was his flat head. But Grandma's excitement was contagious.

"When this summer?" I asked.

"They don't know the exact date," she said and opened the letter and began to read. After a sentence or two, my mind went to Junior's flat head.

He was just a baby when they visited last, a few years before, and the back of his head looked flat as a pot bottom. Mama and Grandma said it flattened out because Aunt Louise always put him down on his back to sleep. They thought babies should sleep on their tummies, so they wouldn't choke if they spit up. The other benefit, of course: a well-rounded noggin. But Aunt Louise didn't take their well-meaning advice. Every time she put Junior down, she laid him on his back.

Grandma didn't hold a grudge against Aunt Louise for ignoring her advice, though. I never heard her utter a bad word about her daughter-in-law. Actually, I don't remember that I ever heard her say anything bad about another person, period.

Most letters from Indiana ended with "Love, Harold and Louise," but Grandma recognized who wrote them. Aunt Louise often mentioned her own family, including her sisters—Virginia, Sadie, and Elgin—and her brother, Al. Grandma even received a few letters from Sadie and Elgin, people she never met, and one of them sent her a set of colorful china cups, which Grandma had displayed on her buffet where they collected trinkets and dust.

Aunt Louise's family seemed very close. She said some of them shared a house in Indiana: one family lived on the main level, and another lived in the basement. I'd never heard of a basement, but Grandma explained it was built underground underneath a house, with stairs going down to it. I couldn't imagine living underground with no windows for light.

In every letter, Aunt Louise said they hoped to visit soon. "Unfortunately," Grandma often said, "*soon* never comes." But she always seemed as proud as a cat with a caught mouse when she found a letter from Indiana in the mailbox, and even happier when Aunt Louise enclosed photographs of Sheilah and Junior.

In all those pictures, my cousins were wearing coats, knitted caps, and mittens. Most photos showed them playing in snow, so I thought it snowed all the time in Indiana. I wished I could see it. The only snow I'd ever seen was the artificial kind that failed to stick to our Christmas tree.

When Granddaddy Rye came in from the field and heard Grandma talking about our cousins coming that summer, he shook his head from side to side, and looked sad. "I wish they'd quit saying they're coming. Promises. Promises."

As it turned out, they came that summer, as promised. Not only did *they* come, they brought along Aunt Louise's brother, mother, and her mother's husband.

I noticed right away that they all talked funny, especially Aunt Louise's mother, Mrs. Petrosoft, and her husband. I could hardly understand a word they said. Only later would I learn that the Petrosofts had come to America from Turkey when Aunt Louise was a baby.

While everybody was busy hugging and exclaiming how happy they were to see one another and to meet Aunt Louise's family, I kept trying to get behind Junior, who was now three years old, so I could check out the back of his head. To my disappointment, it looked normal.

Their arrival coincided with watermelon season. So we celebrated that same afternoon by cutting open three melons on an outdoor table under the big oak trees next to my grandparents' house.

Left to right, back row: Granddaddy Rye, Grandma Rye, and Great-Granddaddy Tip. Front row: Anetha, Patsy, Junior, Sheilah, and me (holding the doll I got for Christmas).

Daddy could tell when a melon was ripe by thumping it with his fingers. "If the thump sounds flat," he said, "the melon is still green. If it sounds hollow, it's ripe." He demonstrated it to everybody, but to my ears all thumps sounded the same. Evidently there was something to his method, though, because I never witnessed Daddy cutting open a green melon. Each always had a slight crack between the seeds in its pink heart, the best part. Everybody gathered around and took the slices Daddy cut.

"Don't eat the white part," he said to Aunt Louise after she'd finished the red meat of her slice and started to eat near the rind.

"But it's good too," she said. "Reminds me of cucumbers."

"Well, we got plenty of melons and plenty of cucumbers, so you don't have to eat that."

I expected her to set that piece aside and get a fresh slice. But just as she had paid no attention to Grandma and Mama's advice about laying Junior on his back, she paid no mind to Daddy. She ate all the way to the green skin of the melon.

Truly, there was no need to do that. Melons were being hauled daily from the field by the trailer load. Granted, the melon buyers were a bit particular about the melons they bought. They didn't load for shipment any melon with a blemish like a sun spot, or any melon not perfectly shaped. But the rejects—culls, Daddy called them—were just as good to eat as picture-perfect melons. So even after a field had been picked over for market, we had enough culls remaining in the field to feed us all summer. In fact, we often ate only the heart and tossed the seedy part back into the field for the crows.

"Mama, will you make us some watermelon teeth?" Anetha asked.

"Sure," Mama said and borrowed Daddy's pocketknife.

"What are watermelon teeth?" Sheilah asked.

"I'll show you," Mama said as she took Anetha's leftover rind. She cut off a thin strip of the white about the size of a stick of gum and sliced into one side to form individual teeth. Anetha took the set of teeth from Mama and slipped them between her lips and her own perfectly-straight front teeth.

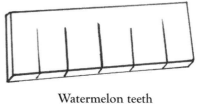

Watermelon teeth

"Yook at me," she said with her new buck teeth.

"Aunt Ethel, I want some!" "I want some teeth!" Sheilah and Junior begged. So, before long, Mama had made teeth for all of us kids—even for Aunt Louise.

Unfortunately, the watermelon teeth combined with their strange accents made it impossible to understand our visiting relatives. They couldn't understand us either. We soon grew tired of saying "Huh?" So we took out our teeth and threw them away. Everybody, that is, except Aunt Louise, who promptly ate hers.

55

Different

When I started second grade, Mrs. Johnson's room looked different. The door to the cloakroom was gone. Sealed up. Painted over. Over the summer, the cloakroom had been turned into a girls' restroom, complete with a white porcelain sink and three flushable commodes within private stalls. We entered through a door off the hallway.

Plus, an addition out back included a porch and a boys' restroom with a long trough where several boys could stand and pee at once. I know because my sisters and I got a glimpse of the thing one Saturday when we went to school with Mama to prepare for a Home Demonstration Club potluck supper. While Mama was busy inside, my sisters and I went out to investigate. Unfortunately, just as we stuck our heads in that door, Mama came out and told us to get back inside and help her sweep up. Consequently, I never got an up-close look at that pee trough, or what the adults called a urinal.

The back porch also featured a water fountain, and it was much nicer than the water fountains we sometimes drank from in Mc-Crory's dime store in Live Oak. The one in town accommodated only one person at a time. Ladyland's white porcelain fountain, resembled the boys' long pee trough, except it contained several spouts with chrome knobs to turn the water on. No longer did we have to get a buddy to pump water for us at the iron pump in the schoolyard. Each person simply twisted his or her own knob and cool water gushed from a fountainhead. When our faces were red and sweaty after recess—and if no teacher was watching—we could even cool off our faces there.

Another difference between the McCrory fountain and Lady-land's was that we had no sign above it that read "Whites Only." Rural colored students, so Daddy said, had their own school over at Bakersville, about five miles away. I didn't know then that it was *the law*—that black children in our area couldn't go to Ladyland even if they wanted to, just as we country kids couldn't go to primary or elementary school in town, even if we wanted to.

Not only did Ladyland School look different when I started second grade, I looked different, having lost two front teeth over the summer. When my teeth first began to loosen, I'd rock them back and forth with my tongue. This grossed Mama out. She threatened to tie a string around the loose teeth, tie the other end to a door knob, and slam the door. She'd tried that on Patsy's first loose tooth a few years before, but when she started to tie the string around the tooth, Patsy had a conniption. She kept dancing around as Mama tried to attach the string, and the loose tooth came out on its own.

It surprised me every time one of us woke up to find a dime in place of a baby tooth we'd tucked under our pillow the night before. I didn't question how the Tooth Fairy could fly from house to house during the night, collecting teeth from boys and girls all over the world, since I knew Santa flew his sleigh all over the world. And just as I imagined what Santa's home at the North Pole looked like with elves scurrying about, I imagined the Tooth Fairy's house. I saw it as a stone-looking cottage, like the one shown in the story of Hansel and Gretel, but I figured the tiny stones were actually teeth. Even the cobblestone streets and stone fences were no doubt made of teeth. What puzzled me, though, was how the Tooth Fairy could take a tooth from under my pillow without waking me up. *That* was almost impossible to believe.

I was, of course, thrilled each time the Tooth Fairy left me a dime in trade for my tooth. A dime for a Sugar Daddy off the rolling store. Yummy. But that summer, after loosing two teeth, I soon got sick and tired of people calling me "snaggle-tooth" and asking me to sing, "All I Want for Christmas Is My Two Front Teeth."

For years, Granddaddy Tip had sung to me, telling me I was the "prettiest little girl in the county." But soon after I started to second grade, a boy at school set me straight.

"You've got rabbit teeth!" Truett Johnson said, grinning as he pointed at my mouth.

My new teeth were coming in notched, like saw blades.

In the days that followed, Truett kept calling me "Rabbit Teeth," and the other boys began picking it up. I now felt like I was the ugliest little girl in the county.

I tried to stop smiling so my teeth wouldn't show. If I couldn't stifle a grin because something was funny, I covered my mouth with my hand.

When the school photographer came to take pictures, I was determined not to crack a smile for the camera. He set up shop in the middle of the classroom—a big square backdrop, a short stool, and a three-legged contraption to which he attached his camera. We students lined up, to take turns sitting on the stool long enough for him to snap a picture. As I stood in line, waiting my turn, I shifted from one foot to the other, nervous because everybody was watching, just as they watched when we lined up for shots.

"Look right here, and smile," the photographer said, tapping the camera as I perched on the stool. I looked but didn't smile.

"Say cheese," he said. I didn't.

"No smile for me?" he said. "Is that because you had turtle eggs

for breakfast?"

I grinned.

Flash!

"Okay, sweetie. Next?"

I got up and stomped back to my desk, mad at myself that I'd let him trick me.

A few weeks later, Mrs. Johnson handed out packets of pictures for us to take home to our parents. Everybody started looking at theirs. When I opened mine, all I could see staring back at me were my ugly rabbit teeth.

On the walk home that afternoon, my sisters and I looked at each other's photos. I was surprised that neither of them said one word about my ugly teeth. Then Pasty asked, "Why'd you button up your sweater like that? Your collar is all wrinkled. And I can't believe you didn't comb your hair."

I felt the ugliest I'd ever felt. I wanted to cry, but kept from it.

When we got home, we handed our picture packets to Mama. She opened each one, saying, "These are good"—even when she looked at mine. Until that moment, I didn't know Mama needed glasses.

56

After the Cakewalk

The sun slid behind the tall pines, spindly scrub oaks, and sweet gums, casting long shadows on Ladyland School's baseball diamond. As the sun set, folks from the community filed through the school's front door. Adults toted layer cakes, steaming pots of butterbeans and acre peas, and pressure cookers of pirleau. We'd arrived at the school for a nighttime fundraiser sponsored by the Ladyland Home Demonstration Club. The group had already raised money to buy draw curtains for the stage, several new leather catcher's mitts, and many other useful items.

As the menfolk milled around the school, the ladies set containers of hot food on Mrs. Johnson's big desk and placed the cakes on a nearby table. After a crowd gathered in the room, one of the men said the blessing, and everybody formed a long line.

While waiting in line, I stared at the table filled with cakes—Mama's with seven-minute frosting and coconut, some with dark chocolate and chopped pecans, and others that looked equally yummy. I wished I could start with the cake table. A few cakes had been cut for dessert. Others, including Mama's, were uncut, reserved for cakewalk prizes.

Earlier that afternoon, my sisters and I had helped draw the cakewalk diagram on the wood floor with chalk. The circle, made up of hopscotch-like squares, covered a large portion of the floor. A number on each square corresponded with a number written on a tiny slip of paper inside a small paper sack—numbers to be drawn for cakewalk winners.

To participate in the cakewalk, you paid a dime and stood on a numbered square. Before long, a person stood on every number, and the music started. We marched around and around the circle, keeping time to the music. When the music stopped, we stopped, and someone not playing the game pulled a number from the paper sack. The winner could choose any cake to take home. They could, of course, slice up the cake right then and there and share it,

> **Home Demonstration Clubs**
> Home Demonstration Clubs grew out of the Smith-Lever Act of 1914. The act mandated that each state establish a Cooperative Extension Service through the state's land-grant university. The Extension Service hired professionals who served as agents in rural areas to educate and demonstrate improved methods of farming and homemaking. Home Demonstration Clubs met monthly in members' homes to learn about gardening, canning, freezing, sewing, community outreach, leadership, etc. Mama's club raised money for our school through suppers and cakewalks, and by getting together to make quilts which they raffled off.

if they chose to. But few people did, since they'd then go home empty-handed.

I marched and marched, using up all four of the dimes I'd saved up, but didn't win. I was glad when Daddy won, knowing he would share his cake at home. I wasn't surprised when he chose Mama's coconut cake. Everybody knew Mama had baked it, and the men made all kinds of comments, ragging Daddy about taking his wife's cake. He seemed to get a kick out of all the kidding. You'd think Mama would have been flattered that Daddy chose her cake, but Mama looked embarrassed. She never liked to be the center of attention.

Usually when we had a supper and cakewalk at Ladyland,

everybody left soon after all cakes had been won and the room had been cleaned up. But that night, Mrs. Hunter, then the president of the Ladyland Home Demonstration Club, asked who wanted to stay and play "Kiss the King's Ring." I'd never heard of this game, but for once I wasn't yet sleepy and was glad Daddy said we'd stay.

"All you men go out and wait in the hall while we get set up," Mrs. Hunter said. But as the men left for the hallway, she pulled one burly man back into the room, saying she wanted him to act as the king. Another lady guarded the door to make sure the men didn't peek. We could hear them in the hall asking one another, "What do you think they're up to?" and one yelled out, "You ladies, hurry up in there!"

Meanwhile, Mrs. Hunter told the king to sit on the throne, which was Mrs. Johnson's chair that had been placed in the center of the cakewalk diagram. Mama draped a big towel around the king's shoulders—his robe—and another lady set a yellow construction-paper crown on his head. The women rolled up one of his pants' legs, positioned his bare outstretched hairy leg on a short stool, so his heel rested on a red pillow, and placed a clunky gold-colored ring on his big toe—the ugliest big toe I'd ever seen. Mama slipped a similar ring—it looked like Daddy's Suwannee High School class ring—on the ring finger of the king's right hand.

With everything set, Mrs. Hunter went out to the hall, blindfolded a man with a white handkerchief, and led him into the "king's chamber."

"To gain admittance to the king's court," she said to the man now standing blindfolded before the king, "you must bow low before the king and kiss his ring."

As the blindfolded man bowed, the king held his right hand over his foot so the kisser's lips touched only the ring on his finger. Then the king folded his arms to hide the ring on his finger. When the blindfold came off, the man who'd kissed a ring stared at the ring on that big ugly toe, made a face and looked as if he wanted to spit. He wiped his mouth with his hand and shook his head. But afterwards, he got to stay in the room and watch the next man's reaction to kissing the king's ring. Nearly every man acted the same way, wiping his mouth and shaking his head as he imagined he'd kissed the ring on his fellow farmer's ugly toe.

As the room filled with men who'd been tricked, they roared at the reactions of all the others when their blindfolds came off. Before long, those in the room clamored to act as king. Mrs. Hunter obliged, switching kings a few times. The game continued until every man in the hallway had been properly admitted into the king's chamber.

Unfortunately, the last man to kiss the ring never got to see the humor of the situation.

57

"Put Your Shoes On"

Mama was always reminding us to do stuff. "Go wash your hands before you eat." . . . "Put on your sweater or you'll catch a cold" . . . "Put your shoes on. The ground's wet."

"Do we have to?" I asked one day when she told us to put our shoes on. It had just rained and I liked the way the wet ground felt—smooth but crunchy on the soles of my feet. And many of the games we played outside worked better on rain-packed sand. We could get sharper lines when we drew hopscotch blocks. If playing marbles, the shooter rolled faster.

Mama answered me with a question. "Do you want to catch ground itch?"

I put on my shoes. That day. But it seemed to me that Mama was overly worried about diseases I'd hardly heard of. We'd had all kinds of shots and vaccinations at the Suwannee County Health Department in Live Oak before we started to school. Each of us had a brown scar to prove we'd been vaccinated for smallpox. We'd also had shots for diphtheria, tetanus and whooping cough. I had scars to prove that too. Nobody knew why my arm reacted to certain shots, leaving behind scars within deep dimples.

Now, once a year, a nurse from the Health Department came to

Ladyland School and gave all of us kids booster shots.

"Take this home and ask one of your parents to sign it," the teacher said one day as she passed out permission slips.

I hated getting shots at school. If you cried, other kids made fun of you. "Crybaby, crybaby," the boys teased.

I'd been thinking about the dreaded "shot day" ever since Mama signed my permission slip. "Do you think the nurse will come today?" I asked Anetha and Patsy as we walked to school one morning. They shrugged like *they* weren't scared.

Sure enough, that was the day.

Dressed in white from head to toe, the nurse set up shop in the middle of Mrs. Johnson's classroom. She positioned her chair next to a table, now covered with a white cloth. The table held jars of cotton balls, a large bottle of alcohol, tiny glass bottles with red rubber stoppers, and several glass hypodermic syringes.

Mrs. Johnson told each row to line up. My line inched forward. I wiped my sweaty palms on my skirt as my heart beat faster. I got a whiff of the alcohol, and suddenly I was up next.

"Okay, sweetie, pull up your sleeve."

My sleeve up, I stood like a soldier at attention as the nurse swabbed my upper arm with a cold, alcohol-soaked cotton ball. "Relax your arm," she said as she pinched up the skin, "You'll feel just a little sting."

Relax? Who could relax?

As it turned out, the shot didn't hurt as much as I'd expected, and I thought that was it until next year. But before the nurse left that day, she handed a large box to the teacher and whispered something to her. When the bell rang at the end of the day, Mrs. Johnson took cardboard tubes from the box and handed one to each student.

"At home, take the metal cap off and follow the instructions inside the tube. It's a test for hookworms."

Hookworms? What was that?

The tube resembled the tube from an empty roll of toilet paper, except it was stiffer—couldn't be crushed. One end was sealed up; the other end had a metal cap.

At home, Mama read the instructions and said we should follow them to the letter:

Step 1. Complete the form below.

Step 2. Collect a stool specimen, place it in the enclosed bag, and seal it tight.

Step 3. Place the sealed bag in the cardboard tube along with the completed form, attach the enclosed label, and mail the tube by parcel post.

I suspect the instructions also included information about hookworms and what would happen if the problem wasn't treated.

On Saturday morning, after all of us had done our "jobs," Mama capped the tubes, put the labels on them, and told us to take them to our grandparents' house and put them in the mailbox. As Patsy raised the red flag on the big mailbox, I wondered if Mr. McNeill, our postman, would know what he was picking up.

> **Hookworm Disease**
> Widespread in the moist tropics and subtropics . . . the disease can indirectly cause the death of children by increasing their susceptibility to other infections. The larvae (immature form of the worm) penetrate the skin, where an itchy rash called ground itch may develop. The larvae migrate to the lungs via the bloodstream, enter the airways and cause coughing. After traveling up the windpipe, the larvae are swallowed. When the larvae are swallowed, they infect the small intestine and develop into adult worms. Iron deficiency anemia caused by loss of blood may result from heavy infestation. (*The New York Times*)

In a few weeks, the test results arrived and Mama looked shocked.

"Y'all have hookworms," she said.

Worms? We've got worms? How could that be?

Mama reminded us that we hadn't always worn shoes when we should have. "It's a lot easier to catch ground itch when the ground is wet," she said. "The literature said that 'moist skin makes it easier for the larvae to enter the soles of your feet'."

I was humiliated that I had hookworms and didn't want kids at school to know, even if they were taking the medicine too.

After that episode, Mama didn't have to tell me twice to put on my shoes. Unfortunately, she wasn't around to remind me to wear shoes when I visited the McPhatters.

58

The McPhatters and the Turpentine Camp

We'd been friends with the McPhatters since shortly after they moved into the community. Tonnie McPhatter and Patsy started first grade at Ladyland the same year, and the two of them hit it off right away. Smart, they both completed the first- and second-grade readers and spellers by the end of the year, so Mrs. Johnson said they could go straight to third grade. As it turned out, Mr. and Mrs. Mac refused to let Tonnie skip a grade. So the next year when Anetha started to school, she and Tonnie were both in Mrs. Johnson's room. They too became buddies. The McPhatters also went to our church, so our whole family soon got to know them.

Mr. Mac reminded me of Granddaddy Rye—small in stature but lean and tough as if he'd spent years in a saddle. Grandmotherly and plump, Mrs. Nellie McPhatter was an American Indian, Mama said, though I don't know how Mama came to that conclusion unless it was Mrs. Mac's dark hair and complexion. Tonnie resembled her father. Skinny as a rail, she had red hair and more freckles than Mama's pincushion had pins.

Mr. Mac was perhaps the only man in the community besides the preacher who didn't farm. Instead, he oversaw the turpentine camp, which some called *The Quarters* and old-timers called *The*

Rye Camp because Mama's Great-Uncle Billy Rye had served as the boss there for many years.

The turpentine camp was a dilapidated looking place, but the house the boss lived in was pretty nice. Its shape and size reminded me of my grandparents' house, but its walls were unpainted like ours. Behind it, several barn-like buildings stood. Or leaned. They'd seen better days. Boards were loose or missing, and the tin roofs were brown with rust and littered with leaves from oak trees. Several run-down cabins dotted the back of the camp. Anytime we passed there, we'd usually see a few colored people milling about and children playing under the shade of the big oaks. Tonnie had no brothers and sisters her age, and she enjoyed playing with the children who lived with their families in the camp.

Tonnie told us that one of the buildings at the camp was "the commissary," where you could buy tobacco supplies, candy, more candy, chewing gum, and other stuff. Off to one side of the camp, alone in the bright sunlight and in stark contrast to the rest of the old camp, stood the colored people's church, as white and bright as paint could make it.

"Why don't you stop at the camp and hire somebody?" I asked Daddy one day when we were about to pass the camp. He was on his way to Bakersville, the nearby colored community, to see if he could hire a man to help him put up a new wire fence.

"The men that live there are all 'under contract,'" Daddy said, and kept driving.

In time, I learned that the men at the camp worked long hours among the pine trees all over the county, harvesting pine tar for turpentine. Granddaddy Rye knew all about the process since his Uncle Billy had once been the camp's boss.

Using a tool called a "hack," the workers slashed the tree trunks at an angle. The slash, an inch or two wide, near the base of the tree, removed an eight-to-ten-inch strip of pine bark. Another slash was made from a different angle so the two bare streaks formed a *V*. Below the *V*, they nailed a piece of tin, and below that, a tin trough or box that was about a foot long and a few inches wide and deep. (In earlier times, they'd used clay cups or pots to hold the tar, but tin was "the latest.") The amber pine tar would ooze out of the tree and run into the trough, drop by sticky drop. It could take weeks to fill the trough. The men at the turpentine camp then collected the gooey tar and transported it back to the camp. The tar eventually ended up in another county for processing into turpentine.

One tree could be tapped several times, and each new *V* was made just above the other. Gradually, each pine tree would have a bare space a foot wide and several feet high up its trunk. People called the bare spot a "cat face" but it reminded me of a badly scraped leg.

Granddaddy Rye owned a hack like the workers at the camp used to create those cat faces on the pines. It weighed as much as one of Mama's wrought-iron skillets and its curved blade was scary-looking. Granddaddy said he got it

Granddaddy Rye's hack

while working for his Uncle Billy at the camp.

That was back when the state leased prisoners to the turpentine camp, he said. Granddaddy said his uncle hired him—when he was a young man—to guard those convicts. Daddy said that the use of convicts was outlawed in the 1920s because of the Martin Tabert Case, and after that, the owners of the camp got colored men to live at the camp and do the work for a small amount of pay.

According to Daddy, most of the tar being harvested around us was converted into rosin and turpentine that went into products such as soap, paint, varnish, and even medicines.

Mama said turpentine was also good for killing head lice. But she didn't have any on hand the day Anetha and I were sent home from school with a note saying we should be "treated for lice." She used kerosene instead.

> **Martin Tabert Case**
> In 1921, the brutal case of Martin Tabert, a white man from North Dakota who died while incarcerated and forced to work as a laborer, brought attention to convict leasing. *The Panama City Pilot* detailed his story and death on Feb 2, 1922, headlining the article as "Florida's disgrace." As a result, Governor Cary Hardee (who was from Live Oak) signed bills to outlaw convict leasing in Florida, though it was not completely abolished until 1923. *http://www.dc.state.fl.us/oth/timeline/1921.html*

I'm glad Daddy wasn't a smoker and standing nearby when Mama doused our heads. We then used nearly a whole jar of Lustre-Crème shampoo to get that kerosene smell out of our hair. Thank goodness, after that one treatment and Mama's warning not to share our combs at school, we never had to endure that again.

Another use for turpentine, Mama said, was to mix it with lard and use as a chest rub. "That's what my mama did when I was a little girl and got a cough," she said. Mama hated that treatment; that's why she rubbed our chests with Vick's salve, which just *contained* turpentine.

One Sunday during church, Tonnie McPhatter invited Anetha to go home with her to spend the afternoon. We kids often took play clothes to church in case we got invited someplace, and then

Workers slash pine trees to collect tar for turpentine.
https://www.floridamemory.com/photographiccollection/

331

following our afternoon visit, we'd meet up with our parents that night at the evening church service.

Anetha didn't know when she headed home with Tonnie that day just how exciting her afternoon would turn out to be. Tonnie later described it to Patsy and me in detail as Anetha nodded her head in agreement at every word:

> *"We were sitting at the dining table eating, still in our church clothes, when a man from the quarters came up to the back door and called to Daddy, wanting him to go outside. Daddy told him we were eating, that he'd see him later. So the man left.*
>
> *"When we finished eating, we all got up from the table, and Anetha and I went out to our porch to play. Daddy headed down to the quarters to the man's house. He was a single fellow. Mama sometimes fixed food and took it to people in the quarters when they got sick, and I played with their children, so I knew who was married, who had kids, and who didn't.*
>
> *When Daddy got close to the man's house, he called the man's name. I was standing on our back porch steps and saw the man come out on his porch. He and Daddy started talking, but then they got into an argument over something—maybe it was some dealings at the commissary, I don't know—but he evidently thought Daddy hadn't treated him right. Before my father could explain or do anything, the man reached inside his door for his rifle, aimed it at Daddy, and pulled the trigger. Either Daddy shoved the barrel away or it misfired because Daddy didn't get shot. But the man then hit him over his back with the gun—broke it in two— and Daddy fell to the ground.*
>
> *"Daddy normally carried his .38 pistol—a Smith and Wesson—with him. He seldom went to the quarters without it. I think he was always thinking there might be a fight or revolt.*

But that Sunday, he'd left his pistol at the house. It was probably a good thing too. 'Cause if he'd had his pistol, that man would be dead.

"When I saw what was happening, I ran inside and told Mama that the man had hurt Daddy. She got his pistol—tucked it under her apron—and headed down there. By then, Daddy was up off the ground. He met Mama about halfway to the house, but the man had run off.

"Mama told us kids to go in the house and get Anetha's play clothes 'cause they were going to take us over to the Warrens' house to stay until church that night. Anetha and I were scared witless, and I wanted to stay right by my daddy, but he told me everything would be okay and for us to go on in the house and get Anetha's stuff. So, we got her clothes off my bed, and they took us to the Warrens' house while somebody else went to town to get the law.

"After the sheriff came out, Daddy said they put the dogs out and those dogs tracked the scent of that man to my bedroom window. They think he crawled through it because they found his boots in my closet. He was probably in there when we went and got Anetha's clothes off my bed—right next to that closet! While in the house, he'd changed into a pair of my daddy's shoes. That confused the dogs.

"After I got home from the Warren's late that night, I was still scared. So, Daddy let me stay by his side. I even went with him and the sheriff back to the woods with the dogs for a little while. The sheriff—knowing the man had tried to shoot Daddy—kept saying, 'Mac, you ought to be dead.'

"They tried all night long to track that man down, but never did find him."

After that experience, it was a wonder Anetha wanted to go back to Tonnie's house, but she did, and I wanted to go too since I'd never been. I was overjoyed when, one Sunday, I got the chance. Tonnie invited both of us to spend the afternoon at her house. By then, I think Patsy thought she was too grown up to be with us so she didn't go.

At Tonnie's house, I immediately took to her mother because she cooked grits for dinner. After we finished eating, we changed into our play clothes and spent the afternoon exploring the quarters. Close to dusk, we heard music coming from the church at the edge of the camp.

"You want to go watch 'em?" Tonnie asked.

Mrs. Mac, nice lady that she was, didn't keep real close tabs on us, and we didn't take time to ask if it was okay. We ran toward the church, ducking behind palmetto bushes and cat-faced pines. When we got there, we ran around to the other side, out of sight of the McPhatters' house, and crouched low as we crawled up under one of the open windows. Gospel music spilled out, filling the air. The three of us eased our heads up so we could get a look inside. People of all ages were shouting as they moved their bodies and stomped their feet to the rhythm of the music as if dancing. But surely they weren't dancing. Daddy said dancing was a sin—because of the thing it could lead to, though Daddy would never explain the thing it led to. The music coming out that window made me want to dance too.

Suddenly the music stopped and we heard Mrs. Mac calling, "Tonnn—e-e-e."

Can we get back to the house without Mrs. Mac seeing us?

The answer was no.

On the way to church that night, I wondered if Mrs. Mac would tell Mama what we'd done. To my surprise, she didn't. More and more, I liked Mrs. Mac. Not only did she cook grits for me, she didn't tattle.

After that, my sisters and I spent many Sunday afternoons at the turpentine camp and were disappointed when we learned one

Sunday that Tonnie would be moving. Her father had accepted a job in Mayo, across the Suwannee River in Lafayette County.

"But we'll still go to Philadelphia to church," Tonnie assured us, "so we can still visit."

We were all racing around barefoot in the McPhatter's backyard in Mayo a few weeks after they moved. The ground was wet and they had no lawn. I was grinning from ear to ear because I was gaining on my sisters and Tonnie. Suddenly, a sharp pain shot through my right foot and I screamed, "Oww!" I thought I'd cut off my big toe, but I looked down and it was still there. I didn't even see any blood, but it hurt something awful. I fell to the ground, pulled my dirty foot up to my face to look at the sole of my foot. I had a deep, gash on the bottom of my big toe. Blood ran down my foot and dripped from my heel, soaking into the dirt, next to a half-buried broken Co-Cola bottle. Seeing that I was bleeding, the others came running back and Tonnie yelled, "Mama! Susanette's hurt!"

Mrs. Mac hurried from the house to see about me.

Will I lose my toe? Will I need stitches?

"I think we can fix that up," she said. I expected her to lead me into the house, wash my dirty foot with soap and water, pour something like Listerine on it like Grandma did for our scrapes and cuts, carefully wrap my big toe with sterile gauze, and secure it with white adhesive tape. To my surprise, Mrs. Mac reached down, grabbed a handful of black dirt, and clamped it around my big toe and held it tight.

"This will stop the bleeding," she said, gripping my foot.

She was right. With that grip, no blood could flow to my toe.

That night, I couldn't wear a shoe on that foot to church. And when Mama saw my toe covered in gritty dirt and dried blood— her mouth fell open.

"I can't believe she didn't clean up that cut," Mama said to Daddy on the way home from church. "I guess that's an old Indian

remedy, using dirt to stop the bleeding. But I'm afraid Susanette's gonna get a bad infection in that toe. I'm glad she's had
a tetanus shot."

My cut toe healed perfectly, with barely a scar.

Years later, I learned that Mrs. Mac had no American Indian
blood in her veins whatsoever. She was Jewish, like Uncle Itchy.

59

Ailments, Accidents, and Mama's Remedies

We seldom went to the doctor. If we got hurt at home or came down with some ailment, Mama usually had a remedy for it. If we caught impetigo from scratching mosquito bites, for example, she cured the infection with a stinky salve that the druggist, Dr. Culpepper, had mixed up. When we came down with sore eyes—gnats were bad in the summertime—she'd put drops in our eyes—yellow drops from a little green eyedropper bottle. Never mind that the drops turned our eyelids yellow and streak-dyed our cheeks; they cured our sore eyes. If I got an earache, something I got pretty regularly, she dropped in some warm oil. Only if Mama's remedy didn't work did we go to a doctor.

We didn't go to Dr. Price anymore, the one who delivered my sisters and me. He now limited his practice to a few patients who waited their turns in the dimly lit foyer of his stately two-story home on Pine Avenue. We'd been going to Dr. Adams for nearly as long as I could remember.

Daddy said that Dr. Adams moved into town the year after elderly Dr. Price delivered me. Right out of medical school, Dr. Adams set up his new practice on Ohio Avenue in the Parshley building, the same building where Daddy then worked as assistant county

337

agent. Daddy bumped into the new doctor on the sidewalk one day and welcomed him to town. Daddy told Mama about the new doctor and they decided to switch, since Dr. Price was seeing fewer and fewer patients in his home office.

Only a few days later, they had to take Anetha to Dr. Adams when she had a stomachache that Phillip's Milk of Magnesia didn't cure. Boy! I hated that stuff—like drinking liquid chalk. But complaining only caused Mama to say, "Be glad it ain't asafetida or nasty-tasting castor oil like I had to take when I was a little girl."

At that time, Daddy still owned his old Model A and drove us to town in it. He dropped us off at Dr. Adams's office before going to his job in the agricultural office. I was a baby then and know about this only from hearing my parents talk about it.

Mama had made no appointment, not because we didn't have a telephone—which we didn't—but because doctors in Live Oak didn't make appointments then. Patients waited their turns in one of the two waiting rooms, *white* or *colored*, until the nurse called their names.

Mama said the nurse put Anetha on the examination table since Mama had me in her arms. Patsy, then about three, stood beside the table. Dr. Adams walked in with a big smile on his face and asked, "What seems to be the problem today?"

Nodding toward Anetha, Mama said, "Her stomach is tore up."

Patsy whirled around, jerked up Anetha's dress to look, and said, "Mama, 'Netha's stomach ain't tore up!"

I always giggled when Mama told that story since Patsy was supposed to know everything.

A few months after Anetha's first visit to Dr. Adams, she had to go back for a real emergency.

"She started out with a sore spot on her stomach," Mama said. "Then she got one on her *fanny*." I giggled when I first heard Mama say the word fanny and wondered how Aunt Fanny Nabb, Grand-daddy Rye's niece who lived in Macclenney, felt about being named

Fanny. We'd visited the Nabbs once and played with our cousins Raleigh and Lissie—and Lissie's paper dolls. How I wished we had our own paper dolls.

"When Anetha first complained about the sore spots," Mama said, "I thought she had just bruised herself. But the place on her stomach turned into a hard knot and started swelling. Then, she got really sick and we knew she had to see a doctor."

The day Mama and Daddy rushed Anetha to Dr. Adams, they left Patsy and me with Grandma Rye.

"By the time we got Anetha to Dr. Adams office," Mama said, "her stomach looked like it would bust. After he examined her, he said she had abscesses that had grown inward and she needed surgery right away."

As Mama repeated the story, Daddy chimed in. "Problem was Live Oak had no hospital—this was 1945, and we didn't get a hospital until '48.[6] The nearest hospital was up in Valdosta [Georgia]. We didn't have good transportation either. I'd just sold my Model A and hadn't bought another vehicle. I'd borrowed Mr. Rye's old truck to get to town. When Dr. Adams saw Anetha's problem and found out what I'd driven to Live Oak, he went and got his own car, which would go a lot faster, and rushed us to the Little Griffin hospital in Valdosta. A doctor there by the name of Johnson—Dr. Alton M. Johnson—operated on Anetha.

"After the emergency surgery, Ethel stayed with Anetha," Daddy said, "and I rode back to Live Oak with Dr. Adams. Later, I drove up to Valdosta in Mr. Rye's truck and brought them home. The truck was reliable, just not fast."

The operation left Anetha with a two-inch scar on her stomach and a smaller one on her fanny, but she'd survived, thanks to Dr. Adams's rushing her to the surgeon. Our family would be forever

---

[6] The Suwannee Hospital was the first hospital built under the 1946 Hill-Burton Act, which provided funding to improve U.S. hospital services.

indebted to him.

Anetha recovered fully, but the extra attention she got while sick must have spoiled her. "She pitched a little tantrum one day," Mama said. "She got mad about something and hauled off and threw her drinking glass. It broke when it hit the floor. Not thinking straight, I told her to "clean it up." When she went to pick up the glass, she knelt down on a shard that cut her knee bad. I felt awful about it. I should have known better than to make her pick up that glass."

Around the time Anetha started to school, she hurt herself again. Mama had told her to take leftover cornbread, still in the heavy iron skillet Mama cooked it in, and dump it for the chickens. Instead of dumping it all at once, Anetha stood on the front porch and tossed tiny bits to the ground so she could watch the chickens fight over each little piece. Engrossed in the chickens, she tripped on an uneven porch board, lost her balance, and fell off the edge of the porch, which was several feet off the ground. The little finger of her right hand caught under that heavy iron skillet when it hit the ground and she landed on top of that skillet. She got up screaming and held up her hurt finger. A piece of flesh dangled by a thread and blood streamed down her hand and arm. From all the blood, I thought Anetha might bleed to death like the little Richardson boy, the one that got shot. But after Mama took a look, she just washed the blood off, dabbed Anetha's finger with Mercurochrome, and bandaged it with gauze and adhesive tape. The wound healed just fine, though it did leave a permanent scar on Anetha's pinky.

Scarred-up Anetha had another accident a year or so after that, and this one led to a doctor's visit. She and Patsy came home from school one day with plans to make paper dolls like Lissie Nabb's, using pictures cut from a *Sears and Roebuck* catalog. Patsy got Mama's sharp-pointed scissors and was wielding them when Anetha got too close. The point of the scissors stuck one of Anetha's eyes. She screamed and Mama came running. Daddy happened to be nearby, so he and Mama took Anetha to the doctor in Grand-daddy's truck after leaving Patsy and me with our grandparents. Although I liked spending time there, I hated not being in the doctor's office to see with my own eyes what was happening to Anetha's injured one.

When they returned, she had a big bandage over that eye. She said Dr. Adams put salve in it. Mama made her keep it covered except when Mama added more salve or changed the bandage. An-etha wore the patch for several days and would never see quite as well after that.

As for Patsy and me, we saw Dr. Adams due to sickness a few times, but never for injuries—not that we didn't get hurt. Like I already mentioned, Patsy burned her foot bad on a hot brick. She also stepped on a rusty nail while barefoot. After both foot inju-ries, she recovered, though that rusty nail did leave some rust in her foot.

One injury left me with a C-shaped scar on my right pointer fin-ger. Mama said I acquired that scar before I could walk. I crawled over to her Singer treadle machine while she was sewing and got too curious about the spinning flywheel. She didn't know my fin-ger had gotten stuck between the belt and wheel until the damage was done.

My second scar resulted from striking a match at age five. I'd begged Mama to let me strike it when she prepared to light the oil lamp because the electric lights had gone out.

"Well, I guess you need to learn," she said, "but let me show—"

"Mama, I know how," I protested for I had seen matches struck all my life. She and Daddy struck them when they lit the fat lighter'd to start a blaze in the fireplace. Granddaddy Rye used matches to light cigarettes. And Granddaddy Tip constantly relit his pipe un-der my nose when I sat in his lap. So I knew how to strike a match and wished everybody would stop treating me like a baby.

A bit reluctantly, Mama gave me the box of kitchen matches. I held the box with my left hand, and took out a match with my right. I scratched the tip hard on the sandpaper side of the box. As I did, the end of that match exploded. Its blazing tip broke off and landed between the fingers of my left hand. I screamed as I dropped the box. Matches scattered across the floor as I fanned my hand back and forth, fingers wide, to cool it off, not knowing I was making the flame between my fingers grow bigger. Mama threw a dishtowel over my hand, smothering the flame, then brushed the smoking, charred bit from between my fingers. *Owwwww!*

"Baby! Baby! Oh, honey," Mama said as she ushered me to the water shelf in the open hall. At that moment, I didn't mind being called Baby. Mama turned on the spigot so the water might cool the burn but it kept burning, burning, burning.

Daddy didn't come home until dark. By then, I had stopped crying and a puffy white bandage of gauze and adhesive tape encased my left hand.

"She wanted to learn to strike a match," Mama explained to Daddy when he asked about my bandage. "The match she struck must've had a big glob of sulfur on the tip. I didn't even think to check the match before I let her strike it."

"With your hand padded up like that," Daddy said to me, "you can be a boxer like Joe Lewis." He playfully jabbed at me with his fists and made me laugh.

But a few days later, I frowned when a neighbor saw my bandaged hand and warned Mama. "Them burned fingers bandaged together like that will grow together. That young'un will have a hand like a duck's foot."

Mama wasn't sure the woman knew what she was talking about, but without consulting a doctor, she feared taking a chance. She removed the bandage, smeared greasy salve on my blistered, raw skin, and rewrapped my fingers separately. This made them hurt more, but I knew I had to grin and bear it if I didn't want a duck's foot for a hand.

My third scar resulted from jumping off the back of Daddy's tractor. I was standing on the drawbar—a *U*-shaped bar behind the tractor used for connecting a piece of farm equipment like a plow or trailer. The drawbar had some haywire wrapped around it, which Daddy sometimes used to further secure the tongue of the equipment to the drawbar. I didn't notice that a sharp, jagged end of the wire stuck out from the drawbar a half-inch or so. When I jumped backwards off the drawbar, I didn't quite clear the point of that wire. It cut a streak from my knee all the way up my leg. It left a scar the size of a long-leaf pine needle, which would always be more prominent when my legs tanned.

All of us caught the chicken pox and measles, but these didn't require a doctor's visit. With chickenpox, all of us broke out at about the same time. Anetha got off light. She had only three tiny pox on her whole body. Patsy's case wasn't severe either, but I had pox all over, including on my scalp and in my thick eyebrows. One left a scar in one eyebrow like a cowlick.

When we caught German measles, Anetha had the worst case. She had bad chills and a high fever. Since the fireplace heated the living room, Mama let her sleep on the couch. Anetha shivered so hard her teeth rattled, even after Mama covered her with several quilts. Finally, Mama shoved the couch from under the glass windows on the north wall to the interior wall next to the kitchen. Anetha finally stopped shivering.

I don't even remember having measles, but I do remember the earaches I got regularly. And as I grew older, they got worse. Sometimes my ears throbbed so much that I had the urge to bang my head against the wall. I had trouble falling asleep, though once I did, I slept soundly and woke up to find I'd had another accident. I didn't know what I wanted most now—to stop having earaches or to stop waking up wet.

The last earache I'd had, soon after I turned seven, lasted several days. The oil Mama dropped in made it feel better for just a minute or two and then the pain returned. So she finally took me to see Dr. Adams. He looked in both my ears, then told me to open my mouth wide and say *Ahhhh*.

"Her tonsils are quite enlarged and need to come out," he told Mama. "I recommend you have it done before she gets much older. Getting the tonsils out should help with the earaches. I suggest you take her to Dr. Johnson in Valdosta."

Back at home, Mama told Daddy what Dr. Adams had said. He seemed to agree. "Yeah, you know I had my tonsils out when I was a kid. In the orphanage, they took everybody's out—mine, both my sisters' and Ira's."

But I still hadn't seen Dr. Johnson and I still had my tonsils.

60

The Germany Question

Uncle Raz and Aunt Katy hardly had time to sit down on my grandparents' front porch before Granddaddy Tip asked Uncle Raz the question he'd been asking everybody lately.

"Aye, God, Buddy, have you ever been to Germany?"

Uncle Raz rubbed his chin and responded with a question of his own. "Why do you ask, Uncle Tip?"

"Aye, God, Buddy, folks say you gotta cross an ocean to get to Germany. But it ain't so."

"Is that right?" Uncle Raz scrunched up his eyebrows and cocked his head.

"Yep. The only water I crossed was at the back of C.G.'s field. I crossed it on a ten-foot log, and then I was there."

Even I knew that Germany wasn't behind Daddy's field. I knew it was overseas. Where *exactly* overseas, I wasn't sure, but I knew Cousin Thomas Lee Boatright had been captured and held prisoner there during the war. I also knew the only water beyond Daddy's field was the Suwannee River, and it was way wider than ten feet. Plus, if you crossed it, you wouldn't be in Germany. You'd be in La-fayette County near Mayo, where Uncle Raz and Aunt Katy lived.

They weren't really my aunt and uncle, but my sisters and I

had been taught to call them that. Aunt Katy was the daughter of Granny Dosia's brother Sammy. So that made Aunt Katy and Grandma Rye first cousins, and us kids—well, I don't know what that made us, but we liked Aunt Katie and Uncle Raz. They sometimes brought candy when they dropped in.

Some visitors, when asked the Germany question, tried to change the subject. Others let Granddaddy ramble on as Uncle Raz did, acting interested. But within a minute or two, they'd hear the same question again.

"Aye, God, Buddy, have you ever been to Germany?" followed by "Aye, God, Buddy, folks say you gotta cross an ocean to get to Germany. But it ain't so."

And if they stayed ten minutes, they'd hear it again and again, like a broken record. Eventually, even those who tried to act interested at first would finally shake their heads in bewilderment.

Granddaddy Tip might, on occasion, ask some other question when a visitor first walked up, like, "Aye, God, Buddy, how ya doin' today?" or, "Aye, God, Buddy, do you think we gonna get any rain?" But that didn't mean the Germany question wasn't coming. Friends and family tried to set Granddaddy Tip straight about Germany's location, but Granddaddy Tip thought he knew better.

From time to time, I overheard adults discussing Granddaddy Tip's "state of mind," but nobody talked about it with us kids. Not even the day a woman visitor showed up at my grandparents' house "to check on him."

The afternoon she arrived, Mama and Grandma were in the kitchen washing dishes after dinner. Granddaddy and Daddy were out back somewhere. Granddaddy Tip was in his usual spot on the front porch. Patsy, Anetha, and I were playing follow-the-leader and attempting cartwheels in the front yard when we heard a car coming. It slowed and pulled off the road near the front gate.

"Grandma! Mama!" we yelled toward the screened door. "We got company! A lady! All by herself!" A woman behind the wheel was an unusual sight. Neither Mama nor Grandma knew how to drive.

"Get out and come in!" we yelled to the visitor, our normal greeting to anyone who stopped at our grandparents' gate, or ours.

Grandma and Mama came out to the porch and stood wiping their wet hands on their aprons as the lady stepped out of the car wearing high heels and a hat, as if she'd come from church. She smoothed her skirt, smiled at us, and said, "Hello."

Once on the porch, she reached out her hand to Grandma, saying, "I'm Miss Dix—Dorothy Dix." She shook Mama's hand too, then looked over at Granddaddy Tip and smiled as she added, "I was Mr. Lanier's nurse in the state hospital."

Hospital? When was Granddaddy Tip in the hospital?

"I happened to be in this area, Mr. Lanier," she said to Granddaddy Tip, "so I wanted to stop by and see you. How are you?"

I don't remember what anybody said back to her, but Granddaddy Tip had the biggest smile on his face, like he was really pleased to see this nicely dressed woman asking how he was.

Granddaddy Rye and Daddy soon pushed open the screen door and came out onto the porch dragging chairs so all the adults could sit. After more introductions, they sat around laughing and talking for what seemed like forever while my sisters and I horsed around in the yard, listening to snippets of adult conversation.

Later in the afternoon, Miss Dix said she had to be going. But before she left, she asked Granddaddy Tip to walk out into the yard with her, where they posed for a picture. Mama snapped it and handed the camera back to Miss Dix. A few weeks later, Grandma received a copy of the photograph in the mail.

My sisters and I never did find out exactly when Granddaddy Tip was in the state hospital in Chattahoochee, though we eventually learned that Grandma Rye decided she had to have him committed after he'd threatened Granddaddy Rye with a knife. Mama would admit, years later, that friction always existed between those two. She said Granddaddy Tip never thought her daddy was good enough for her mama, the precious daughter he sometimes called Queen Delma. Mama said that after she and Daddy married, her grandfather even said to her father one day during a heated argument, "You ain't half the man C. G. Howell is."

But at the time, I knew none of that. From time to time, my sisters and I asked questions but we usually got vague answers. We found out more just by eavesdropping on the adults when they didn't know we were listening. They said it was interesting that Granddaddy Tip's

Dorothy Dix poses with Great-Granddaddy Tip.

nurse had almost the same name as the famous *Dorothea* Dix, from the Civil War days—the "crusader for the mentally ill." They thought that what Miss Dix had told them—that one of Granddaddy Tip's doctors in the state hospital was German—might have something to do with his thinking he'd been to Germany. And they wondered what he did that caused them to confine him in a straitjacket. By the way they talked, I knew this jacket was not just an ordinary jacket.

One day we asked Daddy about it. He said it was a canvas-like bag with straps and buckles that kept a person from moving. The more Daddy explained this jacket, the more I wished he wouldn't. I didn't like the picture that formed in my head of Granddaddy Tip strapped down so he couldn't move. And no matter how I tried, I could never erase that picture from my mind.

But at least Granddaddy Tip was home now where he could sit in his rocking chair all day, smoke his pipe, watch the squirrels chase one another, and ask visitors if they'd ever been to Germany.

As time passed, Granddaddy Tip slept more and more while sitting in his rocker, his crooked stem pipe dangling from his lips. My sisters and I would watch him sleeping, expecting his pipe to fall from his lips any moment.

When he awoke, he'd take out the small box of matches he kept in his sweater pocket and try to relight the pipe. After striking several matches and swearing under his breath, he'd ask us to dump the drool-dampened tobacco. One of us would take the pipe to the edge of the porch, bang its bowl against the edge of the concrete floor until its soggy contents fell into Grandma's flower bed, and give it back. He'd refill its bowl with fresh tobacco, and before long, he'd be puffing away.

He didn't sing as much now as he used to. But then I didn't sit in his lap much either.

"Papa," Grandma Rye said one day when she came to the porch as Granddaddy Tip was trying to relight his pipe. "Don't start that nasty thing up again. I want you to come inside and take a bath."

"I don't need no dang bath," he replied.

"Yes, you do! It's been two weeks now since you bathed and I've already drawn the water in the tub for you."

The two of them argued back and forth a while, but finally he stood. Mumbling and grumbling, he followed her into the house, shuffling his feet down the hall and into the bathroom. By the time he reached the bathroom door, my sisters and I had crept inside the house. After Grandma shut the door behind him and went into the kitchen, we sisters hovered nearby, listening.

First, we heard him talking to himself, then we heard water splashing, and finally he began the song he sang every time Grandma made him bathe: "Way, down upon the Suwannee River, far, far, away. That's where my heart is turning ever, that's where the old folks stay."

Part VI

Change in the Air

61

The Old Touchton Place
1952

In the spring, my sisters and I got the surprise of our lives. We overheard Mama and Daddy talking about building a new house. This wasn't the first time they'd mentioned wanting a new house, but always before, their talk sounded more like a dream than a plan. This was different.

"After the good crop we had last year and the way things are looking this year," Daddy said to Mama, "I think it's time that we go ahead and build a new house. This summer."

What? This summer? My sisters and I couldn't believe our ears. We made our presence known and began to bombard them with questions. Where? What would the new house look like? Who would build it? How long would it take?

"Well, it didn't flood this spot in '48," Daddy said, "so we're gonna tear this house down and build the new one right here."

"Well, where are we gonna live when you tear our house down?" Anetha asked.

"With Grandma and Granddaddy!" I answered. Where did Anetha think?

"No." Daddy said. "Curtis and Loiselle Johnson said we can live in their old house on the old Touchton place."

I much preferred to live with Grandma and Granddaddy, but I knew pouting never changed Daddy's mind.

"We've been saving these blueprints for seven years," Daddy said as he began to unfold map-size sheets that showed the layout of the house. "We ordered 'em from the *Farm Journal* magazine when Susanette was just a baby."

I liked that Daddy said "was" just a baby.

We counted the rooms on the house plan—*nine*, and not one but *two* bathrooms. I didn't know anybody who had *two* bathrooms.

Daddy said he'd talked with builder Leo Dunham in Live Oak.

"Leo said he can build the house in six weeks—after we finish puttin' in the tobacco." By puttin' in, Daddy meant after we had gathered, cured, and sold the tobacco. "The new house will be finished about the time you girls start back to school in September."

I couldn't believe my ears until Daddy took us one day to see the place where we'd live while Daddy tore down our old house and the new one went up. Although the Johnsons owned the place and had lived there several years before building themselves a new house a mile or two away, everybody still called it the old Touchton place.

The house sat in the woods, about a quarter mile off the road we traveled to Live Oak, about two miles north of our grandparents' house. Outside, the house resembled ours: old and weathered. But it had no open hallway like ours. As soon as Daddy's Jeep rolled to a stop, we hopped out to look around. We entered through the unlocked front door. Inside, the layout reminded me of my grandparent's house in reverse. Bedrooms on the right instead of the left. But there was no paint on the walls and no bathroom like theirs.

It all happened so fast, there was hardly any time to think about all the change that was taking place.

At the end of July, with the tobacco crop "put in," we moved out of the home I'd lived in all my life and up to the Touchton place. I felt excited yet sad. Mama called that day "Bittersweet."

62

Shocking News

As we got settled in the old Touchton place, Daddy worked nearly every day at our old house—tearing it down.

"We're saving some of the old heart-of-pine lumber to use in the new house," Daddy told Mama one night at supper. She seemed pleased. He also told her they salvaged the square porcelain sink he'd installed in her old kitchen. "We'll put it in the utility room so your new washing machine can drain into it."

A washing machine? I couldn't believe my ears.

I pictured it with lots of tubs sitting around it like Grandma's Speed Queen wringer washer, not knowing Daddy and Mama planned to buy the latest "spin-dry" washer, which required no extra rinse tubs.

The first Sunday afternoon in August, Daddy took us back to our old "house," now just a pile of lumber and tin. Even the doodlebug homes in the sand under the old house were gone. I found only large footprints where the doodlebugs lived.

We were still there looking around at the mess when a neighbor drove up and delivered bad news. He said Dr. Adams had been shot that morning.

"How is he?" Daddy asked.

"Dead. Shot dead in his office."

Most doctors didn't see patients on Sunday, but Dr. Adams did. *Why would anyone kill Dr. Adams—the doctor who had saved Anetha's life?*

We didn't see the article that came out in the *Florida Times Union*, the Jacksonville newspaper, but we saw a similar article that appeared in the next issue of the *Suwannee Democrat*, with a large headline that read: *Dr. Adams Slain by Negress.*

The murder was all anybody talked about for the next few days. Rumors flew about the *why*.

We didn't go to Dr. Adams's funeral, but we heard the big First Methodist Church in Live Oak couldn't hold all the people who showed up.

> LIVE OAK, Aug. 3—Dr. C. LeRoy Adams, State Senate nominee from the 17th District, was shot to death in his office here late this morning by a Negro woman who was arrested and whisked to the State Prison at Raiford for safekeeping, Sheriff S. P. Howell* reported. Howell said the woman, Ruby McCollum, 32-year-old wife of a "fairly well to do" Negro farmer and mother of three, apparently shot Adams during an argument over a medical service bill. The 42-year-old doctor was found clutching $100 in his hand the sheriff said. Two bullets from a .32 caliber revolver had entered his body, one near the heart and the other in his left shoulder. Howell said there were four spent shells in the woman's pistol. A murder charge will be filed against the McCollum woman tomorrow. Howell said she admitted the shooting, but did not give a reason.
>
> —*Florida Times Union*
>
> *Sheriff Howell was no relation to us.*

I felt really bad that Dr. Adams had been killed, but I couldn't help but hope that this meant I could keep my tonsils. After all, I hadn't had a bad earache in several months now, and the more I thought about having my tonsils cut out, the more it scared me.

63

Exploring, Sliding, and Wishing

One night while we were living at the Touchton place, Daddy's cousin Thomas Boatright came over with his wife Marie and daughter Elaine. After supper, we kids were playing when we heard a sound from the woods, "Whoo, whoo, whoo . . . whoo, whoo." Elaine ran to her mother crying, "I'm scared!" and buried her face in her mother's lap.

Mama jumped up from her chair and said, "Oh, let me just turn my apron inside out and that ol' owl will quit his hooting."

The hoots continued as Mama untied her apron, turned it wrong side out, and slowly tied it back—but after she sat down, the owl did *not* hoot another time! Not once! *How did Mama know how to make that owl stop hooting?* Elaine quit crying and we resumed play, unaware that the habit of owls is to hoot just a few times before stopping.

During summer days at the Touchton place, my sisters and I often explored the woods around the house, since we had no playhouse, jump board, or swing there. One day we came upon a bush covered with strange-looking burrs. We picked a few and took them to show Mama. She said they were chinquapins—had nuts inside—and that we could eat them. So for the rest of our time at the Touchton place, we spent hours and hours in the surrounding woods, searching for chinquapins to eat on the spot.

About once a week that August, Daddy took us back to our old place to see the progress being made. On an early visit, we saw that Mr. Dunham had dug trenches, poured cement, and mortared together concrete blocks to form an *L*-shaped foundation.

A week or two later, two-by-four studs formed rooms and the roof went up. We traipsed around the shell of the house, inhaling the scent of raw wood. "The rooms seem smaller than I expected," Mama said to Daddy. "Where'd the 1900 square feet go?"

"It'll look roomier when the Sheetrock goes up," Daddy said. That didn't make sense to me, but a week later I saw that Daddy was right. When we could no longer see through studs into other rooms, each room did appear roomier.

Finally, the outside was covered with gray shingles. No surprise there. For years Mama and Daddy had admired the Cundiff place, a gray-shingled house on State Road 51, the road we always traveled to Live Oak. Daddy seldom failed to slow as we passed it, nestled among dogwoods and tall pines entwined with wisteria vines that showed off lavender blooms every spring.

By the end of August, our new house was almost ready for us. We went there early one day so Mama could measure windows and do some cleaning. While she and Daddy looked in the bedrooms, my sisters and I slid around on the gleaming hardwood floors. Barefoot, we'd get a running start, land on our butts, and slide five or six feet before coming to a stop. If we'd tried to do that in our old house, we'd have picked up splinters galore.

When Mama and Daddy came back to the living room, I expected them to tell us to stop our sliding, but they didn't. Daddy just said we should never slide on the floors with our shoes on because the shoes and sand would scar the wood.

"While y'all do some cleaning" Daddy said then, "I'm gonna run to town; I won't be gone long." And off Daddy went in his Jeep.

We helped Mama sweep and wipe up some construction dust, then went outside. Under the carport, we climbed the poles (metal pipes, three or four inches in diameter), which supported the roof. How perfect that Mr. Dunham had installed not two but *three* so we didn't have to argue. We each claimed a pole and came up with several competitions: who could reach the eave first, who could stay at the top the longest, and who could slide down the fastest—like firemen. Climbing up and staying there was hard. Sliding down to the dirt floor of the carport was fun.

Later that day, we were clowning around on the screened porch when we heard a car coming down the road. It didn't sound like Daddy's Jeep. Thinking it was company, we called to Mama, "Somebody's coming."

A shiny black car rounded the bend in the road and we saw that *Daddy* sat behind the steering wheel.

"Your Daddy's bought a new car!" Mama said as she stepped out onto the porch. We sisters jumped up and down.

Daddy drove the car under the carport and braked. We stood staring, jaws dropped.

"They allowed me $800 for the Jeep," he said to Mama. "I paid them another $700 for the Plymouth, and they let me drive it home. It's last year's model, a '51, but brand new." Indeed it was.

A brand-new car sitting under the carport of our brand-new house! Did Daddy rob a bank? Strike gold? Or what?

Patsy swung the front passenger door open and folded the seatback forward. Anetha and I crawled into the back, and Patsy slid into the front passenger seat. The three of us sat there looking at the car's interior, inhaling the newness, each by her own window. Little did we know that the desire to have a window seat in that new car would soon lead to trouble.

Back at the Touchton house the next Sunday evening, we prepared to leave for training union and church. I liked training union better than Sunday school because Mama taught our class and she really knew how to tell stories. She'd recently told us a story called "The Coat of Many Colors." As she told the tale, she moved cutouts of people and animals across a flannel board as if they were crossing a desert—like it was a little movie.

Ready for training union, now, Mama sat in the front passenger seat, and Anetha and I sat in the back, each of us next to a window. Our new black car was extremely hot, having sat in the sun all afternoon. My church clothes felt scratchy as we waited in the heat. Daddy started the engine and put his right hand on the gear shift to slip it into first and head out—but we had to wait for Patsy, who was still in the house. Patsy seemed more like Daddy every day. We were always waiting for him—it was usually for him to finish a conversation. Now we always had to wait for Patsy to finish getting dressed. Patsy was now ten, and the older she got, the longer she took to get ready.

"Hurry up. Get in the car," Daddy yelled to her as she came prancing down the steps of the house. "We're gonna be late."

"Scoot over," Patsy said to Anetha as Daddy leaned forward to let Patsy crawl into the back seat.

"Get in the middle," Anetha said. "It's my turn to sit by the window. Not yours."

Anetha didn't move and Patsy stood, hunched over, half in, half out of the car with Daddy leaning forward, his chest against the steering wheel.

"I said, 'get in the car!'" Daddy yelled at Patsy again.

She crawled over Anetha and plopped herself down in the middle. Daddy slammed the door shut and eased the car forward.

"Ou-u-u-u-ch! Anetha screamed. "Mama, Patsy pinched me!"

Daddy stomped the brake and we lurched forward. The engine died as he told Patsy, "Get outta the car and go back in the house!"

Oh, my. I knew by the tone of Daddy's voice that Patsy was gonna get it, like Anetha and I got it when we made Daddy mad that night in the open hall of our old house.

Daddy would probably have whipped Patsy right there by the car if he'd had on his belt, but he'd evidently forgotten to put it on. He went up the steps, across the porch, and through the front door. Patsy followed. After they disappeared inside, we heard licks of the belt and Patsy's crying.

She was still crying when they got back to the car, and by now Anetha and I had tears rolling down our cheeks too. Anetha slid over next to me to let Patsy sit by the window.

After Daddy told us to "dry it up," no sound came from anybody. Just total silence. In my head, I was calling Daddy "turtle," the name the three of us called him behind his back. We'd heard Granddaddy Rye say, "When a turtle hooks onto something, he won't let go till it thunders." When Daddy whipped us, he didn't know when to stop. Once, years before, when he kept hitting Patsy with the belt, Mama spoke up, saying, "C.G., that's enough," and he stopped. I wished Mama had gone back in the house that night. Maybe she'd have stopped it sooner.

"Okay, girls," Daddy said to us about five minutes down the road, "here comes the thrill bump." As the car hit the dip in the road, we bounced so high our hair brushed the car's ceiling. We usually giggled when Daddy hit that bump, but none of us so much as smiled that night. I don't know what my sisters were thinking, but I kept calling Daddy a turtle and thinking about his belt. I wished he wouldn't whip so hard for so long. I'd been wishing and praying for that for as far back as I could remember. Just as I'd been wishing and praying I wouldn't have nightmares, nighttime accidents, and earaches, I had begun to think there was no use wishing upon the first star or praying to God for wishes that never came true. Though, come to think of it, I didn't have as many bad dreams as I used to.

64

A Housewarming

Mr. Dunham completed our house on schedule. In early September, just before school started, he turned over the keys to Daddy, not that we would ever use keys.

On the day we moved in, the men made several trips using Granddaddy's truck. With each load, Granddaddy backed up the truck to the front stoop. Then he and Daddy carefully maneuvered each piece of furniture between the stoop's support posts—white wrought-iron scrollwork, and through the doorway into what was, to us, a mansion: smooth painted walls, light switches at each doorway, overhead glass fixtures that hid bare bulbs, kitchen cupboards for storing dishes, pots and pans, closets for clothes and more closets for linens, running water into the kitchen and into the *indoor* bathrooms—*two* indoor bathrooms. And beautiful floors for sliding.

Patsy, Anetha, and I sock-skated and panty-skidded down the long hallway that led to the bedrooms as Mama showed the men where to place each piece of furniture.

"Move out of the way, girls," Daddy said as he and Granddaddy headed down the hallway carrying iron bedsteads. We followed them into the pretty pink bedroom—ours!—the last room on the right. After they brought in the wire springs and ticking-striped mattress that went with the bed that used to be in the back bedroom of the old house, they set it up. Meanwhile, I glided our closet's doors back and forth on the track. Back and forth, back and forth—with one finger!

"Don't wear the closet doors out the first day here," Mama said, and then told me to make my bed. I looked around and Daddy had set up the cot in the corner of the room. What started out as one of the happiest days of my life—moving into our new house— turned to disappointment—in myself. As I made the bed, I prayed I'd wake up that night if I needed to, and run to our beautiful pink-and-green tiled bathroom.

My cot and the bigger bed were, at first, the only furniture in our room, but within days, Daddy would build us a dressing table to which Mama would add a gathered pink skirt to match the powder pink walls.

Before sundown on moving day, every room in our new home was furnished except the guest bedroom at the end of the hall. You could see directly into it from the living room, so Mama shut its door. We sisters soon opened it, of course, since that empty room provided more space for sliding.

How long that room would stay empty, I didn't know, but I figured it would be quite a while. Daddy never shared money matters with us kids except to tell us we couldn't have something like a bike because we couldn't afford it. I was pretty sure the house, plus the new car, had set Daddy back a few pennies—maybe the house cost as much as a *thousand* dollars. I wouldn't learn for years that the figure was eleven times my guess.

Several days later, Mama was busy preparing food for the housewarming we were having that night when a big truck drove up. Daddy went out the front door to the porch and greeted the two men who got out. "How you fellows doing?"

"Just fine, thanks," the driver said. "We've got your new

furniture, but before we tote it in, would you show us where it goes?"

"You've got the wrong house," Daddy said, "What's the address you're looking for? I can probably tell you how to get there."

"Are you Mr. C. G. Howell?"

"Yeah. That's me."

"Then, we've got the right house—Nice house! Brand new, huh?"

"Yeah—but no, you don't have the right house," Daddy said. "I didn't order any furniture."

"Is your address Rt. 4, Box 245, Live Oak, Florida?"

"That's the address we use."

"Well, Mr. Howell, it's clear that this is your furniture. We've got the right name and address on this receipt." He tapped a paper he was holding in his outstretched hand.

Daddy took the paper, looked at it, then showed it to Mama, who stood just inside the screen door.

"Paid in full," Mama murmured.

"Who paid for it?" Daddy asked the driver.

"I'm sorry, we don't have that information," the man said. "I figured you paid for it."

"No, sir. I didn't pay a dime on it."

"Well, as you can see, the receipt says "Paid in full," and it's got your name on it. So, do you want us to set the furniture here on the sand, or can we take it in your house?"

"Bring it on in," Daddy said. "Here, I'll help you. But who in the world would . . . ."

Daddy's voice trailed off as the rest of us stood staring.

After the deliverymen left, we went to the guest bedroom and ran our hands over the smooth wood of our guest bedroom's matching suite—a four-poster bed, a chest of drawers, a vanity with a big round mirror, and a stool that fit perfectly in the nook under the vanity's mirror. *Who had done this for us?*

Mama took fresh linens from the hall linen closet and had us make the bed while she went back to the kitchen to finish preparing food for the housewarming.

By the time guests arrived at dusk, the dining table was covered with platters filled with goodies. Nearly everybody who arrived brought a gift and made a fuss about our beautiful new home. They oohed and aahed as they looked around the living room at the dusty-gray walls, the blond-brick fireplace, the varnished cabinets that flanked the fireplace, the mantel that spanned the entire west wall, and the picture window that framed the moss-draped oaks out front.

"I love your new couch," one lady said to Mama, gesturing toward our chartreuse couch, opposite the picture window.

"Oh, it's the same old fold-out couch we've had since we married," Mama said. "I just recovered it in that new Naugahyde stuff—real durable—now I can wipe it off with a wet rag."

Our other living room furniture consisted of two modern chairs Mama had found on sale. Their blond-colored legs matched the fireplace brick, and their vinyl seats and back matched the gray walls. I didn't care for them, though. They had no arms and their front legs stuck out. In the short time we'd had those chairs, I'd already tripped over their legs twice.

Our housewarming guests wanted to see the rest of the house, but before everyone left the living room, Daddy opened a cabinet door, to the left of the fireplace, to show off the woodbox that could be filled from a small door on the outside of the house.

Everybody followed Mama and Daddy through the dining room toward the screened porch. The men continued with Daddy to the porch to admire his shiny black Plymouth sitting under the carport. The women followed Mama into the kitchen. Several commented on the aqua walls and cabinets. Others admired the double sink and new electric stove.

After Daddy led the men into the kitchen, everybody followed him into the utility room, also aqua. He stood next to our new spin-dry washer, which had two tubs, and explained. "You put the clothes into the big tub for the wash; then you transfer them to the smaller tub to rinse and spin out the water." He also pointed out the white porcelain sink the washer emptied into, the one he'd salvaged from our old house.

"Our house plan called for a second floor," Daddy said. "We didn't need a second level, so we used the stairwell space for this bathroom here." He opened the plywood door to his shower bathroom. Next, he mentioned Mama's utility-room pantry and closet on the opposite wall. They featured air ventilation to the crawl space under the house. He also pointed out four sawhorses in the closet, and two sheets of aqua-painted plywood sandwiched vertically between the pantry and deep freeze. "I got Leo Dunham to build and paint these to match the walls," he said.

The sawhorses and plywood would convert to a table on the screened porch, a table that would seat about twenty people at once—to be used during the summer on tobacco-gathering days and when we had a houseful of company.

From the utility room, everybody moved into the hall and took a look at our big pink bathroom, complete with a mirrored medicine cabinet flanked by two fluorescent lights. "Wow! It's bright in there," one visitor said as she peeked in.

"Now, this next room was empty until about three o'clock today," Daddy said as he approached the guest bedroom. "Do any of y'all know anything about that?"

Everybody glanced at one another with puzzled looks on their faces, so we still hadn't a clue who had paid for our new furniture.

After looking at the other two bedrooms, our guests made their way back down the hall. We moved dining chairs into the living room, but we still didn't have enough seats for everybody. Our family took seats on the floor along with several guests, and Daddy and Mama began opening gifts. Daddy passed each present to Mama for unwrapping: a gold-rimmed fruit bowl, a matching divided platter, a pair of brown ceramic dogs, several sets of towels, sets of sheets, embroidered pillowcases, crocheted doilies, a blanket, two pink swan vases, and more whatnots.

The empty whatnot shelf that one guest had brought sat in the corner of the living room. The person who brought it and the guests who gave us the whatnots didn't know Mama favorite expression: "If it ain't useful, I don't give it room and board." And they still wouldn't know how Mama felt about knickknacks because, with every gift she opened, she acted as if she loved it.

Eventually, there was only one gift left on the floor. "This smells like fat lighter'd," Daddy said as he lifted it. Instead of handing it to Mama, he ripped off the tissue paper himself, and he was right. It was nothing but a big bundle of kindling tied together with a cord. *What a strange gift*, I thought. Daddy opened the note attached to it and read it aloud.

"This is from Joe and Ruby Hingson, Barney Lanier, Sr., and Monroe and Inez Boatright." Daddy paused for a moment, before reading the rest of the note, a choke in his voice. "We hope you like the bedroom furniture we picked out for you."

Mama's eyes watered and I thought I saw a tear in Daddy's eye, but surely I imagined that, for I had never seen Daddy cry.

65

Third-Grade Lessons

In third grade, everything changed. To start with, I had a new teacher, Mrs. Griffin. She taught third, fourth, and fifth grades, and she was nothing like Mrs. Johnson, who'd taught me for two years. Short and stout, with graying hair, Mrs. Griffin looked grandmotherly.

She wore cotton stockings, held in place with garters. Occasionally, she stuck her hands under the hem of her dress, tugged at her stockings, rerolled the garters, and gave them a twist. I'd seen Grandma Rye make this same adjustment with her garters. I wondered why older ladies didn't wear a girdle to hold up their stockings like Mama did when she dressed up.

Not only did I have a different teacher, the classroom's location and setup were backwards. I had to go into the first room on the left of the hall instead of the last on the right. And seated at my new desk, I faced the back of the building instead of the front. I felt as if I was wearing my dress backwards.

My new teacher didn't help matters when she explained "our world" to us. This happened during a lesson in a new subject I couldn't even spell until Patsy taught me the secret that our Cousin Spessard Boatright had taught her: *George Edith's oldest girl rode a pig home yesterday.*

Until that geography class, I thought the world resembled a giant dinner plate and it had a thick forest around the edge to keep people from falling off. From what this new teacher said, I had it all wrong.

"This globe represents our world," she said as she spun a ball-like object around and tried to explain how the world rotated on an axis. "Here's America, where we live." She'd stopped the globe's rotation and tilted it so America faced the ceiling. She proceeded to point to different directions. Looking back now, I realize when she said, "That's North," she pointed toward the globe's North Pole, but with the way she had the globe positioned, her finger actually pointed South. From that day on, I could never get my directions straight.

One other lesson from third grade stands out in my memory, though I'm not sure which subject we were studying. Mrs. Griffin stood next to her desk holding a shiny golden bud vase about eight inches tall with curves like a woman's figure—one of the loveliest vases I'd ever seen. "What material do you think this vase is made of?" she asked.

Hands shot into the air and she called on several students.

"Gold!"

"Brass!"

"Gold."

"Gold."

"Or, could it be glass?" she asked.

As we pondered the question, she held the vase at arm's length. And dropped it.

Crash! Glass scattered across the rough wood floor. I stared in disbelief. *Did she mean to drop that beautiful vase? Or was it an accident?*

I never knew.

Hurriedly, she retrieved a broom from the cloakroom and swept up the mess. Then she laid a few of the largest glass shards on her desk and had us take turns going to the desk to look and feel. The outside of the glass felt smooth; the inside had been coated with gold paint.

"See," she said as we stared at the pieces on her desk, "appearances can be deceiving."

Sometimes, Mrs. Griffin reviewed things we already knew—like the golden rule, and "Cleanliness is next to Godliness." Every day when we headed for the lunchroom, she reminded us to stop in the restroom to wash our hands.

The lunchroom and attached kitchen were new to Ladyland. Over the summer, an old Army barracks left over from the war had been hauled in by truck. It stood behind the school. This meant my sisters and I no longer had to tote our heavy tin lunch boxes back and forth to school.

Lunchtime at Ladyland School—left to right, standing: Mr. Griffin, principal and teacher, grades 6-8; Mrs. Johnson, teacher, grades 1-2; Clara Mae Jackson, 8th grade student; Mrs. Griffin, teacher, grades 3-5; and Mrs. Corbin, cook.

Patsy is at the table on the left, the fifth student from the far end. Anetha and I are on the far right.

Mrs. Corbin (I think she was Joyce Corbin's aunt), who lived just off the school grounds, did the cooking. And all the students were served in shifts, youngest to oldest.

I didn't always like the food Mrs. Corbin served. I still hated most vegetables. But one day she cooked macaroni and cheese—which I loved—so I rushed to the table as soon as my plate was full and then grabbed a carton of milk. (The pasteurized milk at school tasted much better than the raw milk we had at home.)

I started gobbling up my lunch, then spotted something dark in the macaroni that didn't appear to be black pepper. I'd seen my fair share of weevils in the dry corn we shelled for the chickens, and this tiny thing looked exactly like a weevil. But, being hungry, I used the tines of my fork to drag the thing to the side of my plate and scooped up another bite—*Oops! There's another. And another.* Of course I wasn't the only one finding weevils in the macaroni. Before long, I heard murmuring all round. The boys began counting and comparing weevils as if competing for the biggest pile.

When my sisters and I got home that day and Mama learned we'd had weevils for lunch, she got mad—not at Mrs. Corbin, but at the folks who supplied food to our school. Mama went back to packing our lunches. I didn't mind since those of us who carried lunches still got to go to the lunchroom and eat with all the other kids. Plus, I knew my lunch box would always contain something I liked; Mama usually packed a biscuit with meat left over from breakfast, and grits, though occasionally, I'd find something special, like a catsup sandwich made with *ready-made sliced bread*!

After we ate our lunches at school, Mrs. Griffin sometimes sat on the granite stile in the shade of the oaks and crocheted. She taught some of the girls to chain stitch, something Grandma had already taught my sisters and me. Our teacher also tatted, but that required a shuttlecock which none of us had, so we just watched as she turned plain ol' white thread into the daintiest lace.

Back in the classroom one afternoon, Mrs. Griffin got us to help her make a hectograph, or *jellygraph*,[7] so she could use it to make copies of permission slips and announcements to be sent home to our parents. We mixed up several ingredients to make a clear yellow liquid, which we poured into a shallow rectangular pan. The liquid gradually jelled, like Jell-O does when cooled. The next day, Mrs. Griffin prepared a master sheet. She laid its image side flat on the gelatin surface so the goo could absorb the ink, and then removed it. We students took turns laying clean sheets of paper on the jellygraph, one after the other, to make purple copies.

I don't recall that Mrs. Griffin had any major discipline problems in the classroom. If a student acted up, she'd threaten to send him to the principal, Mr. C. A. Griffin, her husband, who had a reputation for being quick with the paddle. He'd replaced Mr. Patterson.

A skinny man, with dark hair, Mr. Griffin looked as if he'd slept on it wrong and combed it only with his fingers. I never saw the man smile. He had a habit of rolling a pencil up and down from his chin to his nose. I didn't see what Mrs. Griffin saw in him to make her marry him. She once wrote her full name on the blackboard, Mrs. Lois Fitch Griffin, and emphasized that Fitch was her maiden name. In my opinion, she should have stayed Miss Lois Fitch.

Up, down. Up, down went Mr. Griffin's pencil one day as several of us kids stood at attention in the hallway. Jean Evans, Myra Boatright, and I stood side by side with several other girls. We were in big trouble.

"Look at him. This boy's clothes are now sandy and dirty. What were you children thinking? Or were you even thinking?" He patted Duane Hingson on the shoulder. At recess, we had covered Duane with sand, just for fun. But he had agreed to be buried.

Up, down. Up, down went Mr. Griffin's pencil. The expression on

---

[7] Instructions for making a hectograph: *http://blog.lib.uiowa.edu/speccoll/2013/07/16/what-the-hectograph/*

the principal's face was deadly serious. My heart beat faster and faster. I thought my chest would burst as he continued his lecture.

"This boy could have died!"

Died? Was he kidding? Duane could still breathe. We left his head out. Well, at least his nose.

"All right, children," the stern principal eventually said. "You're dismissed—but don't let me catch any of you pulling a dangerous stunt like that again!"

After that scare, I had a closer bond with my friend Jean. I wished I could go home with her. My sisters were always going off to spend nights with friends. Patsy had spent many nights with Alice Faye Allen. And Anetha often went home with Ceil Carver and came home bragging again about sleeping on a feather bed.

Because I still had occasional nighttime accidents, I had been hesitant to spend nights with friends. But one day, after Jean invited me home with her, I asked Mama, and she said I could go. I gave the permission note Mama wrote to Mrs. Griffin the next morning. It said I had permission to board the school bus with Jean that afternoon. I felt giddy with excitement when school let out; I'd never ridden a bus before. At Jean's house, Mrs. Evans gave us cookies, and all of Jean's family members were welcoming. Jean and I talked and played games with her younger brother, Richard, who didn't roughhouse like most boys. Everything went perfectly. Perfectly, that is, until the next morning when I awoke to her mother's voice, "Time to get up for—" and I realized I'd started to pee in my sleep. I quickly tightened my muscles and slid out of bed at the same time Jean did.

"I'll help you make the bed," I said as I pulled the covers up on my side and over the wet spot—*surely it wasn't a big spot!* Jean tugged on the covers on her side and the deed was done. *The bed will dry by tonight,* I kept telling myself. But I knew in my heart I should have told Jean's mother, and I hated myself for what I'd done.

66

An Unforgettable Birthday

Throughout the school day on my eighth birthday, I kept wondering if Alfred Boatright would show up at our house that night for a fried chicken supper and some birthday cake. In the last couple of years, we'd become birthday buddies—celebrating together.

I was born on Alfred's birthday, the year he turned thirteen. His daddy was Grandmama Midgett's brother, which made him and Daddy first cousins. Like I said before, our family saw a lot of the Boatrights, especially during tobacco season, since we traded work. By trading work, nobody had to pay anybody. But I hadn't seen Alfred since the summer tobacco season. Would he remember to come for our October birthday supper?

Maybe. Because Alfred really liked Mama's fried chicken. Daddy was always telling the tale about how I embarrassed Alfred when I was only about four years old and he was eating a meal with us. After Alfred helped himself to his fourth piece of fried chicken, I said, "Alfred, you kinda like fried chicken, don't you?"

It wasn't until Mama scolded me that I recognized I'd said anything wrong. But now, every time Daddy repeated that story—and he repeated it often for company—I wanted to slide down in my chair and hide under the table.

Mama never forgot our birthdays. She always baked us a cake. My eighth birthday was no exception. When my sisters and I got home from school that day, my cake sat in the middle of the kitchen table. I wanted to have a piece right then, but the custom was to wait until after supper.

Patsy, Anetha, and I each found ourselves a cold biscuit, poked a hole in it, and filled it with cane syrup. After eating that, we headed outside to do our chores.

Later, back inside, I kept looking out the front windows for Alfred's car. He still lived with his parents but owned his own car. By the time I saw his dark car coming up the lane, Daddy had already come in for supper, and Mama was in the kitchen, frying the chicken.

I called to everybody. "It's Alfred— and somebody's with him."

When they stopped out front, I realized the person in the car was a girl. Alfred got out of his car, walked around to the passenger side, and opened the door. Out stepped maybe the prettiest girl I'd ever seen. She had shoulder-length reddish-blond hair and very, very fair skin.

At the front door, Alfred introduced the girl on his arm as "my girlfriend, Annette."

Alfred and Annette

While I understood perfectly well that Alfred was my cousin and not my boyfriend, I felt a pang of jealousy. I did not want to share his attention with this girl, especially on "our" birthday.

I don't remember what all was said at the door, but after Alfred and Annette came into the living room, she handed me a pretty package—wrapped in white paper and tied with a bright pink bow. "A birthday present from Alfred and me," she said.

Never in my life had I received a gift on a birthday. Mama always baked us a cake, but gifts came at Christmas. Alfred and I had shared many, many birthdays, and we had never ever exchanged presents. I felt awkward since I had no present for Alfred. I just stood there holding the gift, not knowing what to do or say.

"Open it," Alfred said, as he tugged at the ribbon to loosen it for me. So I pulled the ribbon off, let it drop, and tore off the paper. I now held a gray velvet-covered box. I tried to lift the top, and it sprang open on one side. Behold—on padded white satin—lay a strand of pearls. Pearls! My mouth dropped open like the circle made by the necklace. This? For me?

"Here, let me help you," Annette said as she lifted the necklace, unhooked the silver clasp, and placed the length around my neck. I leaned my head forward, and she fastened it. How different I now felt about Annette. I put my fingers on the necklace, feeling the pearls' smoothness and their sizes, from tiny ones at the back to larger ones in front. This was the most grown-up gift I'd ever received, and future school photographs would show just how much I loved this pearl necklace.

"Can y'all stay for supper?" Mama asked. "I'm frying chicken."

"Sure can," Alfred said.

Wouldn't you know it? At the supper table, Daddy embarrassed me again by telling Annette the story of what I'd said to Alfred when I was only four years old. I slumped in my chair. But after we finished the meal, I perked up because Mama brought the cake to the dining table and lit the candles so I could blow

Me, wearing my new pearl necklace in my third-grade school picture

them out.

I took a deep breath as I made my wish. I was tempted to wish Daddy would stop telling that tale, but instead I made the wish I'd made for as long as I could remember. The one I wanted to come true more than anything else in the world. As much as I loved the pearls around my neck, I would have traded them for my wish to come true.

67

Dr. Adams's Advice
1952-53

It was hard to believe that Dr. Adams had been murdered. It was harder still to believe the rumor we heard during his trial in the fall of 1952—that he, a married white man, and Ruby McCollum, the married colored woman accused of shooting him, had a baby together. Mrs. McCollum was now on trial for his murder.

With our doctor dead and buried, I was sure I'd never have that operation he'd recommended back in the spring. But shortly after Christmas, I ended up with another bad earache. I cried all night with it, and Mama and Daddy decided we should follow Dr. Adams's advice. While I wanted to be rid of the earaches that made me want to bang my head against the wall, I didn't like the thought of having my throat cut on.

But nobody asked me.

In early 1953, I found myself sitting in a hospital gown in the Little Griffin Hospital in Valdosta, Georgia. Mama had explained on the long ride there that I'd be put to sleep with ether and wouldn't feel a thing. Still, I was dreading the operation.

Dr. Johnson came into the hospital room and told Mama and Daddy that everything was arranged.

"While I'm at it," he said, "I should probably remove her adenoids." Mama and Daddy agreed. I didn't have a clue what adenoids were. I was beginning to feel really anxious when a nurse—dressed head to toe in white—dress, stockings, shoes, and a stiff cap perched high on her head—told me that after the surgery I could have all the ice cream I wanted.

Hm-m.m. Maybe this wouldn't be so bad after all. I just hoped I wouldn't have an accident while I was asleep.

Before long, I was moved to a bed with wheels that was pushed out of my hospital room and down a long hallway into a room with a giant overhead light nearly as bright as the sun. I tried not to look straight at it for fear it would put my eyes out like Mama said the sun would if you stared at it.

Several people scurried about. One of them came to the side of my bed and said, "I'm going to place this cup over your nose and mouth. Just breathe normally and count."

"One . . . two . . . three . . . four . . ."

I began to feel like I was spinning. It started off slowly, but soon I spun faster and faster. Panic gripped me. Not only was I spinning, I was sinking deeper and deeper into a dark tunnel. *Oh Dear Lord! Is there no bottom? Am I going to Hell?* More frightened than when wild animals and snakes chased me in my dreams, I screamed.

Did I *really* scream? I don't know. And I don't know how long the surgery took.

The next thing I remember, I was floating in space with giant starfish that had ugly, contorted faces. They began to bump into me and sing in screechy voices, "You can't catch *mee*-eee! You can't catch *mee*-eee!" I didn't *want* to catch them. I wanted to get *away* from them. I wanted them to leave me *alone*! I began to cry.

"Honey, don't cry. It's all over. You can wake up now."

I struggled to open my eyes. A nurse with dark curly hair, pale face, and shiny red lips was looking down at me, gently shaking my shoulder.

"Take a sip of water," she said, offering me a straw, but I floated up and off again into space. This time I saw no dancing stars.

When I awoke again, Mama was there.

"Ma—" I wanted to tell Mama about my scary dreams, but the words stuck in my throat—which throbbed and felt very dry . . . . Dry! Was I dry? I moved my hands around on the mattress to check. My gown was dry. The bed was dry.

"I'm dry," I mouthed to Mama.

"Are you?"

The nurse came in again and told me to suck on a little crushed ice. She placed a cold cup in my hands. I tried, but each swallow felt like a dagger to my throat.

For the rest of that day, nurses fussed over me. I enjoyed the attention, but my throat hurt so much I didn't even want the all-you-could-eat ice cream I'd been looking forward to.

The next morning when I woke up, I was still dry.

"I didn't wet the bed," I told Mama.

"Good. But you haven't had much to drink, and you do need to drink."

After returning home, the soreness in my throat began to wear off, and I started eating and drinking, but I still didn't wet the bed. I don't know who was more astonished, Mama or me. The operation—intended to cure me of earaches—had evidently cured my nighttime accidents! Had the wish I'd been wishing all my life really come true?

It had!

By summer I was sleeping between my sisters—in the big bed.

When I next saw a doctor, Mama told him the unexpected and *blessed* results of my surgery. His explanation? "Maybe with such enlarged tonsils and adenoids, when she finally fell asleep, she slept too soundly to awaken when she needed to."

68

Toasty Toes

Soon after I started fourth grade in September, Mama announced she had a job. She had learned to drive after Daddy bought the black Plymouth. Now, she, along with neighbors Mertis Avery and Clara Neeley, had gone to Lake City, about 30 miles away, and found work. Mrs. Avery and her family lived where Kent and Allie Thomas used to live. Mrs. Neeley was married to Granny and Granddaddy Tip's foster son.

I suppose Mama talked over her decision to find a job with Daddy before she went looking. But her working away from home surprised the dickens out of us kids. She said she would carpool with Mrs. Avery and Mrs. Neeley. The three of them would be working the night shift.

Perfect. Mama would be earning money, yet still be home during the day so she could have freshly baked cookies ready for us to eat when we got home from school, cook supper for us before going to her job at night, and be home in time to cook breakfast for us in the morning. Who could ask for a better arrangement?

"Working on that assembly line's not all that hard," Mama said to Daddy a few days after she went to work, but it does get boring doing the same thing over and over—and it makes my shoulders ache." Other than that, I never heard Mama complain.

After she brought home her first paycheck, she purchased several items we'd always considered luxuries. One was Ipana. *Toothpaste in a tube!* Until then, we'd made our own salt-and-soda paste. Patsy liked the Ipana, but after Anetha and I tried it, we both went back to using salt and soda.

Another item Mama bought, though, was fantastic—an electric heating pad. Perhaps she bought it to soothe her aching shoulders, but we found it ideal for warming cold feet on winter nights. Our fireplace didn't heat the entire house, and once the fire went out at night, the air in the bedrooms felt like refrigerated air—so cold we could see our foggy breath when we exhaled. The heating pad now kept our toes toasty all night since it didn't cool off like the heated bricks or hot-water bottles we'd used in the past.

One freezing winter night as we prepared for bed, Patsy retrieved the heating pad from the linen closet where Mama stored it, plugged it in, and turned the little dial to its highest setting. Before long, we were sound asleep—with me between my sisters— in the big bed.

Sometime during the night, I became vaguely aware that the heating pad felt awfully hot. Every time I put my feet close to it, I jerked them back. At some point, all three of us began to cough, and the coughing eventually caused us to wake enough to realize the room was filled with smoke. Sitting up, still half asleep, I rubbed my eyes. Patsy and Anetha threw the covers back, and with that, the heating pad blazed three feet high. We scrambled to the floor and ran out the door screaming, "Daddy! Daddy! Daddy! Our bed's on fire!"

Daddy, in boxer shorts, bumped into us in the hallway, and seeing the fire, rushed into our room, snatched the electric cord from the socket, and with the cord, jerked the flaming pad to the floor.

"Go get some water!"

We ran to the kitchen, filled pots with water, and ran them back to Daddy fast—but when we got there, no water was needed. Daddy had snuffed out both fires with a patchwork quilt.

Though it was freezing outside, Daddy told us to open up all the windows and doors. The air that rushed in felt like it was coming from a deep freezer. Back in the bedroom, we stared at the hole in the mattress, the pile of burned and scorched linens and covers, and the burned spot on the hardwood floor.

"Y'all can bed down in the guest room for the balance of the night," Daddy said. "Your Mama will help us clean up the mess in the morning."

The three of us were sound asleep in the bed reserved for company when Mama arrived from her job, just before the sun came up.

"Girls! . . . C.G.! . . . Girls! . . . C.G.! . . . Girls!" Mama yelled over and over as she ran through the house.

To my surprise, Mama hugged us. Really, really hugged us! We were not a hugging family, but Mama was evidently glad to see we were okay. She didn't seem a bit upset. Not over the burned mattress and linens. Not over the badly damaged patchwork quilt she'd spent hours quilting. Not even the scorched floor. "When I smelled smoke," she said, "I thought the house was burning down with y'all in it."

Mama's next paycheck was put toward a new mattress.

My sisters' toenails and mine turned yellow from being too close to the heat. Our discolored nails and the scorched spot on the floor reminded us every day of our close call. Smoke detectors were unheard of back then, but on the next trip to town, Daddy bought a two-foot tall copper fire extinguisher that he mounted on the wall in the utility room. Handy for the next fire. Turns out, it was a waste of money. We never had another fire.

69

Beyond Belief

Soon after the heating pad went up in flames, Mama found herself a new *daytime* job. She and her friend Inez became census takers, working as a team—not for the government but for an insurance company. They went door to door in nearby Lake City and Columbia County, asking if people had life insurance. They turned over whatever information they collected to the company, so a salesman could call on the families with little or no insurance and sell them some.

However, Mama and Inez's "cold calling" day job ended after Mama accidentally ran a stop sign in Lake City, broadsided another car, and ended up with a traffic ticket. Only the car and Mama's ego were hurt, but after that, she didn't rush out to look for another job. That's because Daddy had come up with a plan he thought would help pay the bills. In addition to farming our land the next year, he would sharecrop Mr. B. B. Saunders's thousand-plus-acre farm, which adjoined ours.

His property was where we went every Christmas to chop down a red cedar tree. A red cedar now stood in our living room, decorated with colored lights, balls, icicles, and a silver star on top. Under the tree lay six gifts, two for each of us three kids: one from our parents and one from our grandparents. I could hardly wait for Christmas morning when we could open those gifts, plus the ones Santa brought on Christmas Eve night. In the days leading up to Christmas, we'd try to guess what was inside the packages already under the tree by shaking and poking them.

* * *

The year before, as my sisters and I sat beside the tree one day guessing what was inside each gift, I said, "I wonder how many presents Santa Claus will bring us this year?"

"There ain't no Santa Claus," Patsy said.

"There is too!" I said frowning, and looked at Anetha, expecting her to agree. She just looked down at the gift-wrapped package in her lap and said not a word.

"I'll show you," Patsy said as she stood up and then left the room.

I had just turned eight that year. Anetha was going on ten. And Patsy was two months away from eleven.

"There is too a Santa Claus," I said to Anetha as she got up off the floor and moved to the Naugahyde couch. I followed her. Patsy returned holding a *Farm and Ranch* magazine. She plopped down between Anetha and me, opened the magazine, and read a headline, "Yes, Virginia, there is a Santa Claus."

"See, there is too a Santa Claus!'" I said, relieved beyond belief.

"But there *really ain't* one," Patsy said. "You'd know that if you'd read this." She proceeded to read the article out loud. It was long, boring, and it didn't make much sense.

"See!" Patsy said after she finished. "Santa Claus *ain't* real. He's just a spirit, like the Holy Ghost. Mama and Daddy buy the presents that are tagged 'From Santa.'"

"Nuh-uh!" I said, for I knew that Mama and Daddy didn't have *that* much money.

"Let's go ask Mama," Anetha said, getting up off the couch.

The three of us traipsed to the kitchen where Mama stood near the counter with the spice cabinet door open, probably looking for cinnamon, nutmeg, cloves or some other spice she used a lot of around Christmastime. Patsy thrust the open magazine in Mama's hands as Anetha asked, "Mama, is there a Santa Claus?"

Mama walked over, pulled out a chair next to the kitchen table, and sat down as we crowded around. I waited for a *"Yes, of course there's a Santa!"*

"Well . . . " Mama began. But what Mama said after that wasn't any easier to understand than what Patsy had read out loud in the living room.

I left the kitchen puzzled. But that Christmas turned out to be one of the most exciting ever. Daddy bought fireworks, perhaps to celebrate Christmas in the new house. Just after dark on Christmas Eve, we all went to the front yard where he set them off. I poked fingers in my ears before each firecracker popped, but I loved the Roman candles. Daddy knelt on the ground and lit the fuses with a kitchen match, one by one. "Whoosh!" . . . "Whoosh!" . . . "Whoosh!" Light shot from each as they pierced the night sky. Our faces lifted to the heavens to watch. Each cardboard candle burst into hundreds of stars that cascaded above us. "Oo-o-o-o" we said in unison, until the last tiny twinkle flickered out. I'd never seen anything more spectacular.

Around daylight the morning after the fireworks, we sisters ran to the living room to find our stockings overflowing, new packages under the tree, and our grandparents coming through the front door. They came every Christmas to watch us open gifts. I checked each new package passed to me and saw that all of them said, "To Susanette, From Santa." *Why would Patsy think there's no Santa Claus?*

Santa even brought Patsy a baton off her wish list. She seemed thrilled, and over the next few days, she spent many hours trying to get the hang of the thing, tossing it up and catching it. She wouldn't let me or Anetha touch it. But the Sunday after Christmas, having spent the afternoon with her friends from church, Carolyn Johnson and Linda Gail Newbern, Patsy didn't like her baton anymore. She found out Carolyn and Linda Gail had received batons for Christmas too, and theirs contained weights. Patsy quit playing with hers, having decided it was a kid's toy. So now Anetha and I played with it.

* * *

Now, at long last, Christmas was coming again, and one Saturday while Mama and Grandma Rye were in the kitchen, chopping pecans and candied cherries and pineapple for fruitcakes, my sisters ushered me down the hall to the linen closet, pointed to a paper sack, half hidden behind linens and towels, and told me to look inside the sack.

"Santa Claus will give you that for Christmas," Patsy said.

Why would she say that? I didn't believe her. She always thought she knew everything. Still, I couldn't help but peek. I saw something orangey-colored but didn't figure out what it was because Mama called from the kitchen, "What are you girls up to in there?" Patsy slammed the closet door, almost smashing my fingers.

"Nothin'," Patsy hollered back to Mama as she ran and skidded down the hall, snickering.

"Then y'all come in here and help me and your grandma chop up fruit and nuts for the cakes." (When we lived in the old house, Mama and Grandma baked fruitcakes at Grandma's, but now that Mama had an electric stove and a bigger kitchen than Grandma, the annual event took place at our house.)

After the fruitcakes were in the oven, we sisters ambled into the living room and sat on the floor by the tree. This year, we each had three presents instead of two. The extra gifts came from Uncle Harold and Aunt Louise, shipped to us from Indiana. In return, Mama and Grandma would ship them a fruitcake.

On Christmas morning, as usual, we rushed to see what new gifts appeared under the tree. In addition to individual gifts, Santa sometimes gave us a gift to share. I don't remember which one of us opened the "shared gift" that year, but inside we found a View Master along with picture reels of Niagara Falls, the crowning of Queen Elizabeth, and one that showed both the Petrified Forest and the Painted Desert.

From Uncle Harold and Aunt Louise, we each got a dress. Mine was red-and-white candy-striped. My first-ever ready-made dress. Next, I tore into one of the gifts addressed "To Susanette, From Santa." Inside was the most beautiful pullover sweater I'd ever seen—soft as a powder puff—the color of an evening sunset.

Was it what I saw in the sack in the linen closet? I stood up to hold the sweater to my chest to see if it fit, I looked over at my sisters, who both had smug looks on their faces as if to say, "Told you."

70

Granddaddy Tip Leaves His Mark
1953-54

Nobody in our family had ever had a birthday party, and I'd never been to one. But in 1953, when Granddaddy turned ninety, people arrived from far and wide. How they knew Mama had baked a big coconut cake, I don't know, but word somehow got around. With such a big cake—Mama doubled the recipe—I was sure we'd have enough left at the end of the day for us to have seconds, but so many people

Great-Granddaddy Tip
on his 90th birthday

showed up that only crumbs and a few shreds of coconut remained.

Friends and relatives who came probably knew that Granddaddy Tip had once spent time in the state hospital in Chattahoochee, what some called the "insane asylum," but in my mind, Granddaddy Tip was still about as normal as anybody. True, he didn't like to bathe; he took a bath only when Grandma Rye insisted,

388

telling him "You haven't had a bath in two weeks." True, he thought a wool sweater would keep out heat, like it kept out cold. True, he still swore he'd walked to Germany, crossing no ocean. But so what? For as long as I could remember, he'd been a fixture on the front porch of my grandparents' house. He was there waiting for us every day when we went to pick up the mail or when we stopped on our way to and from school. He always had time for us.

Because we stopped in at our grandparents' house so often, it wasn't necessary for them to visit us at our house. But Daddy liked to tell about the time they showed up unexpectedly. My older sisters say I was too little to remember that unexpected visit, but I remember the story.

"We'd planned to go over and visit the George family," Daddy said "and was about to walk out the door when I looked out the front window and saw Mr. Rye's truck coming down the lane. When Mr. and Mrs. Rye got out, I whispered to you girls, 'Don't tell your grandma and granddaddy we was going to visit the Georges.' I knew they wouldn't stay if they knew we had plans to leave."

When Daddy told the story, he never mentioned how we were going to get to the Georges (this was long before the purple Jeep or our new Plymouth). I guess it's possible Daddy still owned his old Model A. Or maybe he planned to drive us there on his tractor. Or maybe, we were to walk. After all, the George family lived just a mile away, not that transportation had anything to do with what happened next.

Daddy continued with his story. "As soon as Mr. and Mrs. Rye walked up to the porch steps, Patsy piped up and said, 'We was going somewhere, but we ain't gonna tell you where we was going!' Naturally, Mr. and Mrs. Rye wouldn't stay."

It was a surprise to me when our grandparents showed up unexpectedly one Sunday afternoon in early 1954 and Granddaddy Tip was with them. If my great-grandfather had ever set foot inside our old house, I couldn't remember it. He certainly had never seen the inside of our new house—not our shiny hardwood floors, not our blond brick fireplace, not our big picture window.

Come to think of it, he never went anywhere, except once or twice a year to church (Patmos Primitive Baptist near Dowling Park) when somebody would drive him there for a preaching service that included a foot-washing ceremony. He never even went to see a doctor. Didn't need to. He was never sick.

The afternoon he arrived with my grandparents, the weather was cool. Logs blazed in the fireplace. As soon as they got inside, Daddy shut the front door so the warm air wouldn't escape. They took off their coats, and everybody took seats in the living room, with Granddaddy Tip sitting in the modern chair nearest the door. After leaning his cane against the wall, he reached in his breast pocket for matches to light the pipe that dangled from his lips. Though Mama and Daddy didn't smoke, they never minded others smoking. But they did mind what Granddaddy Tip did next.

"Uh-uh! Don't do that, Uncle Tip!" Daddy shouted, but it was too late. He'd already tossed the flaming match onto our shiny hardwood floor.

"Look what you did," Daddy shouted, scolding Granddaddy Tip like a child and hurrying over to pick up the now-smoking match that left a sooty mark on the floor.

"Dammit!" Granddaddy Tip shot back, grabbed his cane, and headed for the door.

I stared in disbelief as my great-grandfather stormed out, muttering, "I see I ain't welcome here, so I'll go home."

We all sat in stunned silence until Grandma Rye said. "I'm sorry C.G. I don't know what we're gonna do about Papa."

"No, I'm sorry. I shouldn't have yelled at him."

"His lighting up is getting to be a big problem," Granddaddy Rye said. "It scares us. But you know how he is. You can't tell him a thing. He's always been strong-willed."

"I know," Mama said.

"It's getting to be about as bad as it was before," Granddaddy Rye said, "when we had to take his knife away and put him in Chattahoochee. But right now, I guess we'd better just go get him and take him home."

I tried to wrap my mind around what they were saying as I followed everybody outside, with Mama and Daddy telling my grandparents, "Let us know if you need us—if we can do anything."

I'd never seen Granddaddy Tip throw a lighted match anywhere—he always waved a lit match in the air until the flame went out. And I'd never seen him get mad like that and curse. Oh sure, he got mad with us kids when we didn't mind him—called us hard-headed young'uns and said *dang*—but I'd never heard him actually curse.

Granddaddy Rye's truck stopped down the lane, but Granddaddy Tip didn't get in. He kept walking, so Granddaddy Rye drove along behind him.

Back inside, Mama and Daddy went to the kitchen. I heard them discussing what had just happened.

In the days, weeks, and months that followed, I overheard the adults talking more and more about Granddaddy Tip and what needed to be done, but Grandma Rye kept resisting sending him back to Chattahoochee. She gave in only after having the wits scared out of her.

She was in her kitchen, she said, and thought Granddaddy Tip was in his rocker on the front porch. But when she happened to look out the back kitchen window, she saw him standing in the middle of the cow lot, waving his handkerchief at Granddaddy Rye's newly acquired bull, a white-faced Hereford.

According to Grandma, she flew out the back door, yelling, "Papa, get out of there! Get out of the cow lot!" But Granddaddy Tip kept waving his handkerchief at the bull as if he were a deaf matador. She said by the time she got to him, the bull was pawing the sand. Thankfully, she managed to get her father and herself outside the gate before the bull charged.

Grandma said that after getting both of them to safety, trembling from fear and relief, she admitted to herself that something had to be done. Within a few days, Granddaddy Tip was taken to the hospital in Chattahoochee where Daddy said he was "committed."

Granddaddy Rye's Hereford Bull

I don't remember saying goodbye. But now, when we passed our grandparents house on our way to school, Granddaddy Tip's porch rocker sat eerily still. In truth, I hadn't given him the time of day lately—hadn't sat on his knees for a long time. But now that he was gone, I missed him terribly. I longed to hear him sing "Little Brown Jug," "Froggie Went a Courtin'," and "Prettiest Little Girl in the County O." Sometimes I could almost feel his gnarled hand patting the top of my head.

"When can we go see Granddaddy Tip?" I asked Mama over and over in the weeks and months that followed. She kept saying she didn't know.

After he'd been gone about six months, I asked again, for the umpteenth time, and Mama said, "Soon, honey. Real soon."

71

Today Will Be the Day
1954-55

Our lives revolved around Philadelphia Baptist. Everybody in my family had joined the church. Everybody except me. I wanted to join. I really did. Then I could take part in the Lord's Supper, a ceremony that took place once every three months. But becoming a church member required courage. Something I didn't seem to have. It meant walking down the long aisle in front of the entire congregation to say, "I believe in Jesus." It also meant being baptized, something that scared the bejesus out of me. So when others "partook" of the Lord's Supper, I had to sit and watch like an outcast leper.

At the start of the Lord's Supper, a white cloth hid items adorning a table near the pulpit. To assist in serving the supper, the preacher called on a couple of church deacons—men, because women weren't allowed to serve as deacons. The deacons lifted the white cloth by its corners, revealing silvery trays that held teeny glasses of purple grape juice, and large platters of bread bits. The men carefully folded the cloth, similar to the way we folded the American flag at school, and laid it aside.

Each deacon picked up a platter of bread and made his way down one of the two aisles, passing the platters from one pew to another. As the bread—unleavened, cut in half-inch squares—made its way down the pews, each church member took a piece and held it, hidden in a cupped palm. Not being a church member, I had to pass the platter without taking any. After the deacons served the congregation, they returned the platters to the front of the church where they served one another as well as the preacher. The preacher then lifted his bread bit toward heaven and repeated Jesus's words: "Take. Eat. This is my body that died for you." Everyone chewed and swallowed their bread, most with heads bowed.

Next the deacons passed the silvery trays that held servings of purple grape juice. The jigger-size glasses rattled as the aluminum trays made their way down each pew. Each church member selected one of the dainty jiggers and held it. Finally, the preacher lifted his tiny glass, as if to give a toast, and said, "Take. Drink. This is the blood of Christ that was shed for you." Some took sips. Others downed the "blood" in one gulp.

Before a Lord's Supper took place, one of the ladies in the church prepared it, and that included baking the unleavened bread. Once, when Mama baked it, I sneaked a bit when she wasn't looking. I thought it would taste like a biscuit. It didn't. It tasted yucky. But I still wanted to partake when everybody else did.

When I started fifth grade, I thought more and more about joining the church. By then, it had less to do with participating in the Lord's Supper and more about what would happen to me if I died before I was baptized. Would I go to Hell? According to the preacher, a person had to accept Jesus and be baptized to get into the kingdom of Heaven.

That place behind the pearly gates—a mansion, the Bible said—sounded really nice. All except the streets paved with gold. The metal roof on our barn got so hot in July and August you could fry an egg on it, so I wondered whether people could go barefoot in Heaven in the summertime. Or would gold streets blister the soles of your bare feet? Did Heaven have any green grass or dirt roads to walk on? The preacher never mentioned either.

The thing is, I knew for certain I didn't want to go the other way. My heart raced every time the preacher shouted about Hell being nothing but "fire and brimstone, a place where people gnash their teeth and burn forever." Having burned my fingers while striking a match, I knew what burning flesh felt like.

I became more and more afraid I might die and go to Hell, but I was too scared to walk down the aisle in front of the entire congregation and I was terrified of being baptized—having my whole body, including my head, dunked under water.

I'd heard that some religions sprinkled new converts, but Missionary Baptists didn't believe in that. One revival preacher said, "People who believe in sprinklin' are misguided souls who might never pass through the gates of Heaven." Even Daddy said that "anybody who truly believes will want to be *immersed* like Jesus."

I didn't want to. Did that mean *I* didn't believe?

Both my sisters had joined the church long ago. The afternoon after Patsy walked the aisle, Preacher Hugh Ryals, a short, stocky fellow with a double chin and sandy hair, showed up at our grandparents' house, along with his wife and toddler, to make plans for the baptism. While the adults talked, we kids combed the Ryals' little girl's blond curls.

All baptisms for our church took place in a natural spring that fed into the Suwannee River, or in the case of adults, in the edge of the river itself. (I didn't know then that some modern Baptist churches had something called a baptistery, a tub-like pool behind the pulpit where they baptized their new members.)

Preacher Ryals baptized Patsy at Running Springs. She wore her prettiest Sunday dress and didn't even act scared. Patsy had always been brave.

Soon after Patsy's baptism, Preacher Ryals announced he'd been "called to another church." The man who replaced him, the Reverend Elmer Gaskins, baptized Anetha the following year. Soon, everybody started calling him Brother Gaskins. Mama said she liked his sermons better than all the other preachers we'd had because he stressed God's goodness rather than His wrath. I agreed with Mama, but I wished his sermons were shorter. The pews, built years ago from rough one-by-fours, had no padding.

I envied Brother Gaskins's wife, in that she never sat through the entire hour-long service. Everybody called her Kaye, even us kids. If Kaye's baby began to cry, she would get up and leave, go to the parsonage next door, and not come back. I thought she was just being considerate of others, but there was a rumor that she pinched baby Nancy to make her cry so she wouldn't have to stay through the entire sermon. One Sunday, I took it upon myself to sit on the pew where Kaye sat with Nancy in her lap. I kept my eyes on them, and Kaye never pinched her baby, yet Nancy began to cry. After that, I'd have sworn on a Bible that the rumor about Kaye was false. Except Daddy said that Matthew 5:35 says a person should never swear. So I'd have affirmed it. Daddy said "even the courts will allow you to affirm, instead of swear, to tell the truth."

When Brother Gaskins was called to another church, we hated to see him go—especially Mama, who kept saying he was the best preacher our church ever had, and I don't think her remark had anything to do with his choosing Mama over his wife, Kaye.

It happened one night at a Sunday school get-together at the home of Mr. and Mrs. A. W. Ross. All the adult couples played a game that required the men to be blindfolded. The ladies formed a line and held their hands out in front of them. My sisters and I, along with the three Ross boys, watched expectantly as each blindfolded man made his way down the row of ladies' hands, feeling and rubbing them to decide if he'd found his wife. Everybody was laughing, having a good time. Each man correctly chose his wife's hands, until the blindfolded preacher's turn came. He went down the row, carefully feeling each woman's hands, and was nearly to the end where Kaye stood waiting, when he doubled back to Mama, declaring, "This is my wife."

Mama could hardly contain herself and—boy!—was Brother Gaskins ever surprised when his blindfold came off and he was holding hands with Ethel Howell. The adults would never let him forget that night. But he was a good sport and enjoyed retelling the story as much as anybody.

Preacher W. C. Hall moved into the parsonage in early 1954. One of his daughters, Wilma, and Patsy became fast friends. On Easter Sunday that year, they looked like twins, both wearing navy taffeta skirts and white nylon blouses so sheer they had to wear camisoles under them. Patsy and Wilma were so close that Daddy remarked, "Give one of 'em ex-lax and it'll work on both of 'em." Daddy thought that was funny. I thought it was gross and I'm surprised I repeated it here.

Now that Patsy and Anetha had been baptized, that left nine-year-old me as the only person in our family who wasn't assured a place in Heaven. Yet, nobody in the family acted as if they worried about my going to Hell and burning forever. It was Jewish Uncle Itchy that members of Daddy's family still seemed concerned about. I heard the adults talking about his fate if he didn't "turn to Jesus." I'd learned in Sunday school that it was the Jews who crucified Jesus. But Uncle Itchy wasn't mean and cruel like the people who nailed Jesus to the cross and gave Him vinegar to drink when He was thirsty. Ugh. That story of the Crucifixion always turned my stomach. I couldn't understand how God, who the preacher said could move mountains, would let people kill His only Son like that?

Uncle Itchy was one of the kindest and most generous people I knew. He'd built us that outhouse, and later a shower, when we didn't have one. He'd given us a bike and many other things. He was fun to be around. He didn't deserve to go to Hell. I didn't think I deserved to go there either. *But would I?* It scared me so much I tried not to think about it.

As time went on, all of my friends joined the church, and I kept intending to. Nearly every Sunday morning, I'd say to myself, *This will be the day.*

Sunday mornings were always hectic. While Daddy put on a starched-and-ironed shirt, pleated trousers, and his dress shoes, my sisters and I washed, dried, and put away the breakfast dishes, and Mama hurried around, getting a ham or roast ready to stick into the oven so it could bake while we were away at church. Then we girls and Mama got dressed. For Mama, this meant donning a girdle, nylon stockings, a slip, dress, pumps, and sometimes a hat. Meanwhile, Patsy, Anetha, and I scrambled around, bumping into each other as we dressed in our shared bedroom—or by the fireplace if the weather was cold. In the latter case, Mama would remind us, "Clean up that mess before we leave for church," knowing company would probably return with us from church for dinner. We picked up and put away our nightgowns that decorated the wide mantel, a chair, and the floor.

One Sunday morning in late September, I vowed again to myself, *Today will be the day.* But I immediately began to feel jittery, just thinking about the long walk down the aisle.

As always, everyone first gathered in the sanctuary for announcements and a prayer. Then we went to our respective classrooms: adults into a men's or women's class, and children into classrooms according to age. As usual, the Sunday school lesson focused on a Bible story, after which everybody said a prayer. When my turn came, I mimicked what I'd heard others say: "Dear Lord, thank you for watching over us, and be with the sick and the shut-ins, and guide our missionaries in foreign lands, and protect our men fighting on the battlefront, in Jesus's name. Amen."

Back in the sanctuary for the preaching service, I looked around at all the people, then up at the wall placard behind the choir: Attendance Today, 55; Last Sunday, 52. Courage. I needed courage.

I knew what was on the back wall—the large Church Covenant—an impressive-looking document I'd tried to read once but found the Old English script too difficult. I fidgeted throughout the sermon. When the invitational hymn started at the end of the service, my heart beat faster and faster. Near the pulpit, Preacher Hall stood ready to receive lost souls. But the soles of my shoes seemed glued to the floor.

The song ended. The benediction followed. I had not budged from the pew. Why couldn't I do what both my sisters had done? What my friends had done.

Every Sunday after that, I vowed, *Today will be the day*. And every Sunday, I failed.

When I turned ten in October, I still hadn't joined the church. Before the month ended, preacher Hall left our church for another, and within a few weeks, Brother Gaskins returned as our preacher, along with Kaye and Nancy.

I was still trying to get up the courage to join when the spring revival started. The visiting revival preacher, Reverend Steve Simons, was to preach a sermon every night for a week.

"Please turn your hymnals to page 270 and stand for the invitation," the choir director said one night after the sermon ended.

I stood, clutching the seat in front of me with clammy palms. My heart was pounding. *What page did she say?* The sermon kept playing over and over in my head: "Believe in the Lord, Jesus Christ, and thou shalt be saved! Believe in the Lord, Jesus Christ and . . . "

I flipped through the hymnal, trying to find the right page. I couldn't. But as everyone began to sing, I recognized the song, "I Am Coming to the Cross." I began to sing, and before I got to the words "save me Jesus, save me now," tears were streaming down my cheeks, and I was making my way up the aisle toward the pulpit. Brother Gaskins reached out his hands, put his arms around me, and asked me a few questions. I don't remember what he asked or what I answered. But I knew for sure that I wanted to go to Heaven with the rest of my family.

After the Amen at the end of the benediction, I stood between the two preachers, Gaskins and Simons, and every church member in the congregation came by and shook my hand or patted me on the head. It took forever. I wanted all this to be over. I especially wanted to get the baptism behind me.

On Sunday afternoon, March 20, 1955, Brother Gaskins—dressed the same way Daddy dressed for church, but with shoes off—ushered me down the steep bank and into the cold water at the mouth of Telford Springs. Ugh, this was the spot where I'd once floated into the Suwannee River on an inner tube. It was before I'd learned to swim, so I was scared out of my mind that I was going to drown. I would have preferred to be baptized where my sisters were, in Running Springs, but the water there was now black and too deep; Running Springs was always the first to turn black when the Suwannee River rose, as it did nearly every spring.

Family and church members watched from the bank as the preacher led me into water to my waist and I struggled to keep my dress down. I didn't feel much calmer on this, my baptismal day, than I did the afternoon I'd clung to that black inner tube, crying, as it floated into the river. Whether from my anxiety or the ice-cold water or both, I began to shiver. My heart thumped hard in my chest as the preacher placed his right hand at the back of my waist. With his other hand, he removed a neatly folded white handkerchief from his back pocket and raised his arm toward Heaven. I stood stiff as a soldier as he brought the handkerchief to my face and clamped it over my nose and mouth to keep water out.

"I baptize you in the name of the Father, the . . . "

I closed my eyes and held my breath as he leaned me back. I had an urge to step one foot back to right myself. But I stood rigid as a day-old corpse, knowing that this was what I was supposed to do, having witnessed many baptisms. Water flooded over me. Then suddenly I was upright, wiping droplets from my face. I opened my eyes to the sunlight as Brother Gaskins said, "Amen."

I thought I would feel different after I was saved, after I had become a born-again Christian. And I did. I was freezing. Thank goodness Mama was waiting with a fluffy towel.

72

Excitement Turns to Apprehension

During my three years in Mrs. Griffin's classroom at Ladyland—third through fifth grades—I memorized the multiplication tables (through the tens), learned fractions and long division, and participated in numerous spelling bees. We sang a song every day, so by fifth grade, I knew by heart "Buttons and Bows," "Oh My Darling, Clementine," "Mockingbird Hill," "You Are My Sunshine," "On Top of Old Smoky," "She'll Be Coming 'Round the Mountain," and "I've Been Working on the Railroad."

I also learned a few poems. When Mrs. Griffin wrote the lines of "Trees" on the board, she said it was written by Joyce Kilmer. Thinking Joyce Kilmer was a girl—like Joyce Corbin who was in Patsy's class—I was eager to learn the words:

> *I think that I shall never see*
> *A poem lovely as a tree.*
> *A tree whose hungry mouth is prest*
> *Against the earth's sweet flowing breast;*
> *A tree that looks at God all day,*
> *And lifts her leafy arms to pray;*
> *A tree that may in Summer wear*

A nest of robins in her hair;
Upon whose bosom snow has lain;
Who intimately lives with rain.
Poems are made by fools like me,
But only God can make a tree.

I memorized all twelve lines before learning that Kilmer's full name was Alfred Joyce Kilmer. I felt duped. But I would never forget the poem.

One year, Mrs. Griffin helped us make Mother's Day gifts. She showed the boys how to make baskets using pine needles—stitched together with embroidery thread. And she showed us girls how to make a doll pincushion. We started with a china doll about four-inches long, *nekkid* as a jay bird, that Mrs. Griffin evidently bought for us. Each doll's limbs were held together by twine. We swaddled our dolls with fluffy cotton, fabric, and lace, until they looked like Indian papooses, but we added extra stuffing around their feet to make them stand.

My friend Myra dressed hers in all-white fabric and lace, so it looked like a baby bride. I covered mine with soft, pale blue fabric and trimmed it with white lace. The little doll truly would have made a nice Mother's Day gift. But on the afternoon I took mine home, I reasoned that Mama already had a perfectly good pincushion and wouldn't want to bother taking all her straight pins from her perfectly good pincushion and sticking them into an innocent baby doll. What I did with the doll when I got home, I don't remember, but it never became Mama's pincushion.

By fifth grade, we spent less time at recess jumping rope and playing games like Pop the Whip. Instead, the teachers expected us to team up for volleyball or softball. I didn't care much for either sport since I detested getting hot and sweaty. Plus, sand on the volleyball court was ankle deep. After playing awhile, I'd have to stop and pour a half cup of sand from each shoe. Worst of all was when the ball came straight at me and I had to decide whether to let it hit the ground and get yelled at by teammates or to knock it back over the net and hurt my arms. Some kids acted like hitting the ball with their forearms didn't hurt a bit. *Why was that?* Every time I hit the volleyball, tears formed in my eyes.

At least with softball, we used a bat to hit the ball instead of our arms. But I hated catching fly balls. The school had only two leather mitts for the girls' teams, so most of us didn't get one. When I caught a fly ball, the palms of my hands burned as if I'd caught a hot iron. And if a fly ball hit the tip of a finger and stove it up, the finger stayed sore and swollen for weeks.

My sisters, on the other hand, enjoyed all sports. Patsy, now in eighth grade, and Anetha, in sixth, both played on the girls' softball team, which got to travel to other schools and compete. The only time I got to travel during school hours was when the school went on a field trip.

One of my favorite trips was to the Stephen Foster Memorial in White Springs. The museum had dioramas that depicted Stephen Foster songs— miniature steamboats floating down rivers, trains chugging around a track, hot coals flickering in a fireplace, smoke billowing from chimneys, and Old Joe, the faithful dog, lying on the hearth beside his master, his tail wag-

> "Old Folks at Home," referred to by some as "Suwannee River," was written by Stephen Foster in 1851. Historians say Foster never actually saw the river; he just liked the sound of the name, which he spelled Swanee. "Old Folks at Home" became Florida's state song in 1935.

ging. When it was time to get back on the bus the teacher had to pry me away.

Another time, the school toured the Coca-Cola Bottling Company in Live Oak. I couldn't believe how fast the refillable green bottles danced along the mechanical track, getting washed, dried, refilled with cola, capped, and dropped into wooden crates that held two dozen bottles. Workers touched them only in the beginning, when they placed each dirty bottle on the line for washing.

Back at school, I was also fascinated by the new Co-Cola machine that had replaced the old cooler box. Now, all you had to do was drop in a nickel and press a lever and the six-ounce bottle of Co-Cola was there for the taking—if you wanted it, that is. (I still didn't like it.) That modern machine got a workout when a softball or baseball team from another school visited—teams from Clayland, McAlpin, and Welborn.

Patsy played shortstop and, sometimes, third base. Anetha was looking forward to moving up from the outfield when she got to seventh grade, not knowing she'd never get the chance. Not because she wouldn't be good enough but because change was about to come to Ladyland.

Some parents had not been happy for some time with the education their children were receiving there. Three families— the Boatrights, Curls, and Johnsons—had enrolled their kids in schools in Live Oak at the beginning of that term. But within a few days, the students were sent home and told not to come back to that school. One of the Johnson boys told me he was called to the principal's office at the end of the day, told to turn in his books, and not to return. His parents were out of town at the time and didn't know this was happening—not that any of the parents could be notified since no families in the Ladyland community had a telephone. The three families protested to the school board, but were told that "all students within Suwannee County must attend school within their designated districts; no exceptions."

This ultimatum did not sit well with those parents. They showed the school board that their kids did *not* have to attend school in their designated districts. The Boatrights sent their children to Georgia to live with relatives and attend school there. The Curls and Johnsons drove their boys to a Lafayette County school where they were welcomed.

Then an incident on Ladyland's playground involving Buddy Jackson got other parents riled up. Buddy, a boy in Patsy's class, was mischievous, always testing the patience of his teachers as well as his fellow classmates. No, let's be honest. Buddy was mean. But I don't know anybody who thought Buddy deserved what came his way on the red-clay baseball diamond.

Mr. Griffin, the principal, got mad with Buddy about something. Exactly what Buddy did or said, I don't know—perhaps he cussed, for he well knew how to do that, having learned from his pa (so we'd heard). Whatever it was, Mr. Griffin thought Buddy needed to be disciplined right then and there. Unfortunately, the principal's wooden paddle was in his classroom, so he picked up a piece of electrical wire that had been discarded near the ball field. With that wire, he evermore gave Buddy Jackson a lashing in front of all the other kids. By the time Buddy got home, purple stripes covered his legs and back. News of the beating spread. The community was in an uproar. Several parents went to the school board to demand that the principal be fired, but Mr. Griffin kept his job.

As the school year drew to a close, Patsy was looking forward to walking across the stage to accept her Certificate of Graduation. The next year, she'd be in ninth grade, so she would then be allowed to ride the bus to Suwannee High School in Live Oak.

Mama was in the process of sewing Patsy's white graduation dress when we heard that the Suwannee County School Board had made a big announcement: "At the close of one more school year (1955-56), Ladyland School will be consolidated with Live Oak schools. Parents who choose to do so may go ahead and transfer their children to Live Oak schools this September."

Mama and Daddy made a quick decision. Since Patsy would be going to school in Live Oak that September, they said it made sense for Anetha and me to go there too. Why wait another year?

I wasn't consulted before they decided, but when I realized a yellow school bus would pick us up at *our door*—no walking a mile to school and back every day—I was thrilled.

But wait. I didn't know any kids who went to school in Live Oak. I began to worry. *What will it be like there? In town. I won't know a soul.* My initial excitement soon turned to apprehension.

73

"Yes, Ma'am," I Lied

Throughout the summer of '55, I kept worrying about going to the Live Oak School where I wouldn't know a soul. At Ladyland, I knew all three teachers and every single student in all eight grades. I grew even more apprehensive when Mama took us to register and I saw the size of the building.

A teacher at the registration desk showed us around. Instead of three rooms like Ladyland, this one had thirty, ten on each of three levels. I felt a little better when I found out that Anetha and I would both be on the same floor (the top level was reserved for sixth through eighth graders). But then Anetha's eyeballs nearly popped out of their sockets when the teacher said, "This is your homeroom, but seventh and eighth graders change classrooms for each subject—English, Math, Social Studies, Science, and PE." Later, we learned Patsy would do that too. She would even change buildings for PE, but

Live Oak School

nothing scared Patsy.

After registering, we went to McCrory's dime store to buy fabric for new dresses. McCrory's, an *L*-shaped, split-level store, wrapped around the stodgy-looking Commercial Bank building at the corner of Live Oak's main intersection. McCrory's had three entrances: a double-door entrance off Howard Street (US90), an entrance off Ohio Avenue (US129), and a back door off Warren Street. Mama angle-parked by the back door. Inside, we stopped for a drink at the water fountain, then turned right to go up the eight or ten steps to the upper level to the fabric department. With so many remnants to choose from, the decision was difficult.

"I like this one best," I finally said to Mama, pointing to a pale blue fabric near the bottom of a two-foot high stack.

"Yeah," Mama said as she stuck her hand into the pile and felt the material, then squeezed it with her hand. "That's Bates—won't wrinkle much. And easy to sew."

I knew what Mama was thinking when she said "easy to sew." Easier than sewing silk parachute material. She'd just finished making a blouse for Patsy using fabric from a parachute Uncle Mernest, who was in the service, gave her. He called the thing "no good." None of us thought to ask how he knew. Did a soldier die using it?

Before cutting the apparatus apart, Mama spread it on the living room floor; it billowed out before settling. We could see no defects in the fabric or seams—no holes or rips—and the white silky fabric looked brand new. Mama seemed happy with the amount of free fabric—enough for several blouses, but she ended up making just the one for Patsy. The entire time she worked with that blouse, from cutting the pieces to sewing the last seam, she complained about how slippery it was. It probably didn't help that she was breaking in her motorized sewing machine. She'd recently had somebody add a motor to Granny's old treadle Singer, and it had one speed: fast.

"Yeah, this Bates fabric will be easy to sew," Mama said as she yanked the pale blue fabric from the neat stack without disturbing other remnants in the pile. *How did Mama do that?*

After all of us selected material, we searched the pages of the Simplicity pattern book. Mama no longer made us share a dress pattern. Besides, I was now as big as my sisters. I chose a pattern with a ruffled tiered skirt, puffy sleeves, and a Peter Pan collar. Mama checked the chart on the back of the pattern package for the amount of fabric recommended for my size and deducted a quarter of a yard before asking the clerk to cut off two-and-a-half yards. Mama said the pattern companies always overestimated the yardage needed.

On the first day of school, my sisters and I wore our new dresses. We were first to be picked up.

"Good morning, girls," the bus driver said, as the three of us hurried up the high steps. Inside the empty bus, we scattered, each of us choosing a window seat. As he stopped and picked up more and more students, I recognized a few who had gone to Ladyland— some from Patsy's class—some older. But strangers occupied most seats. By the time we passed the Live Oak city limit sign, an hour or more later, every bench seat held two or three kids.

The driver parked in front of the brick, two-story high-school building. Without saying "Bye," Patsy rushed off toward Suwannee High. Anetha and I walked together toward our cream-colored stucco building. The school bell rang as we neared the steps, so we joined the throng of students, squeezed through the double doors, crossed polished terrazzo floors, and rushed up the stairs to the second level, where we parted to go to our respective classrooms, mine north, hers south.

Near the doorway of my new classroom stood a lady whose hair and style of dress resembled Mama's when she dressed up. "Good Morning! Come right in and find a desk." The teacher's cheery but clipped voice reminded me of my Indiana aunt.

In some ways, my new classroom looked like my old one. Multi-paned windows across one wall invited in lots of light; a wide blackboard stretched the width of the opposite wall; and twenty or thirty desks, lined up in rows, faced the board. But the pale green terrazzo floors gave the room a modern look.

Kids walked about, greeting each other like friends do. Since I knew nobody, I placed my supplies in the cubbyhole under the first empty desk I came to and sat down. Soon, the tardy bell rang, and everybody hurried to their seats. The teacher introduced herself, writing "Mrs. Waltham" on the blackboard, and then began to call the roll. I glanced around, trying to put the names with faces. My heart beat faster as she went down the alphabet.

"Linda Gilmore?"

"Present," said the pretty girl across the narrow aisle from me.

"Susie Jeannette Howell?"

"Present," I said, copying the girl name Linda.

Mrs. Waltham paused her pencil and looked up at me. My heart thumped. What did I do wrong?

"Do you go by Susie?" she asked.

"No, ma'am," I stammered.

"Jeannette?"

"Yes, ma'am," I lied.

A new school. A new teacher. Why not a new name? After all, Jeannette was my real name. Susanette was just a nickname. I'd always wanted to be named after somebody, as Patsy and Anetha were. Now, I had the same name of an artist.

Jeannette Land, who went to our church and served as my substitute teacher in first grade, had completed most of her art training at the Ringling School of Art before being stricken with polio. Though the polio had left her crippled and in a wheelchair, she painted beautiful pictures. She lived in an apartment on the side of her parents' home, complete with a ramp, so she could roll herself out to gather flowers to paint—a handful of yellow black-eyed Susans, a bunch of bright and bold zinnias, a mixed assortment of daisies, purple irises, and Queen Anne's lace. She also painted portraits and murals—most in soft greens, aquas, and blues, of trees shading bubbling springs. The murals served as backdrops for baptisteries. Even Philadelphia Baptist Church would eventually get a baptistery, complete with a Jeannette Land mural. Too bad I'd already been baptized outdoors.

Having paid close attention to the roll call, I knew that Linda Gilmore and Nancy McKeithen were the girls seated next to me—though I didn't know yet that we would become fast friends.

Following the Pledge of Allegiance and the Lord's Prayer each day, we studied arithmetic, grammar, science, and geography, but details of those lessons are a blur. What I remember most is how proudly and carefully I wrote Jeannette Howell in the upper right corner of each paper I turned in to the teacher.

Going by a new name caused only one problem. I wouldn't notice right away when Mrs. Waltham called on me. But I gradually improved my response time. I never bothered to tell my family I had a new name, but Mama found out at the end of six weeks when she saw my report card.

She didn't look at it the minute I got home from school. She had company, friends from the Home Demonstration Club: Lily George, Dot Thomas, Lorene Warren, Renah Robins, Merine Hunter, and Grandma Rye. All sat around a large quilting frame in our living room, putting tiny stitches into a quilt. My sisters and I bounded in, said hello to the neighbor ladies, and ran to the kitchen to help ourselves to a snack. Today, thanks to her company coming, Mama had made egg custard pie. *M-m-m, my favorite!*

After the neighbors left, before Mama looked at our report cards, we explained to her that the Live Oak school gave *As*, *Bs*, and *Cs*, unlike Ladyland's *Os*, *Ss*, and *Us*.

Mama looked puzzled when she first looked at my report card, probably thinking I'd brought home the wrong one. Not because I had all *A*s and *B*s, but because of the name "Jeannette" and of what Mrs. Waltham had written in the comment block: "Jeannette is a perfectionist." This comment had thrilled me when I read it on the bus on the way home. I didn't know then that this was more of a curse than a compliment—that I would never be completely satisfied with anything I ever did because I never thought the result was perfect.

The first thing I noticed when I saw my school picture was that my necklace lay crooked, snagged by a button.

I was ecstatic the day Mrs. Waltham passed out musical instruments she called Tonettes, along with instruction booklets. I'd always longed to play an instrument. Back when Daddy performed (told jokes) at the Suwannee Jamboree, I wanted to play the accordion or banjo like the musicians on stage, who made it look easy. I'd never seen or heard of a Tonette (made of a black, plastic-like material), but I was more than willing to give it a try.

Mrs. Waltham gave us a few pointers and said we could take the instruments home to practice. I worked diligently at the fingering as diagrammed in the booklet. Finally, I learned the notes. But putting them together for a melody, shifting fingers from one set of tiny holes to another while blowing into the mouthpiece reminded me of rubbing my stomach and patting my head at the same time. I finally learned "Mary Had a Little Lamb." Not that I got every note right.

After Thanksgiving, Mrs. Waltham announced that our class would present—on stage to the whole school!—a play entitled, "A Christmas Bazaar." Having never heard the word bazaar, I had no clue about the plot.

"All of you will have a part," she said. "Some will have speaking parts, others will be bystanders. Oh, how I hoped to be a bystander. I had not performed in front of a group since Patsy told me that I "sang too loud and drowned others out" in the children's Christmas program at church.

To my dismay, Mrs. Waltham assigned me a speaking part. Not given a choice, I memorized my lines and tried not to be nervous as Christmas approached.

I never saw the entire script. Only Mrs. Waltham had a copy. But she explained that my role was that of a stuck-up rich lady who had donated items to a charity for resale at the bazaar, and the money raised at this sale would be used to buy gifts for poor children.

Hm-m-m. Donated items for sale.

"So it's like a rummage sale?" I asked, for I had seen rummage sales on the streets of Live Oak. Ladies would gather round the tables, piled high with used merchandise, and paw through the items, mostly clothing, until the table was a big mess.

"Not exactly," Mrs. Waltham said. Your character has donated silver and expensive jewelry to the charity for resale. So when you walk across the stage, spout your lines!" my teacher said, sticking her nose in the air. "Act hoity-toity, like you think you're hot stuff!"

On the day of the performance, I felt shaky inside as I donned my costume: Mrs. Waltham's black leather gloves and heavy wool coat—dark green, with a stand-up fur collar. The coat reached my ankles. I wore Mama's black pumps, with wads of toilet paper stuffed into the toes, and Mama's dark felt hat with a nubby veil, which made me see dots.

On cue, I hobbled from behind the curtain onto the stage, spouting my lines. But my voice trembled and my knees wobbled. Unaccustomed to high heels, I almost turned an ankle before I made it off the stage.

I'm sure I didn't project the image Mrs. Waltham wanted—that

I didn't look like "hot stuff." But in the spotlight under all that leather, wool, felt, and fur, I definitely felt hot.

74

Time of Loss
1956

Granddaddy Tip, the one person who'd always had time for me, the person who used to sing "Prettiest Little Girl in the County O," the one who always made me feel special, was still in the state hospital in Chattahoochee. He'd been sent away when I was ten. I was now eleven.

Some days, when the sun shone bright and everything was going right, I forgot he was gone. Other days, I felt like a piece of me was missing.

Finally, our family went to Chattahoochee to visit him. As we approached the sprawling hospital, Mama said, "Granddaddy Tip might not recognize us."

I was sure Mama was wrong.

Inside the hospital, a lady at the reception desk told us to have a seat in the visitors' area, that members of the staff would bring our relative to us. We found a spot away from other visiting families.

It seemed a long wait. Finally, double doors opened and there he was. Surprisingly, he wasn't using his walking cane. Instead, two men dressed in white, one on each side, held his arms and ushered him toward us.

I stood up to run to him, but Mama said, "Wait, Susanette!

They're bringing him over here. And remember, he might not recognize you."

Granddaddy shuffled his feet and didn't call out to us as I thought he would. *Mama's right,* I thought, *He don't recognize us . . . What's that in his hands?*

He was within six feet of us when he smiled and said, "Hey, young'uns."

With that, I grinned. "Young'uns" was what he'd always called us—that or "*hard-headed* young'uns."

"Hear ya' go, sweetie," he said, holding out a small, reddish box. The words and pictures on the box were so smeared and smudged they were unrecognizable. I took the box and held it.

"Go ahead," he said. "Open it. I've been keeping it for y'all."

One of the men in white leaned over and whispered to Mama, "Mr. Lanier's been carrying that box around every day for months, saving it for his great-granddaughters."

Granddaddy was hard of hearing and didn't seem to notice that they were talking about him.

For months Granddaddy had thought about me and my sisters? And some days I'd forgotten he was gone. I felt sad.

Inside the box? Animal cookies. I chose an elephant and passed the box on to my sisters. The elephant was stale. But sweet.

I don't remember what we talked about during the time we sat visiting with Granddaddy Tip. But the conversation must have bored him. He soon nodded off.

"He tires easily," one of the orderlies said. "We should probably take him back to his room now."

Mama agreed.

"Granddaddy," she said. He opened his eyes. "We have to go now. We'll see you again soon."

My great-grandfather didn't protest as the two men lifted him by his arms and belt. We said our goodbyes and stood watching as the double doors slowly swung shut behind them.

Only a few weeks after our visit, Mama told my sisters and me when we got home from school that Granddaddy Tip had passed away. I cried as I never had before.

The days surrounding the funeral are hazy . . . family and friends gathering . . . hugs, laughter . . . talk of Uncle Alonzo and Uncle Harold . . . would they come from Baltimore and Indiana?

Uncle Alonzo, Granddaddy Tip's only son, came. Mama's brother didn't.

By the time Uncle Alonzo arrived, a casket holding my great-grandfather's body had been placed in my grandparents' living room. Friends and neighbors brought food, lots of it, just as they had done when Great-Granny Dosia died.

The day of the funeral, Patsy, now fourteen, was sick in bed with fever. Mrs. Edith Knight stayed with her while the rest of us went to the church. It was a cold and overcast February day.

After the service, we walked out to the cemetery behind the church and sat under a tent that shaded a hole next to Granny Dosia's grave. Never had my chest and throat ached like it did as Granddaddy Tip's casket was lowered into the hole. I understood, as I had not when Granny died, that Granddaddy Tip was gone forever.

Back at home, Mrs. Knight told Mama that Patsy fainted soon after we left for the church, so Mama and Daddy decided to take her to Live Oak to see a doctor. Turns out, she had scarlet fever. Our whole family had to be quarantined. For over two weeks, Anetha and I couldn't go to school or have any visitors.

During the days we had to stay home from school, Anetha and I were so bored that we went to the bedroom time after time, asking Patsy to stick out her tongue. It resembled a strawberry. Lucky for the rest of us, we never caught scarlet fever. But right after Patsy recovered, she and I came down with mumps. Our throat and jaws swelled so much we didn't look like ourselves. I felt like I'd had my tonsils out a second time. I didn't want to chew, drink, swallow, or even talk.

My grandparents decided to order a tombstone for my great-grand-parents' graves. This led to a discussion between Grandma and Mama about the proper spelling of Granddaddy Tip's legal name. He had always signed his name *A. Lanier.* Mama thought his first name was spelled Asbury, even though his marriage license and his official homestead deed recorded it as Asbery. Grandma Rye, on the other hand, thought it was Asberry, and she's the one who had the name engraved in stone:

Asberry Lanier
June 15, 1863 - February 22, 1956

Granddaddy Tip left behind few material possessions, having al-ready given his homestead away: 80 acres traded for a mule; forty acres to his son, Alonzo; and forty to his daughter, Delma (Grand-ma Rye).

The few items he left behind became precious keepsakes: his yellow-gold pocket watch, a leather wallet, his walking cane, and the 1899 U.S. Patent (homestead) Deed signed by President Wil-liam McKinley.

Inside the wallet, Grandma found a dime, wrapped in a cigarette paper. The menfolk said he'd probably saved the first dime he ever earned. But I thought he was saving it to give to us kids on our next visit.

* * *

Meanwhile, our dog Tommy wasn't well. Sometimes he'd be sleeping quietly and suddenly jerk himself awake as he let out a howl like he was in awful pain. I hated hearing him wail like that. The veterinarian told Daddy that Tommy had heartworms, caught from mosquito bites, and that "any treatment that will kill the heartworms will kill your dog."

Tommy was my age. But in dog years, Daddy said he was an old man. "Dogs don't live to be ninety-two like your Great-Granddaddy Tip," he said.

Tommy couldn't die too! Like Granddaddy Tip, he'd been around all my life. I remembered how Mama said when I was a baby, I would stick my finger in Tommy's eyes, not knowing any better, yet he would never snap at me. True, he did bark and tattle on Anetha and Patsy once when they left home without permission, but that was a good thing. Tommy had walked my sisters and me to school every day when we went to Ladyland. And now he greeted us when we came home on the school bus from Live Oak. He once saved Mama's life too, by killing a rattlesnake she thought was a spreading adder. She was poking the snake with a stick, trying to get it to puff out its head, when Tommy jumped up, pushed her back, grabbed the snake between his teeth, and shook the thing till it was in pieces. Only then did Mama see its rattles.

It didn't seem fair that Tommy was hurting when he'd never hurt anyone. Well, he did bite cousin Michael's jaw so bad that Michael had to have stitches. But two-year-old Michael had tried to take Tommy's hambone.

"Girls, I'm gonna have to ask the vet to put Tommy down," Daddy said one Saturday at breakfast. "He's just in too much pain now." I knew Daddy was right, yet I wanted to protest. On the farm, I'd seen many animals die, but most were slaughtered for food. I was pretty fond of some. But this was different. I *loved* Tommy and I knew he loved me.

Daddy left that same day with Tommy in the car seat next to him and returned with the warm body of our beloved pet in a corrugated box. Daddy unloaded it carefully and carried it the same way the pallbearers did as they carried Granddaddy Tip's casket from the black hearse into the church and then to the cemetery.

Daddy cradled the taped-shut box in his arms as he walked across the yard and set it down gently in the dappled shade of a pecan tree near the tobacco barn. The rest of us watched from a distance as he dug a deep hole, but we drew close when he lowered the box into the grave. We circled around as Daddy shoveled dirt onto the box that now served as Tommy's coffin. Nobody said a word. There was just the sound of the dirt hitting cardboard. I tried to hold back tears by scrunching up my face. But pain swelled from deep in my chest and lodged in my throat.

75

Acceptance

"I'm passing around a list of girls and boys your age," Mrs. Waltham said to my sixth-grade class. "I want you to choose one as your pen pal."

North Dakota could have been at the North Pole for all I knew, but I chose a girl who lived there. Turns out, she lived on a farm like me. But that was about all we had in common. She lived on a *dairy* farm and actually *enjoyed* doing farm chores. As time went on, I wrote less and less, especially after I became friends with Linda Gilmore and Nancy McKeithen. Both lived in Live Oak.

At first, I'd hesitated to invite anybody from town to spend the night, since we didn't have a television like they did, not even a radio that worked. Plus, I had to do farm chores. But on separate visits, they both acted like they enjoyed helping shell corn for the chickens and gather eggs.

When Nancy first visited, I showed her the room I shared with my sisters, and she noticed a necklace on the vanity. Not my pearl necklace that I still kept boxed, but a paper-bead necklace.

"That's pretty," she said as she touched it.

"I made it. Want to make one?"

She did, so I gathered the supplies—a piece of embroidery

thread, a pair of scissors, an old *Sears and Roebuck* catalog—plus a bottle of clear nail polish Mama had on hand to stop runs in her nylon stockings.

We cut twenty-five one-inch triangles of paper from the most colorful pictures in the catalog and rolled each up, starting with the base and ending with the point. We dabbed nail polish under the points to hold them in place. As we worked, Mama walked by and commented that she once made a necklace using dried china-berries. I wished we had some chinaberries to place between each paper bead. Unfortunately, Daddy had cut down our chinaberry tree, saying the berries were toxic to the livestock.

We coated the outside of Nancy's beads with nail polish, and after they dried we took turns threading them onto embroidery thread. I thought our multicolored necklaces rivaled the glass car-nival-bead necklaces sold every year at the Suwannee County Fair, and ours wouldn't break. We wore them to school the next day.

At a later date, when Linda Gilmore visited, I gave her something to take home too. Something we already had on hand.

A stray cat had taken up residence in our packhouse and had four kittens. Daddy didn't mind letting us keep the mother cat. "She'll control the mouse population," he said. But he didn't want the litter of kittens around to trip over. I knew if my sisters and I didn't find homes for them soon, Daddy would cause them to "disappear."

Linda immediately fell in love with a black-and-white kitty and asked if she could have it. "Sure," I said. But at the supper table that night, Mama and Daddy questioned whether her mother and father would approve.

"Oh, my parents won't care," she assured us. So the next morn-ing, Mama found an empty shoebox, which we poked holes into, so the kitty could get air. When we first put the kitten into the box, it mewed with every breath, but on the bus ride to school, it settled down.

Linda took her kitty home at noon when she went to eat lunch and came back without the kitten, so I figured that proved her parents didn't mind. Although when I thought about it later, I realized I was never invited to Linda's house.

Nancy did invite me, and Mama said I could go. Instead of heading straight to her house after school, though, as I expected, we went to a grocery store her mother operated. We walked alongside US 90, past the new Suwannee County Hospital and past a machine and chainsaw shop owned by her father, Harry McKeithen.

When we arrived at the neighborhood grocery, the cash register was going ka-ching, ka-ching, as customers came and went, picking up an item or two. Mrs. McKeithen was very friendly with everyone. After Nancy introduced us, her mother told Nancy to get the broom and sweep the floor. *So, Nancy has chores too.* Mrs. McKeithen then turned to me.

"Jeannette, would you like to straighten the cans of vegetables on that shelf?" I didn't mind at all since I enjoyed putting almost anything in order.

"You girls can go outside now," Mrs. McKeithen said after Nancy put away the broom and I'd finished lining up can after can of vegetables and fruit. "But stay nearby, so you'll hear me call you when I lock up."

Nancy and I wandered into the trailer park behind the store. I was astonished at how close each trailer was to the next. Our nearest neighbors lived a quarter of a mile away, and thick woods separated us. Here, the homes were only a few feet apart. But folks sat around in lawn chairs in clusters, laughing and talking. I noticed one group, all men, drinking from clear glass mugs.

"That's weird that they don't put ice in their tea," I whispered to Nancy as we passed.

"That's beer," Nancy said matter-of-factly. "You don't put ice in beer."

Right. No ice in beer. So that's what beer looks like.

Nancy knew things I didn't, and she seemed to know everybody in the trailer park. We stopped several times to chat with someone. Each time, she introduced me as her friend, "Jeannette," a name I still wasn't completely used to. (Little did I know there was no reason to get used to it, since it would last only until the next year when all of the Ladyland students transferred to Live Oak.)

Upon hearing Nancy's mother call "*Nannn-cy,*" we ran back to the store and got into her mother's car. Her family lived across town on the edge of Sherwood Forest, a new subdivision of mostly ranch-style brick homes. Their house, with its barn-red exterior and a roof that slanted in one direction, stood out as ultra-modern, but inside, it felt warm and cozy. Indirect lighting cast a soft glow on knotty-pine paneled walls.

When Nancy showed me her bedroom, I thought it was kind of strange that she shared it with both her little brother and sister, but then she pulled out an accordion-like room divider that gave us our own private room. *So cool!*

Later, in the dining room, I couldn't help but notice a shiny silver tea service. *Wow! Nancy's family must be rich,* I thought. They were not stuck-up rich, though, like the lady I'd played in "The Christmas Bazaar." Everybody in her family was nice. I felt very comfortable. That is, until the next morning, when Mrs. McKeithen said we were having cinnamon toast for breakfast. I wondered if I'd made a mistake in spending the night with Nancy. I was still a finicky eater, and I'd never heard of cinnamon toast, much less tasted it. *Should I force myself to eat something that might taste awful?*

To my surprise, the toast was sweet, buttery, crunchy, and delicious.

"This is the best toast I ever tasted." I said to Nancy's mother.

"Would you like another piece?"

"Yes, ma'am. I sure would. If it's not too much trouble."

"Not at all."

After this experience, I became more willing to try new foods, and before long, I would even develop a taste for Co-Cola.

A week or so after my first visit with Nancy, Mama received a note in the mail. She looked at the return address and said it was from Mrs. Harry McKeithen. I was anxious as Mama slit open the envelope with a knife. What would it say? *Did I do something wrong at Nancy's house?*

Mama smiled as she started reading, then backed up against the kitchen counter and read it aloud.

> *Dear Mrs. Howell,*
> *I'm so pleased that my daughter Nancy and your*
> *daughter Jeannette have become friends. What an*
> *industrious and polite young lady Jeannette is. You should*
> *be very proud of her. We will be happy to have her visit*
> *again. Anytime!*
> *Sincerely,*
> *Bea McKeithen*

Mama looked at me like she never had before—or if she had, I'd never noticed. When Daddy came home, she showed the note to him. He made a joke, but I could tell the note made him proud too. As for me, I felt as if I'd received an *A* on a very important test. An *A* for acceptance.

Afterword
2017

When Nancy McKeithen (now Chesson) read what I wrote about our visits in sixth grade, she said she remembered my mother making a corduroy skirt for her that featured a bib and straps like one Mama had made for me. I remember mine, but not Nancy's. She also said she shared her bedroom, not with her brother and sister, as I thought, but just with her sister Dawne.

When Linda Gilmore (now Bates-Bump) read the story, she said she thought the two of us were snowflakes in the Christmas play and wore tissue paper dresses she was afraid would come apart while on stage—and that she did not take home *a* cat. She took home *three*!

More and more proof that our memories are collections of half-remembered events. Where the full truth lies sometimes remains a mystery.

If you recall experiences we shared—I would love to hear your version. Please contact me at https://susiehbaxter.com/home/

Mama's Recipes

Updated for Today's Kitchens

Acre Peas

1 quart of shelled acre peas
   with snaps
About a teaspoon salt
Ham hock or 2 strips bacon

Put the peas in a pot and add salt
and pork. Add enough water un-
til you can just see the water (don't cover completely). Bring to a
boil, then cut heat to simmer until peas are tender (30-40 minutes).
Serve with hot cornbread and butter. (Goya ham seasoning may be
substituted for the pork.)

*Note: Acre peas, a variety of field peas (black-eyed peas are another
variety) are also called white acre peas, but pick them when they're
green. Also pick some immature pods so you can snap the pods like
string beans.*

* * *

Bread Pudding

6 biscuits (or about 3 cups crumbs)
Milk to cover crumbs
1 cup sugar
3 eggs
Raisins (optional)
1 teaspoon vanilla

Crumble biscuits into bowl. Pour enough milk over crumbs to

cover. Soak crumbs till soft. Beat in sugar, eggs, and vanilla. Pour into baking dish and bake at 350° F until set. Cut into squares.

* * *

Chicken Pirleau

1 (4-5 lb.) chicken or stewing hen
2-3 eggs (hard or softshell)*
2½ cups rice
Salt and black pepper to taste

Place chicken in large pot, cover with water, and sprinkle with salt. Boil until chicken is tender. Remove chicken from broth and set aside to cool. Add water to chicken stock to make about six cups of broth. Add (prewashed) rice. Bring to a boil. Cover and reduce heat to simmer. Cook twenty minutes. Meanwhile, boil eggs and debone the chicken; then chop them up. When rice is done, add chopped chicken and eggs, and add salt and pepper to taste. Serve with vegetables or salad—and offer sweet pickles on the side.

*If you find softshell eggs inside the chicken when you gut and dress it, use them.

* * *

Chocolate Fudge

3 cups granulated sugar
½ cup white Karo syrup
1¼ cups milk
3 sq. bitter chocolate
½ cup butter (1 stick)
1 teaspoon vanilla
1 cup pecans, chopped

Place sugar, syrup, milk, and chocolate in a heavy pot. Cook over high heat until it boils. Reduce to medium low and continue cooking until it reaches the soft ball stage, 240° F. If no thermometer is available, check the temperature by dropping a dab of it into a cup that is filled with cool tap water. When the mixture adheres together to form a soft ball, it's ready. Remove from heat, add vanilla and butter, and let it cool about five minutes. Beat vigorously until it is satiny, having lost some of its gloss. Mix in the pecans. Pour into a buttered pan. When it sets, cut into 1½ in. squares.

* * *

Cinnamon Rolls

See Yeast Roll recipe (p. 438)

* * *

Cornbread

1½ cups self-rising cornmeal
½ cup self-rising flour
1 egg
2 tablespoons shortening
Milk, enough to make batter the consistency of cake batter

Mix all ingredients together into a large bowl. Pour batter into well-greased iron skillet. Bake in hot oven (about 450° F) until brown. Slice into pie shapes.

* * *

Cornbread Dressing

2 tablespoons lard or vegetable oil
1 large onion, chopped
1 cup chopped celery

Hoecake of cornbread (see previous recipe; bake ahead of time)

4 slices white bread, toasted

¼ teaspoon thyme

¼ teaspoon curry powder

¼ teaspoon black pepper

¼ teaspoon sage

¼ teaspoon salt

1½ teaspoon poultry seasoning

3 hard-boiled eggs, chopped

1 or more quarts of chicken broth (from a boiled chicken or store-bought broth)

If preparing your own chicken broth, do this ahead of time, and bake cornbread and boil eggs ahead of time. Sauté onion and celery in lard or oil. In a large bowl, combine all ingredients except the chicken broth. Then add chicken broth to cover. Let sit for an hour or more to let bread soften. Mix thoroughly, breaking up all the bread, adding chicken broth as needed until the mixture is the consistency of very thick batter. Pour into greased 9"x12" pan and bake at 400° F about 30 minutes or until slightly browned on top.

* * *

Cream Icing

2 cups granulated sugar

1 cup fresh cream (skimmed from fresh, unpasteurized, cow milk) or 1 cup store-bought heavy whipping cream plus 1 tablespoon all-purpose flour, mixed thoroughly

1 tablespoon white Karo syrup

1 teaspoon vanilla

Combine all ingredients except vanilla in heavy pot. Cook on high until mixture boils; then reduce to medium and cook until it reaches the soft ball stage, about 240° F. If no thermometer is available, check temperature by dropping a dab of mixture into a cup that is full of cool tap water. When the mixture adheres together to form a soft ball, it's ready. Remove from heat, add vanilla, and let it cool for about five minutes. Beat rapidly by hand until it loses gloss and looks satiny. Failure to beat rapidly may cause icing to become sugary.

* * *

Custard Pies

Note: This recipe makes two pies: one chocolate and one coconut.

1½ cups sugar for pies, plus ⅓ cup sugar for meringue
6 tablespoons corn starch
6 eggs
4 cups milk
1 envelope gelatin
6 tablespoons butter
2 teaspoons vanilla extract
¼ cup cocoa powder (for chocolate pie)
½ can shredded or flaked coconut (for coconut pie)
2 pre-baked pie shells

Separate all 6 egg yolks from egg whites. Set egg whites aside for meringue. In small pot, mix 1½ cups sugar and corn starch together. Add 6 egg yolks, milk and gelatin. Bring to slow boil, stirring until thickened. Remove from heat. Add butter and vanilla. Divide custard into 2 bowls of equal portions. Add cocoa powder into one bowl and stir well. Add coconut to second bowl, reserving 1 tablespoon to sprinkle onto meringue before baking. Pour each mixture into a pre-baked pieshell.

For meringue, beat the 6 egg whites in a separate bowl until foamy.

Gradually beat in ⅓ cup sugar until stiff peaks form. Spread evenly over custard pies. Sprinkle remaining coconut onto coconut pie.

Bake pies at 350° F for 15–20 minutes or until meringue is golden brown. Cool and refrigerate.

* * *

Divinity

Note: Divinity will not set if weather is too humid. Do not make on a rainy day. Also, you will need to use a mixer on a stand or have another person help you.

3 cups granulated sugar
⅔ cup water
⅓ cup Karo syrup
3 egg whites
1 teaspoon vanilla
1 cup pecans, chopped

Cook sugar, water, and syrup until it reaches the hard crack stage, 290° F. If no thermometer is available, check temperature by dropping a few drops into a tin (or stainless steel) cup filled with cool tap water. When the dab forms a lump that will make a cracking noise when tapped on the side of the cup, it's ready. Remove from heat, add vanilla, and let it cool while beating egg whites to form soft peaks. To the beaten egg white, add hot syrupy mixture very slowly in a steady, thin stream while continuing to beat egg whites vigorously. By the time you finish adding syrupy mixture to egg whites, the mixture should have lost its gloss and be satiny. Stir in pecans. By now, mixture should be getting stiff. Quickly drop by teaspoonfuls onto a sheet of waxed paper (or non-stick foil). Candy should be stored in a loosely covered (unsealed) container.

* * *

Oatmeal Cookies (Crispy)

1½ cups brown sugar (packed)*
¾ cup butter
6 tablespoons buttermilk*
½ teaspoon salt*
¾ teaspoon baking soda*
1½ teaspoons vanilla
1½ cups sifted all-purpose flour*
3 cups quick-cooking oats
1 cup chopped pecans

Combine ingredients in order given. Mix thoroughly. Shape into balls about 1" diameter and place on greased cookie sheet. Press with fork to flatten. Bake at 375° F about 10 minutes or till light brown. With pancake turner, carefully transfer to cooling rack.

*If you wish to use sweet milk, add a tablespoon of vinegar. If you use self-rising flour, omit salt and baking soda.

* * *

Pancakes

1 package active dry yeast
½ cup warm water
1 egg
2 tablespoons vegetable oil
2 cups unsifted self-rising flour (all-purpose flour works too, but
    Mama told me self-rising works best)
1 tablespoon sugar
Milk

Dissolve yeast in ½ cup warm water; set aside. In another cup, mix oil and egg together. In mixing bowl, mix flour and sugar together.

Add yeast water, oil and egg, and enough warm milk to make a thin batter. Set aside for 30 minutes. Bubbles will begin to form on top and batter will thicken up. Cook on hot (about 400° F) oiled griddle.

* * *

Pickled Pigs' Feet

Several pigs' feet
Salt
2 quarts vinegar
Pickling spices (tied up in a piece of muslin)

Scald, scrape, and clean feet thoroughly. Sprinkle well with salt. Let stand 4 to 8 hours (overnight). Wash the feet again in clean water. Place them in pot of hot water and cook until tender but not until meat can be removed from bones. Take feet out of pot. Remove and discard hooves. Place vinegar and pickling spices in pot; bring to a boil. Meanwhile, pat the pigs' feet dry and pack in quart or half-gallon jars. Fill jars to a half-inch from top with the boiling brine. Remove air bubbles. Wipe jar rims. Add lids and process in water bath.

* * *

Pickles (14-day, Sweet)

Choose young cucumbers (cukes), 1½ inch diameter or less. If you prefer whole pickles, choose same-size cukes, 4 to 5 inches long. "Burpless cukes" make good pickles. "Pickling cukes" are even better; they shrink less and hold their crispness longer. This recipe begins with 2 gallons (4 pounds) of cukes, and it will produce about 7 quarts of pickles.

Ingredients for the 14-day period

4 pounds (two gallons) cukes

2 cups salt (not iodized; bagged, pickling salt is best)

4 gallons water (more or less, over the 14 days) plus water for rinsing

3 tablespoons alum powder

12 cups apple cider vinegar (with at least 5% acidity)

20 cups white granulated sugar

⅔ cup pickling spice

2 tablespoons whole celery seed

Equipment needed

Food-safe, wide-mouth container(s), glass or crock, to hold two gallons of cukes

Cheese cloth for making spice bag

A 2-gallon stainless steel or enamel pot for heating liquid

Clean glass jars (14 pints or 7 quarts) and lids that seal

Day 1: Scrub cukes. Do not peel. Cut off stem end and discard. Use whole, or slice the cukes into ¼-inch slices. Place them in wide-mouth container(s). Prepare brine solution in large stainless steel or enamel pot by adding 2 cups salt (non-iodized) to 1 gallon of water. Bring to a boil. Pour this brine over cukes to cover them. Weight with cup/saucer to keep cukes submerged, and cover them. Attend them every day as follows.

Days 2-7: Each day, skim scum off top and discard it.

Day 8: Drain brine solution from cukes. Rinse them in water. Prepare alum solution by boiling 1 tablespoon of alum powder in 1 gallon of water. Pour it over cukes. Weight and cover.

Day 9: Repeat day 8 process.

Day 10: Repeat day 8 process.

Day 11: Tie up ⅔ cup pickling spice and 2 tablespoons whole celery seed in a bag made with 3 layers of cheese cloth. Put the bag of spices in a stainless or enamel pot. Add 12 cups white vinegar and

10 cups white granulated sugar. Bring mixture to a boil to melt sugar. After draining cukes, pour the hot solution over drained cukes. (Note: Save the spice bag and any extra solution. It can remain in the pot, since, during the next three days of processing, the liquid will be drained into this pot and all the liquid will be reheated with the bag of spices.) Weight and cover.

Day 12: Drain the syrup from cukes into the stainless steel or enamel pot. Add 4 cups white sugar. Bring to a boil. Pour over cukes. Weight and cover.

Day 13: Repeat day 12 process.

Day 14: Wash canning jars (pints or quarts). Drain the syrup from cukes into the stainless steel or enamel pot. Add 2 cups white sugar. Bring to a boil. Transfer the drained cukes into the hot vinegar syrup solution in batches (2 quarts at a time). When it comes back to a boil, transfer the cukes and vinegar syrup into clean jars, packing cucumbers tightly. Wipe rims, add lids and tighten. After jars seal, store in a dark cupboard. Best if refrigerated before serving.

* * *

Seven-Minute Frosting

1½ cups granulated sugar
1 tablespoon white Karo syrup
2 egg whites (unbeaten)
6 tablespoons cold water
1 teaspoon vanilla

Place sugar in top of double boiler. Add white Karo syrup and unbeaten egg whites. Stir until thoroughly mixed. Add cold water. Stir. Place over boiling water and stir occasionally until sugar is melted. Add vanilla. Beat at high speed until it stands in peaks.

For a coconut cake, spread frosting between two yellow cake layers and on sides and top, and sprinkle generously with flaked coconut.

* * *

Sour Cream Pound Cake

1 cup butter

3 cups sugar

1 cup sour cream

1 tablespoon vanilla

¼ teaspoon soda

½ teaspoon salt

6 eggs

3 cups sifted cake flour (sift flour, then measure)

Cream butter with sugar until well blended and creamy. Add eggs one at a time beating well after each. Sift dry ingredients together and add to batter. When all ingredients are added, beat well until well mixed and fluffy. Bake in large tube pan (or two pans: one Bundt, one loaf). Bake at 300-325° F an hour or more until done.

* * *

Yeast Rolls

This recipe will make more than four dozen rolls. Mama usually made the full recipe, making half into cinnamon rolls and freezing some. If freezing the rolls, bake only until light brown.

2 packages of active dry yeast

¾ cup warm water for yeast

1 large or two small potatoes, boiled (save liquid)

¼ cup sugar

2 teaspoons salt

3 tablespoons shortening

9 to 10 cups all-purpose flour

Peel and boil potato. Remove potato and mash; save water and add enough water to make 2⅔ cups warm (not hot) water. Dissolve yeast in ¾ cup warm water from tap. In large mixing bowl, mix together the yeast water, the potato, the 2⅔ cups warm water that includes potato water, and sugar. Then gradually mix in enough flour to make a batter like pancake batter. Let this rise until light and full of bubbles. Next, add remaining ingredients. Dough will be rather stiff. Turn out onto floured surface and knead until smooth. Grease inside of a very large bowl. Place dough in bowl and grease top. Place dough in warm place and let rise till double in size. Knead again. Let rest for 10 minutes. Now you are ready to make your rolls. Cut off pieces of dough (each about the size of a walnut). Dab each piece in flour so the dough doesn't stick to your hands as you roll each into a ball. Place balls of dough in greased pan, leaving a little space between. Grease tops with melted butter. Let rise again and bake at 350-375° F until brown.

Cinnamon Rolls

Start with the instructions for yeast rolls above, but do not cut the dough into walnut-sized pieces. While the dough is rising in the bowl, assemble ingredients for filling:

Filling:
1 cup butter, softened, plus butter to grease pans
2 cups granulated sugar
6 tablespoons cinnamon
2 cups raisins (optional)—or nuts if you prefer

Mix sugar and cinnamon together and set aside. Grease several pans with softened butter. Roll each batch of dough out on a floured surface until each is about ½-inch thick. Generously smear softened butter on each rolled-out rectangle (about ¼ cup butter per rectangle) and sprinkle on about ½ cup of the sugar/cinnamon mixture. Add ½ cup raisins and/or nuts if desired. Roll up. Slice off

½-inch thick pieces and place cut side down in buttered pan, sides not quite touching. Grease tops with melted butter. Let rise again until double in size. Bake at 350-375° F until brown. After removing rolls from the oven, mix up the glaze.

Glaze:

¼ cup butter

1 lb. powdered sugar (10x)

1 teaspoon vanilla extract

6 tablespoons hot water

Mix all ingredients together, drizzle over tops of rolls, and serve warm.

Made in the USA
Columbia, SC
21 November 2018